THE
SUPREME
COURT

THE SUPREME COURT

A C-SPAN BOOK

FEATURING THE JUSTICES

IN THEIR OWN WORDS

EDITORS

BRIAN LAMB,

SUSAN SWAIN, AND

MARK FARKAS

PublicAffairs
New York

PublicAffairs books are available at special discounts for bulk purchases in the U.S. by
corporations, institutions, and other organizations. For more information, please contact
the Special Markets Department at the Perseus Books Group, 2300 Chestnut Street,
Suite 200, Philadelphia, PA 19103, call (800) 810-4145, ext. 5000, or e-mail
special.markets@perseusbooks.com.

Editorial production by the Book Factory.
Book design by Jane Raese
Text set in 12-point Minion

Library of Congress Cataloging-in-Publication Data
The Supreme Court : a C-SPAN book featuring the justices in their own words / editors,
Brian Lamb, Susan Swain, and Mark Farkas. — 1st ed.
    p. cm.
Includes index.
ISBN 978-1-58648-835-2
1. United States. Supreme Court. 2. United States. Supreme Court—History. 3. Judges—
United States—Interviews. I. Lamb, Brian, 1955– II. Swain, Susan H. III. Farkas, Mark C.
KF8742.S895 2010
347.73'26—dc22
2010005270

FIRST EDITION

10 9 8 7 6 5 4 3 2 1

To my "gal pals," a family by choice,
for their incredible friendship.
And, to RGK, the best ongoing
business partner imaginable.
—S.S.

To Paige, Sydney and Meghan for all of
their unconditional love and understanding.
And to Terry—whose instincts
always lead in the right direction.
—M.F.

The judicial power of the United States shall be vested in one Supreme Court, and in such inferior courts as the Congress may from time to time ordain and establish. The judges, both of the supreme and inferior courts, shall hold their offices during good behaviour, and shall, at stated times, receive for their services a compensation, which shall not be diminished during their continuance in office.

—ARTICLE III, SECTION 1
CONSTITUTION OF THE UNITED STATES

CONTENTS

PART TWO: SUPREME COURT EXPERTS

PART THREE: SUPPLEMENTARY MATERIAL

INTRODUCTION

The thing that makes our system of government unique is that it's bound by the rule of law, by a written constitution that lawyers and judges have to interpret. So you need to appreciate that something different is going on here than what goes on in the Capitol building or in the White House, and you need to appreciate how important it is to our system of government.

—CHIEF JUSTICE JOHN ROBERTS
C-SPAN INTERVIEW, JULY 2009

THIS BOOK IS REMARKABLE in recording the only time that all the living Supreme Court justices, the nine sitting members and their two retired colleagues have granted interviews to a single television network. They did so in support of a feature documentary created by C-SPAN in the fall of 2009.

We began this project with the idea that we'd focus on the history of the building, not knowing how many justices would agree to participate. But as more of them signed on for interviews, it became apparent to us that we were being given an incredible opportunity to learn about what happens inside the Court, the branch of government least visible to the public, through the eyes of the justices themselves.

This project would not have been possible without the assistance of Chief Justice John Roberts, C-SPAN producer Mark Farkas, and the Court's chief public information officer, Kathy Arberg. What follows is the story within the story of how the Court came to terms with television cameras, if only briefly.

Kathy Arberg, the Court's chief public information officer.

Historically, the Supreme Court and its members have distinguished themselves for their aversion to the publicity—lifeblood to many Washingtonians. Lifetime appointments give justices little incentive to be in front of the public. Indeed, justices over the years have described the pains they take to insulate themselves from public life so that their rulings are reached independent of popular opinion. Yet the Court is not a cloister. Earlier justices may have been somewhat monastic in their habits; by contrast, today's top jurists routinely dip their toes into the waters of public life, beginning with the high profile gauntlet of today's judicial confirmation process. Justices in the modern era routinely accept speaking engagements, take on teaching assignments, write books, and undergo the rigors of publicity tours. Some, by no means all, grant infrequent interviews with print and television organizations.

Because Court policy bans television cameras from covering the seventy-five or so public arguments scheduled for each term, C-SPAN tries to have cameras in front of the justices whenever possible outside their marble home on Capitol Hill. Over the years, many of the justices have welcomed C-SPAN cameras, likely seeing our coverage of speeches and panel sessions as part of a broader, ongoing effort to involve and inform the public about the Court and its work. In particular, justices O'Connor, Breyer, Kennedy, and Thomas have participated in C-SPAN produced programs such as *Students and Leaders,* a series that introduces high school students to history makers. In all of these cases, justices will talk about their jobs, how the Court functions, and its role in society. Needless to say, they refrain from discussing prior cases or issues that may come before the Court.

Others emulate recently retired Justice David Souter, noted for his quip that cameras would come to the Supreme Court "over my dead body." Justice John Paul Stevens, the Court's longest-serving member, rarely speaks in public; at the other end of the age spectrum, Justice Samuel Alito, among the most recent additions to the Court, has done little to cultivate public visibility since his 2006 Senate confirmation hearings. Justice Antonin Scalia, a longtime and vocal opponent of cameras in the Supreme Court, has sometimes been known to carry that opposition to events far from the Court. While Justice Scalia has granted occasional television interviews, there are a few times on record when the arrival of a C-SPAN camera crew at one of his events had an unhappy sequel: Our would-be chroniclers were led to the door.

Though cameras are not permitted in the Court's ornate marble courtroom during oral argument, technology has been allowed a modest toehold there. Since 1955, the Court has created audio recordings of its hearings, which are later turned over to the National Archives for future research by scholars and journalists. The contested presidential election of 2000 affected this practice in a significant way. As that bruising contest made its way to the Court for resolution, C-SPAN requested permission to televise the arguments in *Bush v. Gore.* Other media organizations quickly joined in the petition. After review, then Chief Justice Rehnquist said no to television but citing the heightened public interest in the case agreed to immediately release the Court's audio recording. On December 11, 2000, just minutes after the case was heard, the Court released its audio file. Radio and television organizations, including C-SPAN, instantly carried the file in its entirety, giving many Americans their first exposure to the rapid-fire intellectual jousting of the Court's oral argument.

Precedent counts for a lot around the Supreme Court. The heightened public interest standard provided a framework for additional requests for same-day release of the Court's audio tapes, which then Chief Justice Rehnquist continued to review, as does Chief Justice Roberts. Since 2000, C-SPAN has been permitted to broadcast twenty-one such cases. However, a decade of experience with audio recordings has not opened the door to television coverage of the Court. In 2005, when John Roberts was chosen to succeed Chief Justice Rehnquist, C-SPAN suggested a demonstration of digital technology that could allow unobtrusive coverage of oral arguments. The chief politely demurred. More recently, even as this book neared completion, the Roberts Court reiterated its distrust of cameras in the courtroom with a 5–4 decision that had the effect of blocking a ninth circuit federal district court from posting video of a trial involving California's recent ban on same sex marriage onto the popular video website, Youtube.

Such was our experience with cameras and the federal judiciary when in March of 2009 C-SPAN approached Chief Justice Roberts with the idea of a documentary on the Court building. We entrusted our appeal to Mark Farkas, a twenty-five-year C-SPAN veteran, who had earlier completed video histories of the United States Capitol (2006) and the White House (2008). On March 23, 2009, Mark wrote to the Court on C-SPAN's behalf, asking permission to bring HD cameras into the 1935 landmark to record, through its art and architecture, much more than a building's story. Inside C-SPAN, anticipation built. A week went by with no response, then two. Then, during the second week of April, Mark received a call from Kathy Arberg, the Court's chief liaison to the media. The chief would allow our cameras into the Court. The project was on.

The narrative of the Supreme Court building is far briefer than that of the White House or the Capitol. Until 1935, justices met inside the Capitol in quarters they had long since outgrown. It's fair to say that their majestic building, first occupied at a time of major national and constitutional stress, owes its existence to one man, William Howard Taft, the only American ever to serve as both president and chief justice. Taft put the full force of his personality behind the building project, hiring Cass Gilbert, one of the most noted architects of the day. Taft died in 1930 before he could see the completion of the $9 million building he had championed. It fell to his successor, Charles Evans Hughes, to preside over the cornerstone-laying ceremony for the Court's new home in 1932.

In telling this story, we set an ambitious production schedule geared to the opening of the Court's fall term on the first Monday in October 2009. As it happened, Justice Souter had just announced his pending retirement, setting the stage for President Barack Obama's first Court appointment and summer confirmation hearings. If all went according to plan, Justice Souter's replacement would be on the Court with the opening of the new term. More than ever, people would be interested in the Court, some passionately so. We had a deadline to meet.

Our first day of taping at the Court was April 29, 2009. May and June brought a flurry of activity for C-SPAN camera crews. Mark Farkas's technical partner, crew chief Bob Reilly, assembled a small team of talented technicians for the project. Together Bob Young, Bill Heffley, Jon Kelly, Ben Sorenson, and Mike McCann brought decades of experience shooting in C-SPAN's style. Reilly, who's been at the network almost as long as Mark Farkas, was the main "shooter" for our Capitol and White House features. He brought to the Court project HD production experience and an instinctive appreciation for what it takes to move television gear through public rooms filled with priceless artifacts of national significance.

White House and congressional staffs long ago grew accustomed to television cameras in their midst. Not so in the Supreme Court. Camera crews are rare there, which means we were sometimes met with skepticism. Kathy Arberg's willingness to run interference coupled with Mark Farkas's flexibility and overall good cheer enabled the C-SPAN team to make significant progress throughout the early summer months. Extra production sessions on nights and weekends produced hours of raw video as our cameras went into places rarely or never before seen by the public. One day, it was the Lawyers' Lounge, where attorneys make their last-minute preparations before argument; another time we visited the justices' Robing Room, where nine fine wooden lockers affixed with nameplates hold each jurist's black robes—the world's most exclusive locker room.

In the core of the building sits the majestic courtroom, undoubtedly the most moving production experience for our crew. Scanning the nine empty chairs of the justices, it was possible to hear the echoed arguments that for three-quarters of a century have defined the law and shaped the course of American democracy.

We shot twenty-six hours of interior and exterior production video. The Supreme Court Curator's Office combed their files for historic photographs to augment an emerging storyline. In the end we received permission to take cameras everywhere we requested, save two locations: the Conference Room, where the justices gather without staff to discuss the cases before them. (It is so exclusive a setting, in fact, that when the justices convene there, it falls to the most junior member to answer the door.) As it happens, we were able to secure video of the Conference Room shot in the mid-1990s by a production company. The other place off limits was the top floor basketball court, known affectionately throughout the building as the "highest court in the land." All in all, we were granted incredible access for which we were—and are—greatly appreciative.

Our *Capitol* documentary had included top congressional leaders. *The White House* featured interviews with President and Mrs. Bush. It seemed appropriate to try to enlist each of the justices for interviews. One by one, they began to say yes, and then some. Justice Stephen Breyer agreed to a video tour of his chambers. His interview, our first, showed Justice Breyer, in full educator mode. Standing in front of shelves filled with color-coded briefs, he offered a detailed explanation of the process by which the Court reviews petitions to hear cases. Later, sitting before a fireplace, his office windows framing perhaps the best view of the Capitol in Washington, Justice Breyer described the differences between the Court and the Congress.

Later that same day, another bit of history was made when the laconic jurist from New Hampshire, David Souter, sat down with us for what we believe was his first-ever television interview. Our gear was set up on the west plaza's portico, amid the Court's famous columns. Our interview was short, only about twenty minutes. Truth be told, Justice Souter seemed less than comfortable with the cameras and microphones, and yet he spoke with obvious affection and knowledge about the building he would soon vacate. Here, he described the experience of sitting on the bench in the courtroom, surveying the attorneys and other interested parties ready to make their case, and, perhaps, history in the bargain:

> One of the amazing things about that courtroom, despite its splendor, is the intimacy of it. On the one hand, it's not that big a room, but the real intimacy comes in the relationship between the lawyer who is arguing at the podium and the Court that he's arguing to. And if you stop to think of it when you go in there, I would tell a visitor, you will see that if one of us leaned over the bench as far as we could lean, and the lawyer arguing at the podium leaned toward us, we could almost shake hands. And that is a very important thing because it means that when the arguments take place, you are physically and psychologically close enough to each other so that there is a possibility for real engagement.

Unfortunately, you won't be able to read more of David Souter's comments in this book as he was the only justice to graciously, but explicitly, decline our request to publish the full text of his interview.

As the month progressed, more of Justice Souter's colleagues signaled their willingness to give us interviews. Chief Justice Roberts's promised half hour before our cameras pleasantly turned into fifty minutes; senior Justice John Paul Stevens toured us around his chambers. We accompanied Justice Ruth Bader Ginsburg to her temporary chambers, where she spoke of the challenges of being the lone woman on the Court. Antonin Scalia gave us a lively thirty minutes in which he praised his law clerks and decried a national surplus of lawyers. Sandra Day O'Connor recounted her first oral argument. Clarence Thomas described his travels around the country in a motor home during the Court's summer breaks. Anthony Kennedy talked of the adrenaline rush he still gets from debating cases with his colleagues in conference. In each of these encounters, we got a vivid sense of the justices' personalities, intellects, and love for the institution they serve. Something else became clear as well—all of them spoke of the collegiality that enables the Court to function even through the toughest cases.

The summer was evaporating. While Brian Lamb and I were taping interviews with the justices, Mark Farkas and our colleague Connie Doebele (an earlier court producer in her long C-SPAN career) interviewed individuals who would add their own knowledge of the Court to our production—journalists Joan Biskupic and Lyle Denniston; former Solicitor General Drew Days; attorney and former Rehnquist clerk Maureen Mahoney; the clerk of the Court, General William Suter; and a Court historian, James O'Hara. In time, we had accumulated nearly fifty hours of video and interviews to process into an eighty-five minute documentary. It was time to get into the editing room, and still no word from one serving justice—Samuel Alito.

The day we were scheduled to interview him, Clarence Thomas happened upon our camera crew as they moved equipment through the Supreme Court's garage and stopped to talk. "How's it going?" he inquired. Mark Farkas brought him up to date, then explained that we'd managed to book every justice but Alito. "Let me talk with him and see what I can do," Thomas promised. Soon thereafter, we received word that Justice Alito would, indeed, participate.

And even as we taped, the Court was changing. In mid-July, the Senate Judiciary Committee convened to consider Sonia Sotomayor's nomination to replace Justice Souter. The fifty-five-year-old New York judge would be the Court's third female and first Hispanic American member. If she was confirmed, we knew we'd have to find a way to incorporate the newest justice into our project. Events broke our way: Justice Sotomayor was confirmed by the Senate on August 6 and sworn in by Chief Justice Roberts two days later. Breaking with tradition, the Court was set to convene in early September to rehear arguments in an important campaign finance case. Justice Sotomayor would participate early in her first oral argument. Kathy Arberg agreed to forward our interview request to the new justice just one day after her investiture on the Court.

On September 16, Justice Sotomayor walked through the doors of the Court's West Conference Room, where our cameras and lights were set up and waiting. Making her way to our set, she smilingly shook hands with each member of our production team, then settled into her chair. She made a number of interesting observations over the next thirty minutes, but none of us will forget her recounting "for history" the story of her call from President Obama in which he asked her to serve on the Supreme Court:

> I actually stood by my balcony doors, and I had my cell phone in my right hand, and I had my left hand over my chest trying to calm my beating heart, literally. And the president got on the phone and said to me, "Judge, I would like to announce you as my selection to be the next associate justice of the United States Supreme Court."
>
> And I said to him—I caught my breath and started to cry and said, "Thank you, Mr. President."

We hurried back to C-SPAN with our completed interview. With just days to go, the finishing touches were added to the documentary, which debuted on C-SPAN on Sunday, October 4, 2009.

In thirty-one years of operation, C-SPAN has been granted numerous interviews with presidents, top congressional leaders, and heads of state, yet this project stands apart in its significance. In part this is due to the Court's traditional lack of exposure. Even more, it is the result of access uniquely granted to us by the chief justice and his current and former colleagues. The uniqueness of this opportunity guaranteed that no part of our interviews with the justices would end up on the cutting room floor. To the contrary, all of these judicial and personal portraits aired in their entirety. Each is permanently archived on our video library at www.c-span.org, enabling students of the Court to use them for generations.

We have many thank-yous to deliver, most importantly to Chief Justice John Roberts and his chief of staff Jeff Minnear; to the current and retired associate justices, along with the journalists, Court officials, and former government officials who sat for interviews; to Kathy Arberg and Patricia McCabe Estrada in the Public Information Office and their colleagues Scott Markley, Lauren Ray, Ella Hunter, and Cory Maggio; to Supreme Court Curator Catherine Fitts, and her staff, including Associate Curator Matthew Hofstedt, who tirelessly checked facts and provided rare photographs for our television production and this book. Thanks also to the marshal of the Court, Pamela Talkin, and the many Court security, administration, and technical personnel under her supervision who aided various aspects of our production.

Dozens of people inside our own network contributed to this ambitious undertaking in many aspects of production and marketing/communications. Rick Stoddard was Mark Farkas's partner throughout the production and along with Anna Caulder did most of the editing. As always, Terry Murphy, our vice president of programming, provided a steady hand on the tiller; Bruce Collins, our counsel, lent his special expertise to the project; Rob Kennedy, our co-COO, ensured that the infrastructure was there to make these projects happen. Others at C-SPAN aided greatly with editorial and production issues for this book, most notably Amy Spolrich and Molly Murchie. While space prohibits a full listing of the many fellow C-SPANners involved with various aspects of *The Supreme Court*, their professional contributions and ongoing collegiality are greatly appreciated.

Finally, let me express our thanks to the cable television companies who founded C-SPAN in 1979 and which continue to support our non-commercial operations through affiliate fees and carriage on their cable systems. This summer, industry leader Bob Miron, the guiding light of AdvanceNewhouse Communications, wraps up three years as the chairman of C-SPAN's Executive Committee. Thank you, Bob, for sharing our vision of cable's possibilities, and for being there every time we needed you. That's one verdict that is unanimous.

Susan Swain
January 2010
Washington, DC

PART ONE

THE JUSTICES

CHIEF JUSTICE
JOHN ROBERTS

*C*hief Justice John G. Roberts Jr. was appointed as the 109th member *and chief justice of the United States Supreme Court by President George W. Bush in 2005. After attending Harvard Law School, he clerked for Chief Justice William Rehnquist, served as special assistant to the attorney general, and associate counsel to President Ronald Reagan. He later returned to the Justice Department as principal deputy solicitor general followed by years in private practice. George W. Bush appointed him to the United States Court of Appeals for the District of Columbia Circuit where he served until his appointment to the Supreme Court. Chief Justice Roberts was interviewed by Susan Swain on June 19, 2009, in the Court's East Conference Room.*

SWAIN: Chief Justice Roberts, as we sit in this room today surrounded by some of the famous people who were in this Court before, I'd like to start with some of the history of the Court. The Court today is a modern court. How much is it like the Court that the framers envisioned?

CHIEF JUSTICE JOHN ROBERTS: I think it is in many respects: It's still, as they envisioned, one of the three branches of government under Article III, but I think it's fair to say it plays a much more important role in society and in government than they may have expected. [Consider that] they envisioned a White House for the president, a Capitol building for Congress, but didn't give any thought at all to where the Supreme Court should be based. And for the immediate future, the Court was based in a boardinghouse and then in the basement of the Capitol, which doesn't seem suitable for one of the three co-equal branches of government. But as the Court's responsibilities expanded, it eventually got this beautiful building of its own.

q: As you look along the course of your predecessors, who were the most important in shaping the Court over the years, to become the Court that we know today?

ROBERTS: Well, of course, there's one that stands out above all the rest. We call him the "Great Chief," and that's John Marshall. He really was the first person to take the job seriously. Most lawyers, I think, have this image of him as the first chief, but he wasn't. He was the fourth. The three before him, though—each only served for a couple of years—didn't regard the Court as an important institution. In fact, they spent most of their time doing other things. The first chief justice, John Jay, of course, is most famous for a treaty he negotiated with the English. But John Marshall saw the role of the chief justice and the Court quite differently. He took the job seriously. He served in it for three decades, and he's responsible for establishing the principle that the Court has the authority and the responsibility to review acts of Congress for constitutionality. So he really established the Court in a prominent position as one of the three co-equal branches of government.

q: Among modern chief justices who are the most influential?

ROBERTS: My immediate predecessor, Chief Justice Rehnquist, of course, served also for an extended period, and I think he had a great influence on how the Court looked at legal questions. Earl Warren is

Portrait of the "Great Chief" John Marshall in the Court's East Conference Room.

famous for bringing the Court together and deciding one of its most important decisions, *Brown v. Board of Education*. I think the two of them would have to stand out among the modern chiefs.

Q: How many justices did the earliest courts have?

ROBERTS: I think they started with six, if my memory serves, and it's an interesting thing. It was hard to bring them together early on. The very first session of the Court that John Jay convened had to be adjourned immediately because they didn't have a quorum. I think the second time they convened they did some administrative business then adjourned pretty quickly because they didn't have any cases. So it took a while for the Court to get established. The current number of nine was established—I think—shortly after the Civil War, and it has remained intact since then.

Q: Not without some trying, on the part of Franklin Roosevelt, to make it a bit larger. Do you ever reflect, as you watch the Court and the justices interact, on how it might have functioned if the "court-packing" idea, as it's called, worked?

ROBERTS: Well, it wouldn't have functioned at all, frankly, as a check on the other branches of government. It's an extraordinary episode.

Franklin Roosevelt came into office with huge majorities. He had huge majorities in the Senate and in the House, and the Court wasn't in a very popular position then. It was blocking all of his reforms, reforms that most in the country thought were absolutely critical. He came up with the "court packing plan," allowing him to appoint new justices on the Court—a good number immediately and more over time—in order to get a court that would rule in his favor.

And yet, even with his popularity, the country rose up against it, and the plan really didn't get off the ground. I think the public recognized the importance of having the Court as an independent check on the other branches of government, even if the Court was very unpopular, as it certainly was at that time.

Q: Today, with all of the visibility of the two other branches of government, the Court, I think it's fair to say, is less known by the public than the other two branches. So I'd like to have you talk a bit about what people should understand about the role of this Court in modern society.

ROBERTS: I think the most important thing for the public to understand is that we are not a political branch of government. They don't elect us. If they don't like what we're doing, it's more or less just too bad—other than impeachment, which has never happened, or a conviction on impeachment. It has never happened with the Court. So they need to understand that when we reach a decision, it's based on the law and not a policy preference. For example, if we reach an environmental decision that comes out in favor of environmental groups, you often read in the paper, "Court rules in favor of environmental group," or "Court supports environmental protection." All we're doing is interpreting the law. The decision has been made by Congress and the president. We're just exercising our responsibility to say what the law is; we're not ruling in favor of one side or in favor of another. I think that's very important for the public to appreciate.

Q: What's the role of a modern chief justice?

ROBERTS: Well, in many respects, it's not terribly different from the role of an associate justice. I just have one vote, just as my colleagues do. The chief's responsibility is to preside at oral arguments and also to preside at the conference where the justices vote on and decide the cases. That means I get to initiate the discussion, and I have some responsibility to make sure that all the issues are adequately aired at conference.

My most important responsibility is the responsibility for assigning opinions, once the votes are in. If I'm in the majority, I get to determine who will write the opinion in that case. And that's a very important responsibility because you want to make sure that the assignment is given to the justice whose view commands the most support on the Court. You want to make sure the work gets done on time, so if someone's a little slower than the others, you make sure that person gets assignments, heavy assignments, earlier on. Some cases are more interesting than others. You want to make sure those are fairly distributed. Some cases are harder than others. You want to make sure that's fairly distributed. We get all sorts of different issues. You want to make sure each justice has a nice mix. You don't want one justice just doing criminal cases or something like that. So a lot of factors go into that decision.

The chief justice is the head of the Judicial Conference, which sets policy for the federal judiciary throughout the country, and that also is a very important responsibility. And then the chief justice has very odd responsibilities that don't seem to have anything to do with being chief justice. I'm automatically chancellor of the Smithsonian, for example. So over the past couple of years I have been learning a good bit about museums and research institutions.

Q: Are you also, more or less, the CEO of "Supreme Court, Inc."? I mean, are you responsible for this place and its budget and the people who work here?

ROBERTS: Theoretically, yes. The Supreme Court, from one perspective, is like a small government agency. We have a police and security force of almost one hundred people, for example. We have visitors, and sometimes they slip on the steps. We have to worry about things like that. We have to get a budget to run the Court, but I have very capable people who know a lot more about that kind of thing and help me discharge that responsibility.

Q: Every year, we do see the process by which justices go before the Congress to request the budget. It always is an interesting example of how the branches function. What are your thoughts about that step in the process?

ROBERTS: The Framers appreciated that it's very important that the political branches have control over the purse, how money is spent. In one respect, we're no different than anyone else. We have to go to Congress, hat in hand, and get our budget. As you say, though, it's always a very interesting process. We don't ask for much. We have a very little burden on the federal fisc, but we have to go ask for it, and, when we do, probably because we don't ask for much, the members of Congress have very little interest in budget issues. They view it as an opportunity, I think, to get some of the justices before them. We hear a lot about their views on cases that are before us or cases that we've decided.

Q: And this building itself, let's spend a little bit of time on that because you mentioned that the Court used to be housed in the Capitol itself, which is just across the street from here. What do you think of this place as a building among all the monumental buildings in Washington?

ROBERTS: I may be biased. I think it's the prettiest building in Washington, and it's distinctive. Obviously the Capitol is the grand building, and the White House is the one that most people know about and see on the news. But the Supreme Court building is distinctive. It's a different type of marble, to start with, much brighter, much lighter than the typical government building, which I think is wonderful because immediately, as soon as you see it, you appreciate that this is something different.

It represents that the Court is a different branch of the government, and it really is more monumental. It looks a lot more like the Jefferson Memorial or the Lincoln Memorial in terms of its visual impact, than it looks like another government building. And if you view it as something of a temple of justice, I think that's entirely appropriate.

Q: When it was built in 1935, it was pretty controversial, I understand. Many people have opinions about this building and whether it was appropriate for the Court and the like. When you walk around here, do you think it suits the work that's done here?

ROBERTS: I do. It was a part of a controversy, I think, because it's a grand-looking building, and I'm not sure at the time, in 1935, people thought that type of monumental structure was appropriate. But I do think it's suitable to the notion that here we're not involved in the political process. We are applying the law. The thing that makes our system of government unique is that it's bound by the rule of law, by a written constitution that lawyers, judges have to interpret. So you need to appreciate that something different is going on here than what goes on in the Capitol building or in the White House, and you need to appreciate how important it is to our system of government. Yes, the political branches and the fact that we're a democracy are vitally important, but we're a democracy under law, and in that respect very different from most countries in the world, even those that properly claim that they're democracies as well.

Q: Is its proximity to the Capitol appropriate?

ROBERTS: Perhaps the fact that it's across the street is appropriate. We often refer to that in oral argument, for example, when someone makes what sounds like a political or policy argument, we'll say, "That's something that you should bring across the street."

We are three co-equal branches of government, but obviously there's interaction between us. I think it's very appropriate that we can see the Capitol right across the street, and I think it's very appropriate that they can see us—that we understand that they have responsibility for the policy matters, that that's their job. And they need to understand, as well, that our job is to interpret the Constitution and the law.

Q: Is there communication between you and senior leaders of Congress?

ROBERTS: Well, yes, on a casual basis. We obviously see each other [at events] around Washington and get to know each other on that basis and, of course, as you mentioned earlier, during the budget process. We've got to get money from them, but other than that we communicate very little, to be honest with you. Our job is not to help them as they develop policy, and they don't have a role in helping us as we try to interpret what the law is. We have friendships across the street, but our jobs are very different.

Q: What about that great plaza in front of the Supreme Court, the site of so many public protests over the years? What are your thoughts about the design of the building that has allowed all of that wide public space in the front?

ROBERTS: Well, I'm not sure [architect Cass] Gilbert intended it to be a convenient site for protests, and I'm pretty sure [Chief Justice William Howard] Taft, who was heavily involved in the design and architecture of it, didn't intend it for that purpose either. It is a lovely introduction to the Court.

The protest point you bring up is very interesting. I understand people having strong feelings about some of the things that we do. But it's not a situation where our decisions should be guided by popular

William Howard Taft,
chief justice 1921–1930.
*Collection of the Supreme
Court of the United States.*

pressure. The protests, to some extent, are there as a way for people to express their feelings, but they shouldn't be directed at us. You would not want us deciding what the Constitution means based on what the popular feeling is. Quite often, and many of our most famous decisions are ones that the Court took that were quite unpopular, and the idea that we should yield to what the public protest is, is quite foreign to what it means to have a country under the rule of law.

Q: But are you cognizant of the protests, when the big ones occur?

ROBERTS: Well, sure. You're coming in to work in the morning. You can see that there are a lot of people gathered outside the Court, and you suspect they're not just there to hear a case that happens to be on the docket. But justices appreciate that it's not part of their job to be swayed by popular sentiment.

Q: Let's talk about your interaction with the public as a whole. Justice [Stephen] Breyer told us in our discussion with him, that in the years he has been here the number of tourists has declined from about a million a year to possibly even half that; some of it due to the construction, some of it to the decrease in tourism after September 11. Do you think the Court is visited as much as it should be by the American public? And does the Court actively work to get people here?

ROBERTS: I think everybody who has the opportunity to do so here in Washington should come by and visit the Court. It is an important part of how our Constitution functions and how the government operates, just as important as [what goes on in] the White House and the Capitol. We're kind of tucked away behind the Capitol, but our role in the Constitution is just as vital, so I think people who do come to Washington should visit it. I suspect that the decline is, as you suggested, due more to things like a decline in tourism after 9/11.

We are going through a renovation project. It's the first one in seventy years. It's basically updating. We haven't done anything since 1935. At the time, it was a very big deal that there were going to be telephones in the building, and of course there's so much more in terms of electronic and modern technology. You have to have the infrastructure behind the walls for that sort of thing. Some of it's security-related, I'm sorry to have to say, making sure that things are safer against any type of intrusion. And there is general updating, the usual HVAC stuff as well.

Q: Do you ever run into tourists as you're walking around the building?

ROBERTS: Sure, all the time.

Q: Do they recognize you?

ROBERTS: Sometimes they do, and sometimes they don't. Sometimes they'll stop you, and I'm always interested to find out where they're from. There are a couple of routes around the building when I need to get from my chambers to some other place and [the public areas are] the quickest way. I'm always happy to see that people are here taking a good look at what we do.

Q: How often are you recognized as you travel?

ROBERTS: Oh, it varies with where I am. If I'm going to visit a law school, for example, I'll be recognized a little bit more than if I'm on a family vacation.

Q: Let's move on to the process of how the Court functions throughout the year. You gave us a brief synopsis of it, but I'd like to spend time going into detail, starting with when the Court opens. Basically, give us a bit of a civics lesson on the operation of the Court throughout the year. The Court is about to close, so I'm going to fast-forward to the opening of the new session. Start us on the process of cases coming before the Court and how it all works.

ROBERTS: We get a lot of cases that people want us to hear. Everybody remembers somebody saying, "I'm going to take it all the way to the Supreme Court." I think there are about nine thousand of those cases in the year that we're just concluding. We only hear about one hundred of them, so a big part of our job is going through those nine thousand and trying to figure out what the important cases are. And before we start our term—traditionally as common law courts around the world do, we start on the first Monday in October—we have a long session where we go through those petitions and try to figure out which ones we want to hear. It's an interesting process. We don't just look at the cases that we think are wrong. We don't look at the cases where we think have a lot at stake. Our main job is to try to make sure federal law is uniform across the country. So if you have a lower federal court in California that decides a question one way and the lower federal court in New York decides the same question the other way, we'll pick that kind of case out of a pile and say, "We ought to decide that."

Q: There's a lot more detail in that process, which is called granting *cert*, right?

ROBERTS: *Certiorari*, yes. It's an old Roman law term that people call *cert*, and nobody's quite sure what it means, but that's what has come down from history.

Q: Do you know the history of the starting on the first Monday in October? You mentioned it has a long tradition.

ROBERTS: I don't really know. The courts used to have several terms. We now have one term we call the October term, but I know they used to have the February term and they would take breaks, I suspect, when they had to go travel on circuit as the early justices did. But now we've all condensed it into one. It's called the October term.

Q: The number of cases that you cited, the ones that are petitioned and the ones that are granted, the proportion of that seems to have changed over the past twenty years. There are more requests, fewer granted. Why is that?

ROBERTS: Well the more requests, I think, just comes from the increase in judicial business throughout the country. The fewer granted reflects the growing importance of the Court in the constitutional system. It may seem counterintuitive, the more important, the fewer cases, but in fact early in its history the Court viewed itself as responsible for deciding every case that came up.

In the nineteenth century, for example, most of the cases were admiralty cases, so you pick up the reports and you see hundreds and hundreds of admiralty cases. But as the Court started to have a more important role, they tended to focus on the more important cases for the constitutional system and leave it up to the lower federal courts, basically, to try to get each individual case right. We had a different responsibility.

Chief justices have come from countries around the world and visited here and they've said, "We can't do important work the way you do because we have to decide three thousand cases a year." They spend a lot of time pushing paper and making sure individual cases that don't have a lot of impact are correctly decided. We don't. We try to focus on the ones that are going to be important for how our system of government functions.

Q: And what is the actual role of each individual justice in making the decision about the eighty or up to one hundred that might be heard?

ROBERTS: Well, each one gets a vote, just like anything else, on what cases we should hear, but it only takes four votes to grant *cert* and decide that we're going to hear a case. The Court used to have a lot more mandatory jurisdiction, cases they had to hear. And when they got Congress to pass a law saying that we didn't have to hear all the cases and it wasn't mandatory jurisdiction, the deal we made with the Hill was that you didn't need five votes to hear a case. Four would be enough. The idea is that if four people think we ought to hear a case, we'll hear it, even if it comes out that only four think it should come out the same way.

Q: How much reading do you do on each one of those cases before you vote?

ROBERTS: Well, as you might imagine, not a lot. Nine thousand cases, if we did a lot of reading on each one, we wouldn't have time to do anything else. Our law clerks help us. They write memos on each of those petitions. We look at them. You develop a pretty good eye for what kind you ought to look at more carefully, so that's what I do. I look at the memos, and I'll say, "Well, this one we ought to look at more carefully," and we do that before deciding how to vote on them.

Q: How many clerks do you have?

ROBERTS: Four. I think all the justices have four now.

Q: None extra as chief?

ROBERTS: No. I think I'm entitled to an extra one, but four seems to be about the right number.

Q: And when you are making those decisions, do you instinctively know which ones are going to be the blockbusters of the Court session?

ROBERTS: Well, sure. You can tell if there's a case that's on a particular hot button issue that people are going to give it a lot of attention, but I have to say that doesn't enter into our process of deciding. A lot of our docket is very mundane. You go through the year and say, "We're deciding ninety cases; probably a half dozen are ones that are going to make it to the front page of the newspaper." All of the others are a bankruptcy tax case, a Federal Arbitration Act case, a pension plan case. Those are a big part of our docket, all vitally important, but not anything that's going to attract any interest.

Q: With the scope of work before you, the number of cases that you have to make the go/no go decision about, do you ever pause to think about how many lives are being changed by that "no" decision—"No, we're not going to hear that"?

ROBERTS: Sure. Those are the people who said at some point, "This is so important to me, I'm going to take it all the way to the Supreme Court." And you realize it's the end of the road.

When I practiced law, that was a big part of my job—trying to get the Supreme Court to take my clients' cases, and it's a very sad thing to have to call somebody and say, "Look, they're not even going to hear your arguments. It's not going to get in through the door." But by the time a case reaches the Supreme Court, the litigants have had at least two chances to persuade a court that they're right, in the federal system, sometimes more in the state systems. So, as we put it in legal terms, we are not a court of error. It's not our job to correct every one of those nine thousand cases. We couldn't do it and maintain our position as one of the three branches of government.

Q: In those cases when there are human beings' lives involved, do you ever get letters from people after the fact, when you've made the decision that come to your office?

ROBERTS: I don't get many. Maybe they don't send them in to me, but I haven't seen many. We get correspondence, and I like to look at it, not all of it. Again, most of it is screened, but when you get a nice letter from somebody who has visited the Court from grade school or something like that and they have something to say, you like to respond when you can, even though you can't do it very often.

Q: Now, once the decision is made that X number of cases will be heard in a term, how is the schedule of when they will be heard allocated across the calendar, the timetable for the oral arguments?

ROBERTS: It's a rolling admissions process. When something comes in that we grant, it fills up the next open slot on the calendar, so cases we decide to grant right before October aren't going to be heard in October. They're going to be heard later in the term.

The cases we're going to hear at the beginning were granted the previous spring, so that's how they get assigned to the calendar. The clerk is responsible for that, and he'll allocate them and come in and ask if it is all right, and it almost always is.

Q: Oral argument, the part that people most associate with the Court, how does it work?

ROBERTS: First of all, we'll talk later, I assume, about briefing, which is important, but once all the briefing is done, a case is scheduled for oral argument. Most cases have an hour per case, a half hour per side.

Chief Justice John Roberts in his July 2009 C-SPAN interview.

When you tell that to people they say, "Is that all?" And when you look at some of the other common law jurisdictions, they have a lot more, but a lot of the argument has been laid out in writing. Lawyers are not expected, and even if they expect to, are not going to have the chance to get up and give a speech. A lot of the argument, most of the argument, is devoted to justices' questions. We've read the arguments. We've read the opinions. "You've said this, but what about this? You haven't talked about this case. What about that? You say this is what the record shows about the facts. Well, what about this?"

It's a very, very intense period of questioning. Each of the justices has their own unique style of questioning. We have some people who like the rapid-fire style, others who like to spin out long hypotheticals. It's a real challenge for the lawyers, not only just to answer the questions but to try to do their job of moving the ball in the right direction and defending their clients' interests. It's a part of the process I thoroughly enjoy, because it does give you a lot of interaction with the bar, and through the lawyers, interaction with each other.

It's the first time we learn what our colleagues think about a case. We don't sit down before argument and say, "This is what we think" or "This is how I view the case." We come to it cold as far as knowing what everybody thinks. So through the questioning we're learning for the first time what the other justices' views are of the case. And that can alter how you view it, right on the spot. If they're raising questions about an issue that you hadn't thought were important, you can start looking into that issue during the questioning a little bit. It's a very dynamic and very exciting part of the job.

Q: So you need to listen very intently.

ROBERTS: Very carefully, not only to the questions but to what the lawyers are saying. Their answer might cause you to focus on another issue, appreciating that there's going to be another side of the case as soon as that person's half hour is over. There's a lot going on.

Q: It sounds as if the justices are really communicating with one another through the questions.

ROBERTS: It can be that way sometimes, and this is where you get the justices acting as a devil's advocate. If I think that the lawyer has a good answer to a question that appears to be concerning one of my colleagues, I might ask an aggressive question that looks like I'm hostile. But I know he or she is going to come up with a good answer that might help respond to that other justice's concern.

Q: You mentioned that each justice approaches oral argument with their own style. What's yours?

ROBERTS: I guess it's more the repeated questions, trying to probe a particular point. I don't usually spin out long hypotheticals, maybe because I didn't like them when I was a lawyer, having to answer them. But it's different some other times. If I have a particular view of the case that I think the lawyer ought to have an opportunity to respond to—if my thinking has developed to that level at that point—I might do more of a spinning out, saying, "Counsel, this is how I see the case: You were relying on this statute, but there's this precedent that goes the other way, and this is how you distinguish the precedent. What's your answer to that?" And, hopefully, that lawyer will have an answer; or if not, I'll appreciate the significance of that. But most of the time, it's more rapid fire. Not as much as some of my other colleagues because I like to try to get the lawyer to deal with the particular issue and not say, "Here is a general question." Because he or she will have thought . . . of a good answer to that. You try to throw them off balance a little bit.

Q: You have the particular experience of having been on the other side of the bench, and I am wondering what the difference is. What's the experience like arguing cases before the Court versus your role now?

ROBERTS: Well, it's a lot easier to ask questions than answer them. The big difference is that there is a wonderful Supreme Court Bar and you run into your competitors, both on your side and against you, on a regular basis. But it's still a competition. You still win or lose, as a lawyer, and you still either have to call the client and say, "I am sorry," or call a client and say, "Hurray." And that competitive edge enters into how you approach the job.

It's nothing like that on the bench. Obviously, we have majorities and we have dissents, but I don't think any of us view that as winning or losing, and there is no competitive edge to it. I am very grateful that I had the opportunity to be on both sides of the bench, because they're very different experiences.

Q: Do you remember your first oral argument?

ROBERTS: Oh, sure, yes, absolutely. It was a case called *United States v. Halper.* I was very nervous. But I was very nervous when I did my last oral argument as well. I think if you are a lawyer appearing before the Supreme Court and you're not very nervous, you don't really understand what's going on.

Q: This question is for all the members of the bar out there and for all those attorneys who eventually find themselves lucky enough to have a case before the Court. What is it that you wish you had known about the process when you were on that side that you now know?

ROBERTS: Everybody tells a lawyer in that position, "You have to answer the questions. Don't try to avoid the questions or distinguish your case in any way." And I hope I did that when I was a lawyer. The importance of that is very accentuated. I appreciate it so much more now that I am on the other side of the bench. You have to appreciate that the justices are engaged in the process of trying to help themselves decide the case correctly. So they are going to ask hard questions. They're going ask questions that don't put your case in the best possible light, and you need to appreciate that.

It's good to establish—and I think I didn't appreciate this as much as I should have—some dispassion. Yes, you want to have a certain level of zeal and commitment to your client's cause. The justices know that. But when they ask you a question about a difficult case, it's better to sometimes say, "I appreciate that that case doesn't support my side. I appreciate that that causes us some difficulty. Here is why I think you shouldn't rely so heavily on that case." As opposed to, as soon as we ask, saying, "No, that case doesn't hurt us at all, and here is why." The justices like you to be part of the process that is helping them come to the right result. They understand that you've got a client to represent, and they expect you to do that. But if you can convince them that you're on their side and helping them reach the right decision, as opposed to something that they have to push against to get you to give an answer, I think that's very helpful, not only to the Court but also to your client.

Q: Do you ever change your mind, listening?

ROBERTS: All the time. Partly because you don't make up your mind before you go into the courtroom. It's a continuous process of narrowing your decision window. When you pick up the first brief, the blue brief—they are all color coordinated—you don't have much of an idea how you think it should come out. When you finish it, you say,

"Well, those are good arguments." You pick up the red brief on the other side, and you see that there's another side to the story. You sit down with law clerks and talk about the case: "What do you think about this?" Again, you're moving toward a particular decision. You read the cases that might help; sometimes, it causes you to go the other way. Based on the briefs you're going this way, but you read the cases, and you're going this way. Based on your own thoughts, you're going one way; based on discussions, bouncing ideas off law clerks, you move another way.

So you go into argument not with a totally blank slate, but you've moved a little bit back and forth, and you're more leaning one way than another, but you've got all these questions. How are they going to come out? You learned that others of your colleagues viewed this part of the case as more significant than you may have thought. So, you change your mind as "maybe"—and that happens sometimes too. You begin by saying, "I'm pretty sure I am going to do this," but you end up the other way. It's more a question of helping you get to the point of decision. And then you go to conference, and you talk about it with your colleagues, and that may cause you to move in an entirely different direction.

Q: When cases are argued by the Solicitor General or representatives of the Justice Department, do you have a different mindset about the government because of the co-equal branches and your role as the Court versus the administration?

ROBERTS: No, not at all. When I was a private lawyer I argued against the government. They had very good lawyers, but I thought they were wrong a lot of times, and this was my opportunity to show that. That's really one of the most remarkable things about the process. The government of the United States is one of the most powerful forces in the world, and it has a particular view. And all I have to do, representing just say, one little individual, is convince five lawyers that the government is wrong, and that little individual will win. The government will have to accede. That's an extraordinary thing. It doesn't happen in very many places around the world. It hasn't happened in very many places throughout our history. That's what people mean when they talk about the rule of law. So, the idea that I'm going to, as a justice, defer more to what the government lawyer thinks is inconsistent with the whole process.

Q: Just walk through a typical day when oral arguments are heard. How it is scheduled, and how do you go about it?

ROBERTS: Sure. As I said, the argument process is perhaps more important for me since I had the experience on the other side. It's an exciting part of the process. I'm going to learn what my colleagues think about a case that I've been studying for a long time. For the very first time, I'm going to hear what the lawyers have to say. So it's an exciting day. I tend to get here a little earlier, around 7:30 a.m. That gives me a little more time to go over some last minute things. I will call in the law clerk who has worked on the case just to bounce off some last-minute ideas. I'll say, "What's the problem with this; what's the problem with that; how do you understand this case?" I'll look over the briefs with my notes one last time. And then shortly before argument, we go to the Robing Room. We put on our robes. We meet in our Conference Room, which is right behind the courtroom. We carry on the tradition established by Chief Justice Melville Fuller, more than one hundred years ago: we shake each others' hands before we go into the bench. And we line up outside the bench; we go in. We announce any opinions that we have to announce. We announce any orders that we have to announce. If there are members of the bar or lawyers who hope to be admitted to the bar—we go through that process as well. And then we're off and running. It's exhilarating for me, as I think it is for the lawyers involved.

Q: When you walk out with your colleagues, do you converse about the argument you just heard?

ROBERTS: No. It's, I think, informal protocol; we don't talk about the case. We go to lunch. By then it's lunchtime.

Q: Together?

ROBERTS: Yes, usually. If somebody has a commitment outside the Court, they're not there. But usually on an argument day, most of the justices are there in our dining room. And it is the rule there that we don't talk about the cases.

Q: So what do you talk about?

ROBERTS: My colleagues, who go to the opera, we'll talk about the opera. Some of us will talk about the baseball game or the golf tournament. Somebody will talk about a good movie they've seen or a good book they've read, something particularly interesting their family is doing—the kind of things everybody would talk about at lunch with colleagues.

Q: And then you would hear another case in the afternoon?

ROBERTS: Sometimes we do now. Sometimes we have three cases scheduled. It's usually two cases in the morning. In the fall, it's often three. In the spring, usually two, because we try to frontload the work, so that we can get started on opinions earlier and then spend more time in the spring getting them out.

Q: Talk about the process in conference, please.

ROBERTS: We sit at the conference table in the same places everyday. I sit at one end. Justice Stevens, who is the most senior of the associate justices sits at the other end, and then it wraps around the table in order of seniority. We go in. We sit down. If it's a non-argument day, we have conferences on Fridays when we don't hear argument. We'll shake each other's hand again.

Q: What's the importance of the handshake, do you think?

ROBERTS: I think it's to reaffirm that we're a collegial court, that we're involved in the same process. We've all read the same briefs, read the same cases, are going to hear the same arguments. Sometimes we have very sharp disagreements on matters of great importance to the country we all love, and the handshake shows that we're all involved in the same process, which I think is vitally important.

I initiate the discussion for an argued case. I'll say, "This case is about this. The arguments are so and so, and I think we should reverse or affirm, and here is why." Sometimes in an easy case it will take a minute. In a hard case, it can take a lot longer. Then it goes in seniority. So Justice Stevens would go next. He might say, "I agree with everything, Chief," which is nice. Or he might say, "I disagree. I think it should come out the other way, and here is why." Or he might say, "I agree with the result, but I think the reasoning should be this."

And then it goes on all around. Justice Scalia is next, then Justice Kennedy, Justice Souter, then Justice Thomas, Ginsburg, Breyer, and Alito. It goes around in that direction. And there is a tentative vote as we discuss it: "I think, as I talk about the case, I think it should be reversed," and so on. We keep track of that. And if there is more discussion needed, we have more discussion.

A fundamental rule that helps things work out well is this: Nobody speaks twice until everyone has spoken once. Once everyone has spoken, then we decide if there is a need for more discussion. Sometimes there is; sometimes there isn't. Sometimes we have a lot more discussion and don't seem to be getting anywhere. And at that point, I will say, "We'll work it out in the writing," which means there'll be memos about the case later on, about how we should decide it. I try to make sure that the issues are fully discussed and that both sides have an opportunity, if there are two sides, to get their views out.

Q: You had talked earlier about how you allocate opinions, being fair and giving people different experiences. When do you decide to write it yourself?

ROBERTS: It's a tough part of the job. Obviously, there are good cases, and I'd like to take them all. But you have to be fair. And I'm very conscious of the need to take my fair share of the cases that aren't interesting, my fair share of the ones that are hard, my fair share of the ones that are good and interesting. But it's a hard part of the job.

Q: How do you approach the process of writing opinions?

ROBERTS: I, first of all, do it longhand. I think I was just a couple years too late going through college and law school; the technological revolution was slightly behind me, so I never really learned. I can do it, but I never really learned how to write on the computer. I write out longhand. I have law clerks help if there is something I think they could write part of, saying, "I feel comfortable with this, so you go ahead and draft something up." I will then heavily edit that. If it's a new area that I don't feel I know about, I try to do that myself to make sure I'm getting it right. I like to do a lot of the facts myself, because I think they're very important. And certainly I don't put the opinion to bed until I feel comfortable that it's my work.

It's an ongoing process. You write a first draft. You figure out, "Well, I need to know a little bit more about how this case fits in." You go back and read the case. You're always going back and looking at the briefs, always bringing the law clerks in and bouncing ideas off of them: "What's wrong with it?" It's sort of the continuation of the oral argument process: "What's wrong with this? What's the answer to that?"

And sometimes, memoranda go around to the other justices before that [might say] "At conference, I said this is the reason; as I've gotten more deeply into it, I don't think that's the right basis for decision. I'm going to write the opinion this way," just so they're alerted to that. I like to do a lot of different drafts. Twenty drafts, twenty-five drafts, it's not unusual, changing one thing in one draft and changing something else, sometimes changing it back, and then changing it back again. I like the writing process, so I enjoy that.

When you're ready to send it out to the toughest critics in the world, your colleagues, that's what you do. It's printed up nicely, which always makes it look more authoritative, but it doesn't work with them. They are not restrained on commenting on things that are . . . if they think a particular analysis is different and they want to go that way, they'll send a detailed memorandum about it. Sometimes, it's fine except they say, "I don't like this footnote or I don't like this paragraph" or "Don't cite that case; I don't think it's right." And you make those accommodations if necessary to get their support.

Obviously, if you are just starting out and someone says, "I would like you to change this or that," you're going to be very receptive. When you get eight votes and the ninth one comes in, saying, "Change this or that," you often say, "Well, you know . . ."

Q: "I'm there already."

ROBERTS: Not quite, "Go fly a kite," but the fifth vote is a more critical one. You're more susceptible to making changes than the ninth vote.

Q: What about those 5–4 cases and the process of dissent? Can you talk through, knowing that this is going to be a 5–4 decision, how much extra time you might spend on writing the opinion, crafting the opinion? What's the value of the dissent in that process?

ROBERTS: I don't think I spend more time on a case that I know is going to be 5–4. Whether you got 9–nothing, or something that looks like it's going to be 5–4, it's an opinion that's going to show up in those bound books on judges' and lawyers' shelves and . . .

Q: You're cognizant of that, as you're writing?

ROBERTS: I'm very cognizant of that. Now, dissent is a very valuable part of our process. It shows the thinking of different parts of the Court. It shows that arguments have been fully considered, and it's valuable for the writer of the majority, because we have a healthy degree of skepticism about what we're saying up to the very end. So it's good to see those fleshed out.

Obviously, you don't like it when somebody disagrees with you. But in some cases, that can be very important. Now, not in every case. And, you hope to be able to persuade people. I think it's a good thing if we talk about cases and send memos around and try to come together as much as we can in agreement. But sometimes, we can't do that, and sometimes there is dissent, and you need to respond to it. There is a lot of back and forth. When the dissent comes around, you try to say, "You're wrong about this, this, and this." You try to alter your opinion to, say, "You know, the dissent says this, and here is the answer to that." And sometimes, it goes back and forth a lot. But it's an important part of the process.

Q: Do you ever, as chief, broker dissents that might get too personal?

ROBERTS: I think all of us do. On the court of appeals where I served, a couple of the judges had what I thought was a very good process: When it was all done—and of course, the court of appeals is going to be 2–1—everybody sat down. And the two authors said, "What is there about my opinion that you think is too personal or crosses the line or is not quite right?" And they would say, "Mostly it's taking out adjectives and adverbs." Or maybe somebody says something like, "Oh, the majority ignores this and this." And they didn't ignore it; it's just that they didn't agree that it was important. So you take that out. And [instead you might write:] "The majority is not persuaded by these cases" or something like that.

I thought that was a very good custom. It's not quite so formalized here, but there are times when you sit down with somebody and say, "On reflection, do you really want to be that harsh?" And most of the time, they are surprised, "Oh, I didn't realize that was going to be viewed that way," and they are happy to change it. It's not just me. I think it's all of my colleagues.

Q: Your colleagues had been at this for quite a while when you joined them in the role of chief. What was that transition like for you? How did you get up to speed with the many traditions and operating procedures of conference, so that you felt in command?

ROBERTS: "In command," are the wrong words, and I'm sure my colleagues would correct you on that. It helped that I had been a law clerk here twenty-five years earlier; I had some sense from that how the Court functions.

Q: But you never got to go in that [Conference] room as a law clerk.

ROBERTS: Never. And it helped that I had spent twenty years of my private practice life and in government arguing cases here. You pick up a little bit of a sense about how the Court functions. When I got here, my colleagues were very helpful in filling me in on how things worked—often in contradictory ways. But you do get some sense about what's expected in the process. And then you go in and do it and hold your breath and hope they all don't say at once, "What are you talking about? Why are you doing that?" The real key is that my eight colleagues were extraordinarily helpful in making me feel very comfortable.

Imagine—it's not just that I was coming in as chief and the youngest among the bunch, and in many respects the least experienced as a judge. But they had been together for eleven years without any change. And you can easily imagine that that would be difficult. But every one of them went out of their way to make me feel comfortable in the process, for which I've always been very appreciative.

Q: Let me move to this building, because it's really why we're here, ultimately. When you're here after work is done and you have the opportunity to walk the Court building, where do you most like to go? Where is your place of reflection, or your real sense of history and purpose?

ROBERTS: I like to go sometimes on a quiet night to the conference rooms called the East Conference Room and the West Conference Room—we're not very creative in naming things. The portraits on the walls, eight in one room and eight in the other, are all my predecessors as chief justice. And to some extent you look up at them on the walls with a degree of awe, appreciation for what they've been through. They're probably looking down at me with either bemusement or amazement. But each of them has a special story to tell, not only personally, but with the institution of the Court.

You look up at Marshall and appreciate the importance, for him, of having the Court function as a court. Moving the Court from a situation where each justice wrote his own opinion and instead saying, "No, we're going to have an opinion of the Court," which was vital in establishing the Court in its present form.

Right next to him is Roger Taney, the most unfortunate of my predecessors, the author of the *Dred Scott* decision. And you understand that he saw this great problem in the country of slavery, and he was going to solve it. And this was how he was going to solve it. It was tremendously misguided; it injured the Court for generations to come. So that helps to inform how you look at your own job.

You walk down a little further, and you see Morrison Waite. If you asked one thousand lawyers and law professors, "Who is Morrison Waite?" one of them—maybe a couple of them—would know. That's a good lesson. The job doesn't give you a prominent role or historical significance just because you hold the job.

You look at Melville Fuller, and you understand his role in making sure the Court functioned collegially.

You go into the next room, and you see Charles Evans Hughes, and you recall his vital role in turning back the "court-packing plan." And you think about the importance of the independence of the judiciary and things like that.

Perhaps, I don't do it everyday, don't do it every week, but from time to time, I find [looking at the portraits] a useful reminder of the role of the Court and the role of the chief justice.

Q: Looking at what your predecessors did and how small things like the handshake, for example, can set the tone. Have you instituted changes in the Roberts's Court that help change the way the place functions?

ROBERTS: I don't think so, at least, none that I am aware of. It's hard to say if things have changed when you are not sure about how they were before. So I guess the short answer is none that I'm aware of.

Q: There have only been sixteen people before you to hold this job. When you put your hand on the Bible and took the oath, what was your sense of the responsibilities that you were taking upon yourself?

ROBERTS: That I had an important job to do. I was very grateful that I had eight colleagues. If I had to make all these decisions on my own, I think it would be paralyzing. But we share the burden. We share the responsibilities, and we help each other out in discharging that process.

Obviously I was very excited. We were hearing cases that day. My investiture was in the morning, I had cases right away, and I was anxious to get to work.

Q: As we close here, the Court is in the process of preparing for a new member. Can you give us a sense of what that's like, saying goodbye to an old colleague and not being sure what the process will be like before a new justice is sworn in?

ROBERTS: To some extent, it's unsettling. You quickly get to view the Court as composed of these members, and it becomes hard to think of it as involving anyone else. I suspect it's similar to the way people look at their families: "This is my family; how could it be different?" But you do get new arrivals in both of those situations. It's a tremendous sense of loss.

Justice Souter is just a wonderful colleague in so many different respects, and we will miss him in our deliberations, and we will miss him around the Court. But that's part of the process of the evolution

John Roberts's confirmation hearings, September 12–15, 2005.

of the Court. We will welcome the new member with open arms, and the Court will be richer in the course of history because of the gradual turnover. But you do get used to seeing the same people every day. You get used to having lunch with the same people every day, and it will be an interesting part of the changeover.

Justice White always used to say, "When the Court gets a new member, it changes everything." We move the seats around in the courtroom. The seats are by order of seniority, so there will be a shift there, same in the conference room. But more fundamentally, it can cause you to take a fresh look at how things are decided. The new member is going to have a particular view about how issues should be addressed that may be very different from what we've been following for some time. So it's an exciting part of life at the Court.

Q: And since we are speaking in the summer, does the chief get vacation in the summer time?

ROBERTS: Vacation is the wrong word. Justice Brandeis once said he "could do the twelve months worth of work at the Court in ten months, but he couldn't do it in twelve months." It's good that we get something of a break from each other.

We have work that we continue to do. We continue to pore over those nine thousand petitions that come in. You can't put those off until the fall. You have to keep up with those. We get emergency matters from time to time. But we do get out of Washington; the workload is significantly reduced. I get to spend a little more time with my family than was the case during the sitting.

Q: Well, thank you for spending almost an hour with us, Chief Justice. We appreciate it.

ROBERTS: Thank you, very much.

JUSTICE
JOHN PAUL STEVENS

Nominated by President Gerald Ford, Chicago native and Northwestern Law School alumnus John Paul Stevens was sworn in as the 101st justice in 1975. Today, he is the Court's oldest member and its most senior associate justice. Justice Stevens was interviewed by C-SPAN's Brian Lamb on June 24, 2009, as he gave the network an on-camera tour of his chambers at the Supreme Court.

LAMB: Justice Stevens, what part of your chambers are we in right now?

ASSOCIATE JUSTICE JOHN PAUL STEVENS: We're in the office of two of my law clerks: Lindsay Powell and Damian Williams are working here. I come in a lot and learn about the law from them.

Q: How many law clerks do you have?

STEVENS: Four. Two others are upstairs.

Q: In this room we have some photographs on the wall. One of them in particular seems kind of interesting because you're the only person left on the Supreme Court that served with Warren Burger.

STEVENS: That's correct. I think that was taken the day that Justice O'Connor was sworn in, if I'm not mistaken, taken in the Conference Room that day.

Q: What's the difference between the Court then and the Court now?

STEVENS: Eight different justices make a difference. The eight that were in that picture were all succeeded by my present colleagues.

Q: Is there a difference in the way the Court operates today, and is that determined by the chief justice?

STEVENS: Well, it's determined by how it has been operated over the years; there's much more continuity in the way we do our work than there is change. And there is a change when the new chief justice is presiding at conference. Each chief justice has his own method of presiding at the conference, and the present chief justice is doing an excellent job; there's some virtues that the others didn't have, but that pretty much follow the tradition that's been followed for many years.

Q: We understand that you do about eighty cases a year. Back in those days, were there more? And if there were, why? From your particular perspective, how many cases should you handle a year?

STEVENS: I think that the number we handle a year now is probably about right; maybe we should be up to about one hundred. But there were well over 150 when I started, and that was a very, very heavy workload. There are a number of reasons for the change, one of which is we no longer have the mandatory jurisdiction applied back when Chief Justice Burger was here, so we have more control over our docket than we did then. I think we do a better job, for the most part, in picking cases. Although I think we should take a few more than we do.

Justice John Paul Stevens gives C-SPAN a tour of his chambers.

Q: What is your relationship with the people in this room? And over the years, have you ever counted how many clerks you've had?

STEVENS: Somebody knows, but I don't. But they play a very important role in two or three different ways. One, they review all the *cert* petitions that come in, and prepare memos on those that they think I would be interested in, those that we really have a likelihood of granting. They also work on all the opinions that we produce. Our practice is, I usually write a first draft, in fact I always write a first draft, and then they convert it from a draft to an opinion. They make it much better than it started out.

Q: Let's walk in this middle room. Will you tell us what this room is used for?

STEVENS: My secretary and assistant secretary both are in this office, and there's room for visitors to sit and see what the place looks like.

Q: What kind of visitors do you get over the years, and how easy is it to come see you?

STEVENS: Well, I probably shouldn't say this, but it isn't all that difficult. Usually we're pretty busy; that schedule is governed pretty much by the availability of time. It is a full-time job so you spend an awful lot of time preparing for arguments, reading briefs ahead of time, and talking over the cases. Of course, the major work is in writing opinions and finishing those off.

Q: Did you ever total up how many hours a week you have to read?

STEVENS: I don't know just what it is, but it's a lot more than forty, I'll tell you that.

Q: What's your pattern on a given day?

STEVENS: I'm an early morning person, so I do quite a bit of work early in the morning, and I'm usually pretty well prepared when I come downtown. I have flexibility, on days in which we're not sitting, I can work at home; with what computers do for us, I can work at home on opinions. I can read at home, and I sometimes do. And sometimes I come down; it's a totally optional schedule.

Q: Let me ask you about this portrait over here on the wall. Who is that gentleman?

STEVENS: That's Wiley Rutledge, a great justice of the Court for whom I clerked in the 1947 term. He's one of my heroes.

Q: Who was he?

STEVENS: He was, of course, a justice of the Court here, and before that he had been a judge on the Court of Appeals for the District of Columbia circuit. And before that he'd been the dean of Iowa Law School. Before that he'd been the dean of St. Louis University Law School, and he taught at other law schools during his career as well.

Q: What year did you clerk for him?

STEVENS: 1947 to 1948.

Q: What did you learn from that experience that you still hold on to today?

STEVENS: I learned an awful lot, I have to tell you. I learned to take the time to write out your own draft opinion so you're sure you understand the case before you turn it over to someone else to work on. I learned that every case is important, and not just where there's a lot of money involved and important public issues involved. Every case is important to the people who are involved in it.

Q: Back to the writing of the first draft that you do, is that unique to you?

STEVENS: No. I can't speak for my colleagues; I'm sure some do a first draft, but I'm not sure they all do. One of the reasons I do it is that Justice Rutledge used to write them out on a yellow pad—now I type them on computers rather than using the pad—but he would write out in his own longhand a full first draft. Then the secretary would type it up, and usually that was it. We might supply some footnotes or suggestions, but he did the whole thing himself.

Q: What has been your philosophy of the length of an opinion that you would write and also the dissent that you write sometimes or the concurring opinion?

STEVENS: The length depends on the case. I try to keep them as short as I can, but sometimes you take more pages than people think you should. And I use footnotes regularly because I think footnotes are optional reading. There are some things that should be in an opinion, and I think people might gain from having the opportunity to read them, but they don't always have to read them in order to understand the argument and opinions. I'm one of those old-timers who think footnotes perform a very useful function. Some of my colleagues think you should never use footnotes, and a lot of scholars feel that way, too.

Q: Why do they feel that way, do you think?

STEVENS: Well, they think if it's important enough to be included in the opinion, it ought to be worked into the text, and if it doesn't belong in the text you should save space by leaving it out.

Q: How does an opinion change in length from the first draft that you write to the time it's finished?

STEVENS: Sometimes it doesn't change very much at all. Sometimes it becomes shorter and sometimes longer. I think more often it becomes a little longer, but I'm a fan of shorter opinions if it's possible, but you can't always do it.

Q: Over here on your wall is a number 22 baseball jersey; what's that from?

STEVENS: That was a gift from my law clerks a few years ago. They know I'm a Cubs fan and kind of encouraged my continued interest in the Cubs.

Q: When did you throw out the first ball?

STEVENS: That was about three years ago, I guess. . . . That was the highlight of my career. I had all my grandchildren—not all of them, but most of them—there, and I can tell you I was a hero that day. It was much more important than my job.

Q: Did you make it from the mound to the catcher?

STEVENS: Oh, absolutely. I threw it high and wide. I had to practice, though, to tell you the truth.

Q: Let me go back to the seventh circuit. Where is it located?

STEVENS: Well, it covers Wisconsin, Illinois, and Indiana, and we always sit in Chicago.

Q: What was your learning experience sitting on the seventh circuit?

STEVENS: I learned a great deal. I learned an awful lot about federal law, of course, because I served with some awfully good judges and learned a lot from them. For example, in that picture, Tom Fairchild was a chief judge for years, and I learned a lot from him and others of my colleagues.

Q: What's the difference between a circuit court of appeals and the Supreme Court?

STEVENS: In the circuit court of appeals you are more bound by precedent than you are in the Court here. If there's a decision or even a dictum in the opinion, the court of appeals is required to follow it. Whereas in this Court there are many more open questions that have not really been finally resolved, and you have more of a duty to decide things for the first time that have not been faced before.

Q: Let's go into your main office here. You've been in a lot of different offices . . . does the atmosphere you're working in matter to you much?

STEVENS: Actually, it doesn't. I enjoy the office, and I have a wonderful view of the Capitol from my desk. But the most important part of the office is the computer, which is sitting right next to me. Wherever you are, you spend a lot of time reading and composing on the computer.

Q: Behind your desk are a number of pictures. Can you give us an overview of what's here?

Justice Stevens, 1976.
*Robert Oaks, National
Geographic Society, Collection
of the Supreme Court of the
United States.*

STEVENS: Most of them are family or President Ford, of course, and Justice Rutledge . . .

Q: Give us some background on your parents.

STEVENS: That's a long story. They both lived a long time, but probably the most notable part of their career was that my dad was responsible for building what is now the Conrad Hilton in Chicago. It was then the Stevens Hotel. He was in the hotel business, and also he was a lawyer. He studied at Northwestern back in the days of [Dean]Wigmore.

Q: Now, you were a Northwestern law graduate.

STEVENS: Yes.

Q: It's not that usual to have somebody on the Court from Northwestern.

STEVENS: Well, Justice Goldberg was from Northwestern. And of course I went to law school at Northwestern, and I did my undergraduate work at the University of Chicago.

Q: Is there any difference coming from a Midwestern school when we hear that so many justices are from Stanford and Yale and Harvard?

STEVENS: I think there is. Of course, every school has its virtues and its strengths, but Northwestern really had a fine law school when I went to it, and it still has a fine law school. There are good law schools all over the country. I learned that in hiring law clerks. I've hired law clerks from many, many different schools who have done a magnificent job, even though they're not from the Ivy League.

Q: I read that you were the top student in the history of Northwestern Law School. Is that still the case?

STEVENS: I've been told that was true. I don't know about the record since then, but I was told that that was the case.

Q: With all your experiences, Northwestern Law School, your job as a clerk here, service on the seventh circuit, and a father that was an attorney, where along the way did you get your philosophy of the law?

STEVENS: Of course many, many things combine to give you your views of what the law is. A lot of it's just a result of your reading; a lot of it is your experiences. I know, for example, that my experiences during World War II have shaped my thinking in some cases.

Q: You were in the navy.

STEVENS: I was in the navy, yes. And my experiences as a practicing lawyer have had an impact on the work I've done. My experiences on the seventh circuit affect me here. There are an awful lot of things combined to affect your view of the law.

Q: When you're sitting up on the bench, looking out at the Court during an oral argument, what do you think up there? What do you see that we don't see?

STEVENS: One thing I often remember is the first time I argued before the Court. I was really surprised at how close I was to the justices. I think to myself sometimes, "He is thinking the same thing. He didn't expect it to be quite as close, to have it be quite as intimate an experience as it really is." You're right in the conversation with the people on the other side of the bench. And it's a very, very interesting experience.

Q: Have you been here long enough where the bench itself was straight?

STEVENS: No. Warren Burger made that change a year or two before I got here. Since I've been a justice, it's always been with an angle on the two sides. But when I was a law clerk, it was a straight bench.

Q: Where's your favorite spot in the whole Court; what room do you like the best?

STEVENS: I haven't really thought that through. I suppose that I enjoy the oral arguments; I like the courtroom. I really do. I enjoy my own office, and I always think one of the most interesting places in the Court is the spiral staircase. It's well worth seeing if you can.

Q: Have you spent much time studying the history of this place?

STEVENS: I've picked up a good deal of history, but I haven't really made an independent study of it the way some people have.

Q: What are those books behind you?

STEVENS: Those are the U.S. Reports from—I forget just what—but they're the last maybe forty years of reports. And over there I have reports from the beginning.

Q: What does it mean? What are U.S. Reports?

STEVENS: They're the reports of the decisions by the Court, which of course include all of the majority opinions and all of the dissenting and separate opinions that have been written.

Q: We have read for years that you've figured out a way to spend part of your time here and part of your time in Florida. What's been your philosophy? When did you start spending a couple of weeks a month in Florida and doing a lot of work down there?

STEVENS: I've been doing that for, I don't know, at least twenty-five years and perhaps more. Part of that is the product of the computer, continuing to be in communication with the office here, even though you're working there. And of course, it's the kind of job that you don't have to be in the office to perform. You can read briefs and do other research without being in the office, and you can write opinions without being in the office. So I do just as much work when I'm in Florida as I do here, except I don't hear any oral arguments. Sometimes I read briefs sitting on the beach. I can remember getting a kick out of the fact that I had the briefs on the bench one day and I shook the sand out of them and found that it made my neighbors a little jealous of the way I prepare.

Q: As you know, when you're around Washington, a Supreme Court justice is somebody that everybody knows. I'm sure you've found yourself in the supermarket and someone will say, "Oh, there's Justice Stevens."

STEVENS: Never.

Q: Do you ever get this in Florida? Do they know who you are down there?

STEVENS: The only time that I can remember being recognized, when I'm doing the shopping or something, was while renting a video. . . . The guy who owned the store had been admitted to the bar a couple weeks earlier, and he recognized me. Apparently he's both a lawyer and an entrepreneur. But I'm almost never recognized, which is nice. I just do the shopping and so forth, and nobody knows who I am.

Q: Let's go back to the *cert* pool that we talked about. *Certiorari*. What does that mean?

STEVENS: It's a common law writ that has become a statutory writ. It's the writ that a party who lost in the lower court files in this Court. He files a petition for a writ of *certiorari*, which is a request for this Court to grant review of the case and set it down for argument. I don't know how many thousand *cert* petitions we get every year, but the cases we grant come out of the number that are filed.

Q: How many justices participate in this *cert* pool, and what is it?

STEVENS: That has varied from over the years. When I joined the Court there were, I think, six justices in it. I did not join it because, having been a law clerk years earlier, I had some familiarity with the *cert* process. I thought I could handle cases more efficiently myself without participating in these memos prepared for the group of justices. So there were six then, and after I joined, every justice to join the Court has joined the *cert* pool since then. And so there have been eight. With this one exception that last year Justice Alito decided to do his *certs* independently, too. So now there are seven different justices who share their law clerks and their memos as preparation for the *cert* conference.

Q: Why did you decide not to join the *cert* pool?

STEVENS: I thought I could handle the cases more efficiently independently than as part of the *cert* pool. The memos they prepare are very thorough and very carefully written, but they're a lot longer than I thought was necessary in order to make a decision on whether to vote to grant or to deny.

Q: What does that do to your personal work load or your clerks' work load?

STEVENS: You'd really have to ask them. I think it makes it a little less. They go through every *cert* petition themselves and divide them up, but they don't have to write memoranda in every case. So they read more petitions, but they write fewer memorandums. So it kind of cancels itself out.

Q: How is a *cert* petition accepted here? How does that happen?

STEVENS: [It happens] once a week except when we recess; then we'll miss a week. We have a conference on Friday, we review all the *cert* petitions that have come in since the last conference, and we vote on whether to grant or deny them. You need four justices to vote to grant, then the *cert* petition is granted.

Q: And where do you do that?

STEVENS: We do it in the Conference Room of the Court. All the justices are present at the conference, and no one else is present. The deliberations are entirely off the record.

Q: What is the Conference Room like?

STEVENS: It's a nice big room with a big table in it and nine chairs around the table. Sometimes they have coffee sent in with a sweet roll or cookie or something.

Q: How formal is the meeting?

STEVENS: It's informal in the sense that everybody is congenial and there's a certain amount of conversation, but most of it's business. We are fairly rigid in our rules: We talk in the order of seniority about the case, we go around and vote in turn, and sometimes after we've discussed the case for a *cert* petition we'll talk about it a little further, but usually it's through after one go round the table.

Q: Now you're senior.

STEVENS: Well, second senior. I'm senior in age and years in service, but the chief justice, of course, speaks first.

Q: When you came on this Court did you ever think that you'd be here in thirty-four years?

STEVENS: No. In fact, I had a law clerk named Stewart Baker who was with me in my second or third year here. I asked him to prepare a memorandum for me on the ages of retirement of all my predecessors and to suggest the age at which I should plan on retiring. I thought then—and I still sometimes think—that you're not the best judge of when you should retire. I thought it would be helpful to have that kind of guidance. Well, I didn't follow that recommendation.

Q: When did he suggest?

STEVENS: I can't remember exactly, but the year has long gone by.

Q: Now you're very close to being the longest-serving justice in history or the oldest justice in history. Does any of that enter your thinking right now?

STEVENS: No, I'm not out to break any records, I can assure you of that. I just enjoy the work. Each year I've thought about it, and I've

Justice John Paul Stevens in his chambers for the June 2009 C-SPAN interview.

decided that I could continue to enjoy it and continue to make a contribution.

Q: What do you do at age eighty-nine to stay as healthy as you are?

STEVENS: I play a lot of tennis. I don't play as much golf as I used to because my fore swing is not the same as it used to be. When I'm in Florida, I go swimming every day and play tennis probably three times a week.

Q: Put the Court, for a moment, in perspective for the public in a town like this where we have a president, the Capitol, and this building across the street. What's its role?

STEVENS: It's an independent branch of the government. It has to decide cases of controversies that raise federal questions . . .

Q: Does it do it the way you want it do it?

STEVENS: Sometimes. Sometimes not. It's been true while I've been here, and really throughout the history of the Court, that there are cases that are very difficult in which there was a difference of judgment by different members of the Court. When you're not in the majority, you wish they had decided it the other way and you think the world would have been better off if they decided the other way. But if you don't have the votes, you can't do anything about it.

Q: In your thirty-four years, are there cases that mattered more to you than others?

STEVENS: Oh, I'm sure there are, but if you're going to ask me which one is the most significant, I'm going to have to say the ones I'm working on currently are always the most significant.

Q: Which one over the years created the biggest sensation in the country? You sit here, you write these opinions, they pop out, and all of a sudden they're all over the news. Do you pay any attention to that?

STEVENS: You read the papers, of course. I read the papers both about our work and the work of other courts. But you have to let others decide which are the most significant.

Q: Do you plan when you retire that your papers eventually will be released for public perusal?

STEVENS: Yes, I think I'm going to send them over to the Library of Congress.

Q: Go back to Wiley Rutledge who was the justice that you served as clerk. Were there other justices in history that made a difference to you?

STEVENS: Yes, indeed, because of the quality of their work. There have been some really, truly great justices that sat on the Court. . . . Brandeis and Cardozo are the ones we often mention. Of course, Justice Holmes was an exceptional justice, and my good friends Potter

Stewart and Byron White were great justices, too. There have been a number of great men that have sat on the Court.

Q: In your opinion, what makes a justice great?

STEVENS: The quality of his work is a major thing. You judge justices by the work product that they produce when they're on the Court.

Q: But what's quality in your opinion? What makes good writing?

STEVENS: Well, I don't know. I don't think I can give a lesson in English grammar and all the rest, but you have to able to write clearly and accurately and honestly about what the issues are.

Q: What is your option if you're sitting in a conference and the other justices don't vote your way? What role does your dissenting opinion play, do you think, in the law?

STEVENS: Sometimes it becomes persuasive later on; sometimes it doesn't. But I don't write dissents trying to change the law. I just think it's part of the job of the justice to explain his or her vote in the case. I think the process is an open process in the sense that this is one institution that explains in a public way what it decides and what it does. I think that when there's difference within the Court on how a case should be decided, it's appropriate for those who disagree to explain why they thought the other side had the better of the argument.

Q: You've been active in oral argument. We run an argument a week on our radio station, and I listen to them, and I hear you. What is your philosophy of participation during the actual oral argument?

STEVENS: My philosophy is to ask questions when I think the answer might give me a little help in deciding a case. I don't view the participation of a justice as an opportunity for the justice to advocate one point of view. I think, rather, the questioning should be designed to help understand what the arguments on both sides are in order to enable the justice to reach a decision on his or her own views.

Q: How often do you change your mind on a case after the oral argument?

STEVENS: Sometimes, I can't tell you the number, but it has happened. It has happened when I've been writing an opinion, for example. And that's one reason I think it's important for the justice to do the first draft. When you try to write something out, you sometimes learn things about the case that you didn't fully appreciate or understand before. There has been more than one case on which I have changed my views when I was writing the opinion.

Q: This is a Court that has every member with a history of serving on the circuit court of appeals. They're all circuit court veterans. Is that something that is going to be expected, do you think, from now on for justices?

STEVENS: That's something that future presidents are going to have to decide. I think it's healthy for the Court to have members with different backgrounds. I saw a television program recently in which somebody said there should always be someone who had served in the armed forces on the Court. I think there should always be someone who has had practical experience in litigation. I think experience in other branches of the government such as the legislature would be very, very helpful. For example Justice O'Connor had experience as a legislator, and I think she made a very significant contribution to deliberations because of that experience. In my own case, the experience I had as a staff attorney on a legislative committee taught me a great deal about legislation that I know has affected my work in trying to interpret statutes. I think differing backgrounds is a plus.

Q: What year did you serve on that judiciary subcommittee?

STEVENS: I think it was 1951.

Q: Who was there at the time? Who was the chairman, do you remember?

STEVENS: Manny Celler was the chairman; he was a Democrat from Brooklyn. Chauncey Reed was the senior minority member, and he was a Republican from DuPage County, Illinois. I was hired by Chauncey Reed.

Q: What role does the legislative history, not the law, play when you think about a case that comes to you?

STEVENS: I think it's always significant because I think our job is to try and figure out what Congress intended to do in enacting a statute. I can remember being asked by members of the committee about rather tricky questions that might be presented in the case. I remember explaining to one congressman some of the difficulties that I saw in a case, and he answered, "We'll let the judges figure that one out." It's a cooperative venture. Congress expects the judges to help fill in the holes in statutes as it goes along. And realizing that the job is not just trying to read words on a sterile piece of paper is important for a judge.

Q: Thank you, Justice Stevens.

JUSTICE
ANTONIN SCALIA

A *ssociate Justice Antonin Scalia was nominated to the high court by President Ronald Reagan, and was sworn into office September 26, 1986. Earlier, the 103rd justice had been a law professor, a Nixon appointee, and a judge on the U.S. Court of Appeals. He spoke to C-SPAN's Susan Swain in the Court's East Conference Room on June 19, 2009.*

———————————

SWAIN: Associate Justice Antonin Scalia, in the simplest of terms, would you explain what the role and responsibilities of a Supreme Court Associate Justice are?

ASSOCIATE JUSTICE ANTONIN SCALIA: To try to come out the right way on cases that the Court has agreed to hear. Also, and this is the only respect in which the job differs from the job of a court of appeals judge, to decide on what cases the Court should agree to hear. [There are] essentially two functions, but the latter is prior. First of all, decide what to put on our docket and, secondly, what is on our docket, to try to get it right.

Q: What role do you see the Supreme Court playing in society today? And has it changed over your tenure?

SCALIA: I think the same role it has always played. I don't think it has changed. Its proper role in the democracy is to give a fair and honest interpretation to the meaning of dispositions that the people have adopted, either in Congress in statutes or the people when they ratified the Constitution. It's as simple as that, no more and no less.

I don't think we're a leader of social causes. We're not pushing the society ahead. We are supposed to be interpreting the laws that the people have made.

Q: What do you like best about the job?

SCALIA: I like figuring out the right answer to legal questions, believe it or not—and not everybody does. I think some people who lust to become an appellate judge find the job quite unsatisfying when they get there. You have to have a rather warped mind to want to spend your life figuring out the answer to legal questions. It's a very isolated job. The only time you see, in connection with your work, people from the outside is when you're listening to argument from counsel. Other than that, it's very disembodied and intellectual work. Probably it most closely resembles the work of a law professor, which is what I was before I was here, so I'm no more unhappy than I was before.

Q: After two decades of doing it, is there any aspect of the job that if you had the choice you'd prefer to pass on to somebody else to do or avoid?

SCALIA: I think undoubtedly to my mind the most, what shall I say, onerous and for the most part uninteresting part of the job is ruling on all of the *cert* petitions that come to the Court, and they have increased enormously in the time that I've been here. I think when I first arrived, if I'm correct, it was about five thousand a year. Now it's approaching ten thousand, and every one of them we have to consider. If not by reading the actual petitions—we rarely do that—by reading summaries of the petitions that law clerks have prepared. So, that's ten thousand of those a year. That's not a lot of fun.

Q: With the increasing number of petitions, why only eighty to one hundred cases a year?

SCALIA: Less than that even; we've been averaging about seventy-five recently. That number, by the way, is not out of line with what other Supreme Courts in other jurisdictions do. I think we could do more than seventy-five; we could do one hundred well. I don't think we can do what we were doing when I first came on the Court: 150. I don't think we can do 150 well.

Why? Your guess is as good as mine. I certainly have not changed my standards for deciding what cases we should take, and I don't think my colleagues have. If I had to guess, I would say that what has happened is that in my early years on the Court, twenty some odd years ago, there was a lot of major new legislation that had recently been enacted—the new bankruptcy code, ERISA. There's not been that much major new legislation in recent years and new legislation is the principal generator of successful *cert* petitions because it takes ten years or so to get all of the ambiguities in a statute resolved, and that's our main job, of course.

We don't take cases because we think they were decided wrong. Very rarely would we take a case for that reason—a death case we would. But we usually take cases because the analysis of the courts below reflects a disagreement on the meaning of federal law, and you can't have two different federal laws in different parts of the country. We will take one or both of those cases.

Those disagreements on significant questions simply have been more rare in recent years. It's not as if we sit down at the end of the term and say. "Okay guys, how many cases do you want to take? Let's take 120." That's not what happens. They trickle in week by week, and we vote on those that we think are worthy of our consideration, and the last few years at the end of the term they've been adding up to about seventy-five or so.

Q: When you make those decisions, are you aware at the time which ones are going to be the blockbuster cases?

SCALIA: Usually. I think you could usually tell which ones pertain to a major piece of legislation, legislation that has a major impact on the society, sure.

Q: Does it affect the decision process?

SCALIA: Not mine. You'd have to talk to other people, but I don't think it does. I put in as much blood, sweat, and tears on the little cases as I do on the big ones. If somebody asked me, "What's the hardest case you ever decided while you've been on the bench?" you wouldn't want to know the answer, because it is a relatively insignificant case, but it was very hard to figure out. There's no relationship whatsoever between how important it is and how hard it is.

Q: So, can you tell me now that you've described it?

SCALIA: You don't want to know.

Q: Okay, we've heard so much in talking to the justices about clerks, but I'd like to ask you about their role in what you do. You've had many of them over the years. Do you stay in touch with them after they work for you?

SCALIA: I do indeed. We have an annual clerks' reunion every year, and it's good to see them. It's one of the most enjoyable parts of the job. You work very closely with four young people every year. There are new ones every year. They are full of vim and vigor. They are not jaded; it's all new to them. Their enthusiasm rubs off on you, and you work closely with them during the year. You really become very close, and then they go off. It's like acquiring four new nieces and nephews every year, none of whom will be a failure. They all go off to do very significant things, and it's fun to follow their later careers.

Q: And you do that in fact other than the reunion?

SCALIA: Oh, sure. Sure.

Q: And how do you use them in your job?

SCALIA: I can just say how I do it; what I do is not necessarily what others do. I let them pick the cases that they want to work on. It's sort of like an NFL draft. They have first pick, second pick, third pick. I figure they're likely to do the best work on the cases they're most interested in, so they divvy up the cases. And then I usually discuss the case very briefly with the law clerk who has chosen it before oral argument.

And then after oral argument, I sit down with that clerk and with the other three who know something about the case, although not as much as the clerk who really is responsible for it, and we kick it around for as long as it takes. It could be an hour, it could be two hours. Then if I happen to be assigned the opinion or the dissent, that clerk will normally do a first draft of it. I'll tell them what's supposed to be in it, but he'll write it out. Then I'll put it up on my screen and take it apart and put it back together.

So, I kid you not and I tell them at the reunions, I am indebted to my law clerks for a lot of the quality of the work that comes out of my chambers. I couldn't do as well without the assistance of really brilliant young people.

Q: In a week when the Court is in session, how many hours do you spend in this building in a typical week?

SCALIA: I have no idea.

Q: Is it a forty-hour-a-week job, a sixty-hour-a-week job?

SCALIA: One of the nice things about the job—or one of the not nice things about the job—is you don't have to be here to be working. I could, and I think some judges on the courts of appeals do, only come into court when there's oral argument. I could do this job from home. The main thing it would deprive me of is consultation with my law clerks and it would deprive them of my company, too. So I do like to come in, but that has no relationship to how many hours I'm putting in. I've never counted the hours in the week, but I almost always work weekends, not all weekend, every weekend, but some of the weekend every weekend.

Q: And is there ever really a break in the summertime for example?

SCALIA: Yes, the summertime's a break. We clean our plate before we leave at the end of June, so it is really a summer without guilt. The only work we have to do over the summer is stay on top of *cert* petitions because there's a monster conference at the end of the summer to vote on all of the *cert* petitions that have accumulated over the summer. So you have to stay on top of them, but that's a manageable job. For the rest of it, we have continued to function the way all three branches of the federal government used to function. This town used to be deserted in July and August; there was nobody here. Now we are generally not around in July and August and come back in September to get ready for the arguments in October. During the summer you have time to do some of the reading that you didn't have time to do during the court term and to regenerate your batteries.

Q: You mentioned that the Court has retained some of the tradition that the other branches used to have regarding the summers, but the Court's also quite well known for many of its other traditions. I was just writing down a few that came to mind, including in the courtroom itself, the quill pens, the solicitors in formal dress, institutions in the courtroom. Why do they matter to the process, and why are they retained in 2009?

SCALIA: I think traditions, in a way, define an institution. An institution is respected when it is venerable with tradition. And certainly one of the remarkable things about the Court is that it's been here doing this job for what, 220 years. I think traditions remind people of that fact. I guess we could sit in a bus station and not wear robes but just business suits or even tank tops, but I don't think that creates the kind of image that you want for the Supreme Court of your country.

Justice Scalia. *Collection of the Supreme Court of the United States.*

Q: On the robes, I was looking at a little bit of history before I came in, your earliest chief justices depicted here really didn't wear them.

SCALIA: Didn't wear robes?

Q: That's right; it began around 1800, according to Supreme Court sites.

SCALIA: John Jay, over your right shoulder, was the first chief justice, and that was before 1800, and in that portrait he is wearing a glorious robe not just of black, but of black and red. What you just told me is news to me.

Q: Well, I'll [concede on] John Jay, but it is now 2009 and tank tops aside, what's the symbolism behind the robe, and why is it important for members of the judiciary to continue to wear them in our society?

SCALIA: Well, I'm sure we could do our work without the robes. We could do our work without this glorious building that you're deciding to have this conversation in. What the robes, like the building, impart to the people who come here is the significance or the importance of what goes on here. That's nothing new. Public buildings always don't look like bus stations, and they shouldn't.

Q: This building itself, Justice Breyer yesterday called it the "symbol of American judicial process, internationally." When you come to work here, are you conscious of that, conscious of the Court being a symbol of the American judicial process, after doing it for such a long time?

SCALIA: I can't say it's in the middle of my mind; I'm usually thinking about whatever case I'm going to be working on that day. You get used to it; you get to taking stuff for granted that maybe you shouldn't take for granted. But I take for granted working in this glorious building. I take for granted wearing a robe when I go out on the bench.

Q: When you have the opportunity, when it's quiet around here, are there special places in this building that you might go to reflect on the history of the Court and its predecessors?

SCALIA: Not really. I hang out in my chambers most of the time. The center of the building, what is really the reason the building is here, is the audience chamber where we hear oral arguments. As the august nature of that chamber suggests . . . it has a ceiling so high you can hardly see it from the ground. That's the center of the Court, of course.

Q: Let's talk about what goes on in that room in the process of oral argument. Can you talk about how you use oral argument, and why, in fact, when there's so much paper beforehand on all of the cases, oral argument is even needed?

SCALIA: Yes, a lot of people have the impression that it's just a dog and pony show. [They think] "I read a sixty-page brief by the petitioner, a sixty-page brief by the respondent, a forty-page reply brief, very often an *amicus* brief by the solicitor general. Sometimes dozens of other *amicus* briefs, not all of which I will read. I have underlined significant passages, I have written, at best, nonsense in the margin. What can somebody tell me in half an hour that's going to make a difference?"

And the answer is that it is probably quite rare, although not unheard of, that oral argument will change my mind. But it is quite common that I go in with my mind not made up. A lot of these cases are very close, and you go in on the knife's edge. Persuasive counsel can make the difference. There are things you can do with oral argument that cannot be done in a brief. You can convey the relative importance of your various points.

Sometimes you have four points, and one of them is very complicated. It's not your most important one, but it's an "it takes a third ear" point. Now if I've read your brief a week ago and I come in, I have a misperception of the nature of your case. You can set that right in oral argument. Very often that third point, the difficult point, may be the first point you address in your brief because that's the logical order. You don't put it in jurisdiction last; it has to go first. But in fact that's not your strongest point, even though you discuss it first in your brief, and even though it takes more of your brief than anything else simply because it's the most complicated. So you get up in oral argument and say, "Your Honors, we have five points in the brief. We think they're all worth your attention. But really what this case comes down to is . . . " Boom! You hit your big point, and that can make a difference.

The brief cannot answer back when I write "nonsense" in the margin. [In the oral argument, though] you can ask, "Counsel, is there some reason why this point is not nonsense?" And sometimes they can tell you. So I'm a big proponent of oral argument. I think it's very important, and you'd be surprised how much probing can be done within half an hour—an awful lot.

Q: What's the quality of counsel who come before you, generally?

SCALIA: Well, two chiefs ago, Chief Justice Burger, used to complain about the low quality of counsel. I used to have just the opposite reaction. I used to be disappointed that so many of the best minds in the country were being devoted to this enterprise. There'd be a defense or public defender from Podunk, and this woman is really brilliant. Why isn't she out inventing the automobile or doing something productive for this society?

Lawyers, after all, don't produce anything. They enable other people to produce and to go on with their lives efficiently and in an atmosphere of freedom. That's important, but it doesn't put food on the table, and there have to be other people who are doing that. I worry that we are devoting too many of our very best minds to this enterprise. They appear here in the Court, even the ones who will only argue here once and will never come again. I'm usually impressed with how good they are. Sometimes you get one who's not so good. But, by and large I don't have any complaint about the quality of counsel, except maybe we're wasting some of our best minds.

How can I put it another way? Law firms spend enormous amounts of money to get the very, very brightest—that amount of difference between that guy and the next one—but it's worth it because the law is so complicated and so complex. The legal system probably shouldn't put such a premium on brains, but it does, and our lawyers are really good. I think lawyers generally are pretty smart people.

Q: Can you talk about the next stage—conference—and how it works?

SCALIA: I can't talk too much about it, but I can tell you we sit down together and there's nobody else in the room. I'm not giving away anything because Chief Justice Rehnquist wrote a book about the Court in which he acknowledged that conference is probably a misnomer. It is really not an occasion on which we try to persuade one another.

Very few minds are changed at conference. Each justice states his or her view of the case and how he or she votes. You go right around the table, and if in the middle of somebody's presentation, you disagree with something that the person says . . . if when John Stevens is speaking, I say, "Wait, John, now why do you say that?" That would not

Justice Antonin Scalia before his 2009 interview with C-SPAN.

happen. Or if it did happen, the chief justice would say, "Nino, you'll have your turn. John is speaking now. Let him finish." When we get all around, yes, at the end, you can speak a second time and raise some of these questions.

But it is not really an exercise in persuading each other; it's an exercise in stating your views while the rest of us take notes. That's its function. You take notes so that if you get assigned the opinion, you know how to write it in a way that will get at least four other votes besides your own.

Q: With regard to being assigned the writing of opinions, the chief told us in our conversation that he works very hard to be fair about the distribution of the assignments. You said earlier with your clerks that you try to give them cases that they're interested in because they'll do the best job. Are you able to lobby if you are particularly interested in a certain case?

SCALIA: I haven't done that. I could if I wanted to. On very, very rare occasions have I said, "I'd like that case"—I bet you not more than three times the whole time I've been on the Court. No, I pretty much take what I'm given. Both of the chiefs that I've served under have tried to be fair in giving you good ones and dogs.

Of course, sometimes what they think is a good opinion is not what you think is a good opinion. Chief Justice Rehnquist used to love Fourth Amendment cases involving searches and seizures, and I just hate Fourth Amendment cases. I think it's almost a jury question—whether this variation is an unreasonable search and seizure; variation 3,542. Yes, I'll write the opinion, but I don't consider it a plum. But Bill Rehnquist used to consider it a plum, and if he gave you that, he thought he was entitled to give you a dog. I didn't much like that.

Q: You are a writer. You've written three books now, is that correct?

SCALIA: Two. . . . You don't want to be an appellate judge if you're no good at writing.

Q: Do you enjoy the writing of opinions and the exchange of precise words to make your point?

SCALIA: No, as I often put it, I do not enjoy writing. I enjoy having written. I find writing a very difficult process. I sweat over it. I write, I rewrite, I rewrite again. Before the opinion goes out, the law clerk will say, "It's going out this afternoon. Do you want to read it one last time?" And I'll say, "Yes, let me read it one last time."

I guarantee you, every time I read it I will change something else. Finally, it has to be wrested from my grasp and sent down to the printer. No, I am not a facile writer, but I think writing is a job that is worth the time you spend on it.

Q: Has technology, in the course of your time here, made the process easier?

SCALIA: We had word processors when I arrived, so I can't say that has made it easier since I've been here. I had word processors when I was a law professor. That certainly makes the job of writing, especially writing when you're editing somebody else's first draft, enormously more simple than it otherwise would be. You don't have to write little balloons and what not. You just highlight the part you want taken out, bang! It's gone. And you put in the new part. Bang! It's in. It makes it a lot easier.

Q: When you strongly disagree with someone's point of view, how do you keep the opinion or dissent from being personal?

SCALIA: You criticize the argument and not the person, that's all. An *ad hominem* argument is one that is addressed at the person rather than the argument. I feel quite justified in whacking the argument as hard as it deserves. That's not impugning the individual that made the argument.

Q: Do you have a preference for writing the majority or the dissent?

SCALIA: Of course, I always want to write a majority. Why do you want to write a dissent?

Q: Intellectual challenge?

SCALIA: Well, hey, dissents are more fun to write, I've got to say that, because when you have the dissent, it's yours. You say what you want, and if somebody doesn't want to join it, who cares? "If you don't want to join my dissent, fine, it's my dissent. This is what I want to say." When you're writing a majority, you do not have that luxury. You have to craft it in a way that at least four other people can jump on. Actually you try to craft it in a way that as many people as possible will jump on, which means accepting some suggestions—stylistic and otherwise—that you don't think are best, but nonetheless, in order to get everybody on board, you take them.

Q: You and I are talking at a time when the Court is about to say good-bye to a member and accept a new one. How does this institution change during that process?

SCALIA: The institution doesn't change at all. I think the relationships change; you lose a friend and hopefully acquire another one. I'll miss David Souter; I'll miss him a lot. He has sat next to me for his whole time on this Court. When we go out on the bench, he is always, depending on which side of the bench I happen to be sitting on, he's to my left or to my right. So he's been a rather constant companion, and we chat back and forth sometimes during argument or pass a note back and forth. I'll miss him. He's an intelligent, interesting, good man. I miss a lot of my former colleagues on the Court, from Byron White to Bill Brennan, but that's the process. They go, and new people come on.

Q: In fact, during your tenure I think that there have been, including the chief, seven new arrivals. When you welcome new justices in the system, when they've come from the appeals court, is there an acclimation process, even here?

SCALIA: Not really, it's the same job. It's the same job as being an appellate judge on a lower court. You read the briefs, you hear the argument, you write the opinion. We have the added job of deciding what to decide; a court of appeals judge does not have that burden or that luxury. You take whatever they bring you; you have to.

But except for that additional part of the job, it's the same with maybe one other exception. On the lower courts, if there is a whole line of Supreme Court authority that you fundamentally disagree with, you just say hey, "I think it's stupid, but that's what they say." You follow it. You don't have to worry about whether it ought to be changed; whereas, on the highest court, if it is indeed a stupid line of cases, it's your stupid line of cases. You have to decide, do you leave it alone? Do you simply refuse to extend it any further? Or, do you try to get rid of the whole thing? In other words, *stare indecisis*. You don't have to worry about that on the court of appeals; you do up here.

Q: For people for whom the Supreme Court is just an item in the newspaper, would you like to say something to them about this place, about how it functions and what they really ought to know about the Court?

SCALIA: It's really not a point distinctive to this Court. It's a more general point that applies to this Court and to all others: You can't judge judges unless you know the materials that they're working with. You can't say, "Oh, this is a good decision, and this was a good Court" simply because you like the result. It seems to you that the person who deserved to win, won.

That's not the business judges are in. We don't sit here to make the law, to decide who ought to win. We decide who wins under the law that the people have adopted. And very often, if you're a good judge, you don't really like the result you're reaching. You would rather that the other side had won, and it seems to you a foolish law. But in this job, it's garbage in, garbage out. If it's a foolish law, you are bound by oath to produce a foolish result because it's not your job to decide what is foolish and what isn't. It's the job of the people across the street.

Don't judge judges unless you really take the trouble to read the opinion and see what provisions of law were at issue and what they were trying to reconcile and whether they did an honest job of reconciling them, whether they were interpreting the words of the law in a fair fashion. That's what counts. Unless that's what you want your judges to do, you have a judiciary that's not worth much. You have a judiciary that is just making the law instead of being faithful to what the people have decided. So that's my main advice. Be slow to judge judges unless you know what they're working with.

Q: Justice Antonin Scalia, thank you for spending time with C-SPAN.

SCALIA: My pleasure, thank you.

JUSTICE
ANTHONY KENNEDY

*A*nthony *Kennedy was sworn in as the 104th justice in 1988. A Cali-fornian and Stanford graduate, Justice Kennedy spent many years as a lawyer and law professor and thirteen years as a judge on the U.S. Court of Appeals, Ninth Circuit. He was appointed to the Court in 1988 by Pres-ident Ronald Reagan. Kennedy was interviewed by Susan Swain on June 25, 2009, in the Supreme Court's West Conference Room.*

SWAIN: Justice Anthony Kennedy, you've spent twenty-one years now on the Supreme Court. Since you came from the federal appeals court, is there really such a difference here?

ASSOCIATE JUSTICE ANTHONY KENNEDY: Yes, and it took me a few years to understand that. Sometimes you think you're functioning at a high level, but you're paying attention to the details and not to the larger picture.

I was a judge on the court of appeals, a very fine court of appeals, the United States Court of Appeals for the Ninth Circuit in San Fran-cisco, and I thought I was a very good appellate judge and this was just another appellate assignment. Wrong. This is a different institution. It has a different function, and you must approach it in a different way.

On a court of appeals you can write just for the case that's in front of you so that you have room in the next case to make adjustments, to make qualifications, and to accommodate your colleagues who are also writing in the same area. Here, your function is to try to give some guidance to the state supreme courts or to the federal courts. You're not going to see this kind of case again for maybe at least a few years, and you don't have the luxury of equivocating much.

The other thing is that all the cases are hard. The only reason we take them, as some of my colleagues may tell you, is that other courts are in disagreement most of the time. And that means that other judges and other actors in the legal system have come to differing conclusions. Every case is that way.

Q: You said that it took you a while to realize this. Can you talk through that process of first realizing that you didn't know as much as you thought and when you finally said, "I get this"?

KENNEDY: Of course, you're always hesitant to say, "I get it now." The nature of life is that life is learned looking backward and lived going forward. It would maybe be pretentious to say, "Oh, I know everything about this job now," because of course, if you're not open and willing to learn about the institution and learn about yourself, then you should get a different job.

But my first realization came when I was given my first assignment. The first assignment to a junior justice is usually a simple little case, and this was simple by our standards, and it was terribly difficult. I got into it and said, "Well, maybe this, maybe that." Then I realized, "This is a different job," and that began to sink in.

Also the legal system, and to some extent the press and to some extent the public, is concentrating with great intensity on what you say. You can use different metaphors for the judicial system, different means, allegories to define what this Court is. I like to think of us as teachers that first teach ourselves and then teach others, and we're teaching what the law means.

I was in one of my son's dormitory rooms a few years ago when he was in college, waiting because he had something important to do. And I opened one of his books, *Aristotle's Aesthetics*, and Aristotle gives advice to playwrights. He said, "You can write about what was, what is, or what it ought to be." And it reminded me of the judicial function. We write about what was, what happened, what were the facts. Was it an auto accident or a crime or a dispute among government officials and a private business owner? What happened? What was?

Then what is, what is the law? But we must always write about what ought to be because that is how we teach, and this Court is really a teaching institution when it functions at its best.

Q: What do you like best about the job?

KENNEDY: The best part about the job is that I have the opportunity to try, in my own way, to teach young people, particularly, but I hope [to teach] all judges and lawyers and all citizens and to teach myself constantly, that the law and freedom and what it stands for only survive if you're conscious of what they mean, to you, to America, to its heritage.

When we rebelled against the English, the world was amazed. Americans said, "We want freedom," and the English said, "What do you mean, freedom? These Americans are the freest people you've ever seen. They pay taxes when they want and not when they don't want to. They have all the land that they need. They seem to do quite well. What are they talking about, freedom?"

So we had to give them an answer, right? We didn't have a fax machine or e-mail, but we had to give them an answer back. What did we want? Our first answer was the Declaration of Independence, Jefferson's beautiful preamble, explaining that we owed a decent respect for the opinions of humankind and that we owed an explanation, an answer.

And we gave that answer. That was 1776. Then, some years later, in 1787, the Constitution of the United States was drafted and that was our second answer. The result is that Americans have a self image, a

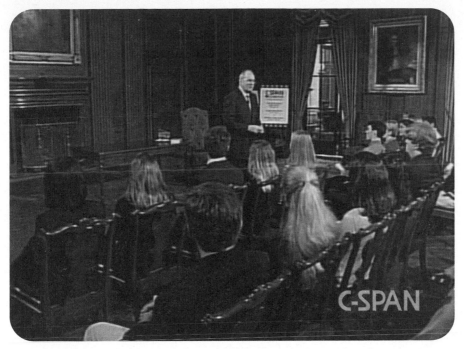

Justice Kennedy, taking questions during a 1999 C-SPAN *Students and Leaders* program.

self identification, a self understanding about who they are by their legal documents.

And this is one of the few countries in the world that's that way. We come from many different backgrounds, many different religions, many different ethnicities, but we have this thing called the Declaration of Independence, this document called the Constitution, in common. They define us. The best part about this job is that you can have a very small part in reminding yourself and reminding the legal system and reminding the public, that this is our heritage, our freedom. And that is only maintained if you understand it and if you transmit it. You know, you don't take a DNA test to see if you bleed freedom. It's taught and it's learned, and teaching and learning are conscious acts. Each generation has to learn all over again what the Constitution means.

And great cases, great teaching cases are the ones in which what the Framers wrote in 1787 and ratified in 1789 has real meaning today.

We had a case some years ago, the flag burning case. Can you burn a flag? Americans get infuriated when you burn a flag. It drives us crazy because we love the flag. This Court said, "That's okay. You can burn it." We said that because of the First Amendment. That gave the Constitution real meaning in our own lives and in our own time, and that's when the Constitution is most important. It's not just some old relic, some old dusty thing you read. It's yours.

Q: In your twenty-one years here, have there ever been, for the institution, any dark days?

KENNEDY: I guess every day when you're not in the majority you think is a dark day. Judges were once lawyers . . . and I've not met too many lawyers that don't think they're on the right side. If you can't convince your colleagues, then you think it's a dark day.

But the nature of the profession is that you go on to the next case, and you respect your colleagues. One of the things you learn when you're a judge is that you're not the only person in the room that is objective, disinterested, detached, knowledgeable, unbiased. Your colleagues feel the same way, and you have to recognize that.

Q: When we asked Chief Justice Roberts about his role, he was very modest in his answer, but as someone who's lived under more than one chief justice, I'm wondering how significant the individual is on the culture of the Supreme Court?

KENNEDY: I'd give you answers on two different parts of that. I have been very fortunate. I knew Earl Warren very well because he was from Sacramento, California, and we were family friends. He was an older man and I was a young boy, but I knew him very well.

Of course I knew Chief Justice Burger, Chief Justice Rehnquist, and now, Chief Justice Roberts. On the one hand, there's not much the chief justice can do. His eight associate justices have a lifetime job. They have a duty to uphold the Constitution. He can't fire them. He's got to get along with them. We have traditions that will outlast any chief justice. And so, the chief justice comes to a court where there are these elements of stability and permanence and protection. We have our tradition, and we have our oath. On the other hand, the chief justice who presides over our conference, and steers us through the mechanics of hearing the cases and calendars, by his personality and his warmth and his decisiveness and his understanding of the law and of the institution of his colleagues, can do a great deal to set the tone.

Q: In the course of our time here we're going to be able to see various rooms, and it will be interesting to hear your take on what happens in those rooms. We've heard about the process of conference from some of the justices, but if we were to have a camera in conference while you were there, which we will never be able to do, what's it like?

KENNEDY: My colleague Justice Breyer made a very interesting comment one day. Somebody asked us—we were together—"Are you nervous before you go on the bench?" He answered, "No, not at all. I'm not nervous when I go on the bench. I look forward to it." Sometimes you'll hear a university professor or a high school teacher say, "Well, it's as hard to give the exam as to take it." Don't believe it. Same thing with attorneys; I was always nervous when I appeared in court as an attorney.

Even not long ago I was in Sacramento, California, I went up the court steps because I was there to visit a judge, and my heart started to beat because I remembered my days as an attorney. Judges don't feel that way. It's relaxed. It's easy. We have to be careful that we're courteous to the attorneys and that we're open-minded and that we do our job. That's a preface to your question about what happens in the Conference Room. Justice Breyer made the observation, very right, that he gets nervous before he goes in the conference, and so do I.

Q: Why is that?

KENNEDY: It's like being an attorney once again. You're arguing your case. I have eight colleagues who've studied very hard on the case, who may have some very fixed views, they may be tentative depending on how they've thought the case through, and I have to give my point of view and hopefully persuade them. I feel a sense of anticipation, whether it's an adrenalin rush or I don't know what they call it, but this is a big, big day for us. We sometimes have as many as six cases, and I have to present the argument—well, usually four —and I have to be professional and accurate and fair. Each of my colleagues feels the same way, so there's a little tension and excitement in the room, but we love it. We're lawyers. We're designed to do that. The job is no good if you can't argue.

Q: You mentioned the traditions in the Court. It seems as though conference is one of those places where many of those traditions come to bear. Will you talk about them?

KENNEDY: I think they're probably pretty well known. . . . Before the case is heard, we have an unwritten rule: We don't talk about it with each other. Sometimes if there's a technical problem I might go to Justice Scalia and say, "Hey, Nino, I think there may be a technical problem in this case." But if we go into it, then we send a memo to everybody about what we've talked about, because we don't want little cliques or cabals or little groups that lobby each other before. We don't do that. The first time we know what our colleagues are thinking is in oral argument, from the questions. And one of the reasons you ask a question is to advise your colleagues what you're thinking or what your concerns are. A good attorney can realize that he or she is engaging in the conversation that the Court is having with itself. So that's the first time we ever get an inkling of what our colleagues' views are. Then we go in the conference about forty-eight to seventy-two hours later. This is the first time in which we give our tentative views on the case.

When we're on the bench, we're beginning to make up our mind, and when we're in the Conference Room, we try to have made up our mind tentatively, depending on what other people think. So as we go around the table, it can be quite fascinating to see how a case is un-

Justice Kennedy is readied for C-SPAN's interview in the Court's Conference Room, June 2009.

folding. It's not just win or lose, reverse or affirm; it's what rationale we use. What principle you use to teach something.

And if the case is close, 5 to 4, and let's say you're on the side that prevailed with the majority, there are not a lot of high fives and back slaps. There's a moment of quiet, a moment of respect, maybe even sometimes awe at the process. We realize that one of us is going to have to write out a decision that teaches and gives reasons for what we do. The point of writing an opinion is to command some allegiance to the result, and we have no army. We have no budget. We do not have press conferences, and we don't give speeches, saying how wonderful my dissent was or how bad the majority. We don't do that.

We're judged by what we write, and we have to write something that shows that we're following the rules and that we're open and honest, that we give reasons for you to believe that what we did was right.

Q: Do you take notes in conference?

KENNEDY: Yes. I never speak from notes, but I take notes from what other people say.

Q: Because they might end up framing an argument to bring someone over to your side?

KENNEDY: You take notes because you might be assigned the case. You don't know who's going to be assigned the case until after the conference, and if you're senior in the majority or the dissent, then you assign it. And you should have notes so that you can remember what your colleagues said because, as I indicated, it's not just what you do, but it's how you do it. And it's fascinating. Sometimes a case will be 9–0, but there will be different points of view on how to reach the result, so that's part of the process.

Q: Is the room well designed for what happens there?

KENNEDY: Well sure. It's not all that exciting. It's a rectangular table; that's about it. I suppose you could have a circular table and what was it, the Korean peace talks where they spent a year talking about the size and the shape of the table? Ours happens to be rectangular, and it works out that way. . . . Although when you're getting into the building, why is it that we have an elegant, astonishingly beautiful, imposing, impressive structure? Is it so that we feel important? I think not. It's to remind us that we have an important function and to remind the public when it sees the building of the importance and the centrality of the law.

Sometimes I'll teach a high school class and I'll say, "Give me one word to describe this building." Cold? Warm? Opulent, arrogant, inspiring, durable, stable? Choose your adjectives. The building is magnificent enough so that you can think about these adjectives as you come to it.

Q: Do you have one adjective you would use?

KENNEDY: I would like to say timeless. It dates from the Greeks, of course, and in fact there are a lot of Greek architectural features to it.

What is the shape of the windows? Rectangle? No, they are smaller at the top than at the bottom. It looks like a rectangle, which we found out to our grief when we were ordering new windows. They came and measured the bottom and they measured the height, but they forgot to measure the top.

So the windows were all wrong because they are slightly smaller at the top. It's not a rectangle. It's a quadrilateral structure, designed so that it looks durable, elegant, imposing, balanced, symmetrical from a distance, which is what the law ought to look like.

Q: You mentioned before we started taping that the steps and the entrance are of particular note to you.

KENNEDY: Again it's symbolic. We like to think of the law and the Constitution and the great documents of freedom as something that you have to respect, and so you should frequently be inspired and have elevated thoughts. That's the idea of the steps.

I was one time, meeting—when I first was here on the Court—with a prime minister from a foreign country who is also an attorney. It was a nice day so I met him outside. I thought it would be courteous to do. We stood looking up at this beautiful building and the steps and above the steps on the pediment is "Equal Justice Under Law." I thought, oh my. He's going to ask me where that comes from, and I don't know. My mind was racing. It wasn't in the Declaration of Independence or the Constitution, not in one of our cases. It had to be before [1935] when the building was built.

So I steered the conversation in a different direction so that he wouldn't ask me something I didn't know. Then I went to the files and I found out. "Equal Justice Under Law" was made up by the architect because the size of the letters and the balance of the words kind of works out. It looks good on the pediment. Now, "Equal Justice Under Law" has become a very, very famous phrase. But the law takes help from wherever it can get it. If we get inspiration from an architect, all the better. You can ask yourself if "equal justice" isn't redundant. Isn't all justice not justice if it isn't equal? But we need reminding. So even if it's redundant, we need reminding. The steps are wonderful.

I guess it was five years ago, that in Washington we dedicated the monument to World War II. The government flew World War II veterans in from all over the country and for two or three days they were walking around the city. These people would have been in their late seventies or eighties. I thought I'd take a walk in front of the building. And two of these obvious vets, they came from the Midwest. They had farming community dress. I stopped and said, "Well, good morning. I guess you're here on behalf of the memorial." And they said, "Oh, the government did something very nice for us." And I said, "Well, you did something wonderful for the nation." And the man said, "Charlie here, my friend, we served in the Pacific together as marines, and we now live a couple hundred miles apart. But we phone each other all the time." And he said, "Now come on, Charlie. That's the Supreme Court. We can make it up the steps."

It's important for the justices. It's important for the attorneys. It's important for the public to make sure that people always want to come up these steps because we're doing the job the right way. Not a day goes by where we must not ask ourselves, "Are we doing this job the right way?" The nature of a judge, the nature of a reporter, the nature of most human enterprises is to ask yourself in an introspective way, "Am I doing this the right way?" The law is designed for that, in a way, because we have to write out and give reasons for what we do. The first justification for that is we have to convince ourselves. When I sit down and write an opinion, the first thing I do is convince myself. There's a lot of stuff that goes in the wastebasket. And then you have to convince others. This Court [building] reminds you of the fact that you have to do this job.

Q: As a local citizen, I've always remarked at the design and how suitable it seems to be for public expression of sentiment, the protests and affirmations that go on at the Court. I'm sure that was not the intent of the architect originally, but what do you think about the fact that it's the site of so many public demonstrations?

KENNEDY: It's very important. The law and the Constitution don't belong to the Court. The Constitution is yours. It's yours. And it's yours to talk about, to explain, to express, to defend. That's why it's so important for people, young people particularly, to know and understand the Constitution.

The president takes an oath to preserve, protect, and defend the Constitution. You can't preserve something you don't revere. You can't protect something you haven't learned. You can't defend what you don't know. As I indicated, you must understand the traditions of freedom, its meaning, the purpose of liberty so that you can hand it down to the next generation. Democracy doesn't have a permanent life expectancy. It has to be preserved from one generation to the next.

Q: Can you ever hear the public on days when there are big protests going on when you're working in your chambers?

KENNEDY: It's interesting; I see the demonstrations sometimes, but I'm on the front of the building. But I don't know which side they're on. I know they're interested, but I don't know which side they're on.

Q: So no consciousness as you're working on an opinion of what might be going on outside?

KENNEDY: Only that it reminds you that you have to be clear and honest about your reasons and try to convince people that you're right.

Q: Let's talk about the actual Supreme Court chamber itself. You've worked in other courtrooms. What do you think of this one with its ornate red velvet drapes, and its touches of tradition from past centuries?

KENNEDY: As I've indicated, its principal purpose is to remind the judges and the lawyers and the litigants of the absolute importance, the essential duty that you have, to follow the mandates of your profession and the mandates of the law. That's what it's for.

When the Iron Curtain fell and we began seeing more Russian judges, they couldn't quite believe that the White House didn't give us a call to tell us how this case should come out. We said, "No, no, no. That's not the way it works. There's separation of power." And then they thought, maybe so but there's some cultural mechanism by which we try to see, get the signal from somebody of what to do. It was quite a task, educating our foreign visitors in that respect. When we took them in the courtroom I said two things. I said, number one, the government sits at this table. The government argues its case just like everybody else. And we have a rule that we don't talk to litigants and we don't talk to attorneys, other than in open in public where everybody can hear what the reasons are. That was a help to them, to know that, number one, the government is just like every other litigant. And number two, the government has to argue before us. That helped teach the lesson.

Q: As a lay person, this hadn't struck me before, but you often have attorneys arguing cases here who have one shot at it in their entire legal career. And the court that you came from is a bar where you regularly see the same lawyers; you know their expertise. What's the quality of oral argument here compared to the ninth circuit?

KENNEDY: It's good. I think we sometimes do a disservice to the profession by complaining too much about the oral arguments. It's good. Look, I've made arguments to judges. And I made up my mind that I was always going to be courteous to the attorney and understand the stress that he is under or that she is under. I'm completely at ease. I know they're not. And sometimes we ask a question just to help the attorney make the point that the attorney wanted to make.

Q: We're talking to you on a day close to the end of session with a number of opinions coming out. We were in the press room earlier today, which is quite a scene on a day like this. A number of the reporters have spent much of their professional career here: Nina Totenburg, Lyle Denniston, and the like. What is your relationship as a justice with the long-term reporters covering the Court?

Justice Kennedy during his June 2009 interview.

KENNEDY: I don't see them on a regular basis other than in the Court. Occasionally, there will be a retirement party at which we meet each other. We have each a professional obligation of keeping a certain amount of distance, a certain amount of independence. We never complain about what they write, even though they sometimes are wrong on the facts.

Q: But you do read what they write, obviously.

KENNEDY: Yes. I don't really rush to do it. I am upset sometimes when I see an editorial, and it's obvious they haven't read the opinion and they don't understand. The reason we write, as I explained, is to explain the reason for what we did. To just write an editorial that indicates that you've made up your mind without reading what we wrote is to me quite silly. But by and large, the people who cover us, I like their work. They, as you indicate, know our traditions, they know the schedule, and they do a very good job of reporting with this observation: The news cycle, the interest, the attention span being what it is, they have twenty-four to forty-eight hours to make the point. Well, we write for a different time dimension than that. It's not just the results. It's what the principle is. The press does a very good job of reporting what we do. It's a little more difficult, for reasons I've explained, to report why we did it. I can understand their problem because they have the twenty-four-hour, forty-eight-hour news cycle. So they have a tough job.

Of course, we do have commentary, and we have law reviews. Every law school in the country, every major law school, has a law review. And this law review is dedicated to explaining, criticizing, analyzing, the opinions of the courts, particularly this Court.

So don't think that it's just the institutional press that does this. We have law students who spend months working with a law professor analyzing our cases, often criticizing them in print in the law reviews. And we look at that with some care.

Q: If you had a child or a grandchild that came to you today and said, "I'd like to be a lawyer," would you say, "That's the direction I'd encourage you to go"?

KENNEDY: Absolutely. I still miss being a lawyer. After some years on the bench, I would be very happy to practice law. I loved it.

Q: What is it about it that you love?

KENNEDY: Well, you have an oath, an obligation, to defend something that is really basic to the American identity to the American ideal to freedom as we know it.

Q: And you felt that fresh out of law school?

KENNEDY: Yes. And you're playing a little part in that when you have a case involving a misdemeanor or even a felony. You're just a little cog in the wheel. But the idea that the government cannot arrest your client without cause, convict your client without proof beyond a reasonable doubt is so impressive.

Half the world doesn't have freedom, A, because it can't, or B, because it doesn't want it. And the jury is out. As to whether or not the rest of the world will choose freedom, we have to make that case. And frankly, it's not being made. I'm not sure that we're picking up a lot of ground.

q: What do you mean by that?

KENNEDY: There are 6 billion people on this earth. Over half of them have to live outside the law. They see the law as an obstacle, not an instrument of progress. They see the law as a threat, not a promise. They see the law as something to avoid, [not] something to be embraced. They don't understand it.

I gave a speech not long ago in which I talked about Solzhenitsyn, the great Soviet writer. He gave a commencement speech in the 1970s: '78. He criticized the United States and the West for being obsessed with the law. I was astounded that this man who I thought understood the principles of freedom, the unyielding, indomitable, human spirit to rise above tyranny, would criticize law. And it occurred to me that he thinks of the law as something cold, a threat. We don't. For us, the law is liberating. And that's a big difference. We have to teach that. We don't teach enough of it.

q: As you look across the justices, because of your lifetime tenure, because there isn't media coverage of this Court in the same way as the elective branches of government, you could choose whether or not you wish to be a public figure, to give speeches, to give commencement addresses, to teach, to do interviews such as this. You have chosen to do this to some degree. Why is that?

KENNEDY: Again, because I think it's our obligation to do our very best to make sure that the institution is understood, to make sure that people know what's at stake. When we say that we want freedom for the rest of the world and that freedom, we think, is the only way to recognize the dignity of man, the dignity of woman, this is something that we can't talk about too much. Americans are busy. They're going to baseball games. They're working. They're raising their families. They don't think about the law night and day. But I'm so impressed, when I go around the country, at how much people do know about their court system, about the respect that they do have for it. And of course that's one reason we have the jury system, which is a whole other subject.

Q: As we close here, you're about to leave for summer. And while you're gone, there'll be hearings for a new justice for the Supreme Court. You've seen others come and go during your twenty-one years here. How much does the Court change when a new justice arrives? Is there a cultural shift? And what do you do to get a new member acclimated, as you talked about in the beginning?

KENNEDY: It's a new court. When I was trying jury cases, which is usually twelve, if a juror had to be replaced because one was ill or something, it was a different dynamic. It was a different jury. It's the same way here. This will be a very different court.

It's stressful for us because we so admire our colleagues. We wonder, "Will it ever be the same?" But I have great admiration for the system. The system works. After the appointment and the confirmation process is finished, if there's a confirmation, the system will bring us a very, very good justice.

It gives us the opportunity, again, to look at ourselves to make sure that we're doing it the right way so that the new justice will be able to take some instruction from our example if we are doing it the right way. I'm sure a new justice can always ask the question, "Well, what are you doing this for?" Then we have to think about whether or not we should continue to do it.

Q: Justice Kennedy, thank you so much for your observations on the Court.

KENNEDY: Thank you for your work.

JUSTICE
CLARENCE THOMAS

Clarence Thomas was nominated as the 106th justice of the Supreme Court by President George H. W. Bush. Born in Pin Point, Georgia, Justice Thomas attended Holy Cross College and Yale Law School. His earlier career included the Equal Employment Opportunity Commission and service on the U.S. Court of Appeals, DC Circuit. He was interviewed in the Court's East Conference Room by Susan Swain on July 29, 2009.

———————

SWAIN: Justice Thomas, we're sitting in a Supreme Court Conference Room for this conversation. Do you have a memory of the first time you ever walked inside this building?

ASSOCIATE JUSTICE CLARENCE THOMAS: I do. I was a Hill staffer in the Russell Senate Office Building in the early 1980s, probably; it may have been even as early as 1979. I loved the city. I would walk over to the Library of Congress, the then-new Madison building. I poked my head in this building one day and was overwhelmed by what I saw and immediately left. I only got as far as the Great Hall.

Q: Why was that?

THOMAS: You know, the Supreme Court is special. It was special when I was a kid; it's special for what it's done, what it symbolizes, and unlike the Library of Congress—I love libraries—it's just interesting. The Supreme Court was awesome in a sense that it was someplace [where I thought] "Maybe I'm not supposed to be here." And, I was relatively young. But that was my first foray into the building, and I didn't come into it again for a number of years. Eventually, I came to a few events here, and just briefly before I was nominated, one of my former law clerks took me on a very brief tour of the building, but that was about it before I came as a member of the Court.

Q: During any of those visits, do you remember feeling aspirational, as in "This is a place I could be someday?"

THOMAS: Oh goodness, no! No. This was not something that I could look forward to or think about. I had not thought about being a judge. The irony was that I had been approached about considering becoming a member of the Missouri Supreme Court in my early thirties. I thought that was far too young, and I did not know whether or not I wanted to be a judge. I didn't think I did.

Q: Why does age matter when you are a judge?

THOMAS: Maybe we all mature at different rates; we probably do. But I do think there are decisions that we make at forty or fifty that we would not have made at twenty or thirty. I think that you have judgment that comes from having had the experiences, and experience that you don't have in your early years.

Q: I was interested in the tour that your former clerk gave you of the building. When you take people on tours, where are the places that you like to take them?

THOMAS: I don't do tours like that. But the whole building is special to me. The people [who work] in the basement of the building . . . every room is special. The various gardens around here are special. I think that if I had to envision what a Supreme Court should look like, this is it. I wouldn't change anything. There are some times, particularly in my early years, when you're here late at night, you didn't have all this connectivity that we have now where you're free to work at home, but you get drained. You are tired. You're wondering, "Why am I doing this?" And I would just simply leave the building and go around front and look at this institution from that side. It's hard not to get goose bumps; it's hard not to realize that this is much larger than me.

I can remember when I first got here, and I was relatively young in those days. Justice Powell and I went to lunch, I believe, at the Monocle, and we were returning, and he looked at this building. At that time, he had retired from the Court and was in questionable health and was rather frail. We were the two southerners on the Court, so we loved to have lunch and to chat. And he looked at this building as we approached it, and he said, "Once you think you belong here, it's time for you to leave." Meaning, that this institution and what it represents and what we do is much larger than us. And I think the building reflects that. It says to each of us that it is much larger than us.

Q: You said it was the perfect building; I'm sure in the course of your work over the years, you've visited both state supreme courts and high courts in other countries. What is it about what the architect captured in this building that symbolizes the work of the Court?

THOMAS: I'm not an architect, and I'm not an artist.

Q: I understand, but it appeals to you, so something about it sings to you. What is it?

THOMAS: Well, it gives you that sense that there's something that transcends the mundane part of the job. That there's an ideal that's beyond the day-to-day, back-and-forth, the disagreements, the opinion work, the reading of briefs. I remember when I first got here, Senator [John] Danforth came over when Chief Justice Rehnquist was swearing me in. He looked at the rows of briefs that had to be read and joint appendixes, and he said, "Clarence, this looks really boring." Maybe the mundane part of it is, but it's for a good reason. And I think this building—just look at it—the architecture, the rooms, the atmosphere, how quiet it is, how serious it is, it says to you that the work is important. I think the danger is that sometimes you can come into a building like this and think it's all about you, or that you're important. And that is something that I don't think works well with this job. I think that's the point Justice Powell was making. But as far as the architecture and the specifics of that, I don't know enough about architecture to tell you. It's just, it gives you the sense of the awesomeness of the institution and the work.

Q: Let's move on to the work done here. Would you describe your reflections on the role of the Court in our society today?

THOMAS: I happen to think that our job is to decide cases. We're Article III judges. And there are so many problems that come our way, and issues and questions that come our way, that sometimes we have a larger role than the Framers envisioned. But it's certainly one of the three branches; we're part of the top of one of the three branches of government. Beyond that, deciding important things about our society, I don't have a particular view that we're larger than life or anything like that.

Q: Can you describe what you do?

THOMAS: I decide cases. That's it.

Q: But there's a lot of process that goes into that.

THOMAS: There is, you're right. And that's the mundane part. You remember years ago there were several TV programs about the Court and they were supposed to be sitcoms. And I just wondered, "Who in the heck's going to watch that?" Because most of it is rather sedentary. You come in; you sit; you get your work done. When I first got here, Justice White said that you have to get a system. So you develop a system to approach every case, because there is nobody to tell you when to start. There's no game plan that's sent out by anyone. There's no timeline. You know when the sittings are, you know what cases are going to be dealt with, you know when we're going to have our conferences. And you must get it done. You must get your *cert* work done, you must get your opinion writing done. I usually divide the work into three categories: You have to decide which cases come here, you decide those cases, and then you write opinions. And you agree or disagree with opinions. That's it. You continue throughout the year, reviewing the *cert* petitions; those are the requests. Most people think they have a right to come to the Court. For the most part, you don't, not this Court; maybe the court of appeals, you normally do; maybe the state courts of appeal and courts that don't have discretionary jurisdiction, the courts of last resort—maybe they have a right to go to those. But here, most of our jurisdiction is discretionary. In other words, we decide if you come.

We receive about nine thousand requests a year. In the last few years, we've taken around eighty cases. Now, there's a process of sorting through that. I like to go through all of those requests. We do that in short memoranda; they're not so short. There are memoranda we call pool memoranda. Two of the members of the Court are not in the pool; in other words, we don't share that memoranda with them, or the memorandum, with them. But I go through all nine thousand of those. That's a regular process. You do that almost every day. During the year, I like to have that done on the weekend before the conference, which is normally on Friday. So, that's a part of your workday that you don't normally think about. It's routine; it's like brushing your teeth. And it's continuous. As far as preparing for argued cases, those are the ones that we've said we will hear. There are two ways that cases are argued: in writing and then in the courtroom; that's our oral argument.

In my view, most of the heavy lifting, most of the work, is done in the written briefs, written arguments by the parties. They're usually over fifty pages per side and . . . [cover] a lot of areas we've worked on before. Whether it's the Fourth Amendment, the Fifth Amendment, the First Amendment, you're getting another iteration of an old problem. You're getting another view, another aspect of it, but it's not brand new. This is not Perry Mason; this is not some mysterious thing going on. We know where the law is going, and this is just another part of it. You read the briefs, and I have what I call, with all four of my law clerks, a clerks conference. We actually debate it back and forth. Out of that, we prepare what I call a "disposition memorandum." That becomes sort of a decision tree of how the case is going to be, my view of the case. We have all of this before oral argument.

You go to oral argument, and I don't find those as useful now, because I think there are far too many questions. We all learn differently. Some members of the Court like that interaction; it helps them learn and process what they have been thinking. I prefer to listen and think it through more quietly. Each to his own. After oral argument, I go back, I meet again with my law clerks and again we think, "Is there anything new from oral argument to add to the equation?" Usually there are a few things, but nothing that totally changes what we've done, based on the briefs. After that, we finalize our disposition memorandum. We go to conference, the cases that we hear on Mondays, that are argued on Mondays, are decided on Wednesday afternoons. The cases that are argued on Tuesday and Wednesday are decided on Friday morning.

I go to conference with this disposition, and that's the explanation for the vote. The senior member in the majority vote—it's normally the chief justice—assigns who's going to write the opinion. You get the opinion, now I already have an outline, together with my notes from conference, and, just like we were taught in the eighth grade, you have an outline for your essay. You already have an outline for the draft opinion. And that's basically the process. You go through the draft, it gets circulated, and then it's finalized.

Q: Do you mind if I pick that apart just a little bit to learn more about those steps?

THOMAS: Yes, you sure can.

Justice Thomas with a student at DC's Banneker High School, during a C-SPAN *Students and Leaders* event in 2003.

q: Let me start with the petitions for *cert*, as it's called, *certiorari*—cases you will decide to hear; the volume versus the number selected. The volume of petitions keeps growing; it seems as though the number of cases heard continues to lower slightly each year. Why is that? Does the Court hear the appropriate number in a term?

THOMAS: We hear what's *cert*-worthy. What four members [deem *cert*-worthy]; it takes four votes to decide what comes up here. When I first came on the Court, we had about 120, about 110 or so. I like that number. I think that's a good number.

q: Why do you like it; what's the difference?

THOMAS: It keeps you busy. You hear four cases a day, rather than two. It really pushes the process. The problem is this: We only take what we call is *cert*-worthy. There has to be a significant federal issue, usually some confusion with the lower courts, with the courts of appeal, state courts of last resort. I can assure you that there may be one or two that I would quibble with per term, but there isn't some huge list to make up the difference. Maybe it's that the courts of appeal are more in agreement; maybe there hasn't been any major legislation that changes the landscape. When I first came on board, you had the bankruptcy act, you had ERISA. But there are not sea changes going on out there. Again, our mandatory jurisdiction has been basically eliminated, or it's minimal now. You don't have that big pocket, so I can't explain it and I don't think anyone can. Anything we say would be speculation. There is no desire to reduce the numbers on my part or, to my thinking, in anything I've seen on the part of any of my colleagues.

Q: Some of the other justices we've talked to have particular areas of review that they find more interesting, stimulating, intellectually challenging. Do you? Are there certain parts of the Constitution that you love to dig into and get another opportunity to visit with a case?

THOMAS: It goes against my nature to want to make big decisions about other people's lives. That's my job. I do it. So I can't tell you that I look forward to wading into these "exciting" areas. I look forward to watching my Nebraska Cornhuskers, but . . . this is about our country and our Constitution. I get my game face on. This is our job. The cases that I am perhaps most excited about are the ones that have the least impact on people's lives. That then relieves you of some of that burden. But the way I try to do it, is not so much to get some exhilaration from it, but to be faithful to the Constitution, to be faithful to the oath that I took to uphold it, to interpret it. And the exhilaration I get is at the end of each term to be able to say that I gave it my best shot.

Q: Will you talk about the recognition that your work affects people's lives? You just said the cases that you prefer are the cases that don't directly have an impact on the ways people live their lives. Why is that?

THOMAS: I think that when you look at our country, some of the decisions that we make, interpreting the Constitution—people win, people lose—[these decisions] have tremendous impact. You have changes in the Constitution. You have cases involving detention. You have cases involving execution of other human beings. You have cases involving our sentencing system, criminal justice system, First Amendment, what can be seized from other human beings, fellow citizens. I don't get joy out of making decisions like that. What I do get a fulfillment from is living up to the oath to do it the right way. And knowing that on behalf of my fellow citizens I've tried to be faithful to their Constitution, to our Constitution. That's where the exhilaration comes, living up to the oath that I took, and the obligations that I have under Article III.

Q: Let me move to argument. You referenced the fact that you listen during argument. Much has been made of that by court observers. We've read and heard from other justices that sometimes the arguments are used for the justices to communicate with one another, telegraphing their opinions through the kinds of questions and areas they explore. Do you find that happening a lot as well?

THOMAS: I have no idea.

Q: Do you pick up cues from other justices about where they're going with a particular case from the questions they ask?

THOMAS: Not really. I view oral argument a little bit differently. I think it's an opportunity for the advocate, the lawyers, to fill in the blanks, to make their case, to point out things perhaps that were not covered in the briefs or to emphasize things or to respond to some concerns, that sort of thing. In other words, to flesh out the case a little better, to get into the weeds a little more. We're here, the nine of us, and we can talk to each other anytime we want to. I wouldn't use that thirty minutes of the advocate's time to do that, to talk to each other. But as I said earlier, we all learn differently. My bride would learn, when she was in school—she's more interactive, I'm not. I was never that way. I don't learn that way.

When I first came to the Court, the Court was much quieter than it is now. Then perhaps, it was too quiet. I don't know. I liked it that way because it left big gaps so you could actually have a conversation. I think it's hard to have a conversation when nobody is listening, when you can't complete sentences or answers. Perhaps that's a southern thing. I don't know. But I think you should allow people to complete their answers and their thought, and to continue their conversation. I find that coherence that you get from a conversation far more helpful than the rapid-fire questions. I don't see how you can learn a whole lot when there are fifty questions in an hour.

Q: Let me move to the process of conference because it still feels mysterious.

THOMAS: It should be.

Q: Because that's the place where all of you are behind closed doors and none of the rest of us ever get to see it. Can you tell me what happens in that room?

THOMAS: It should be mysterious. I can still remember the first time I set foot in that room and those doors closed. I mean, my goodness, it's pretty daunting the first few times. That's where the actual work and the decision making takes place. It's just the nine, there's no staff, no recording devices. And we vote in descending order of seniority. . . . And people are engaged; they actually talk about the case. They actually tell you what they think and why. You record the votes. And there's some back-and-forth; there's more now. When Chief Justice Rehnquist was here, he moved it along very quickly. Now there's more back-and-forth, more discussion. We normally have one break, and there's more discussion, off to the sides, about cases. To see people who are trying their best to decide hard things and feel strongly about their view of it, is fascinating. And the thing that's been great is, I just finished my eighteenth term, and I still haven't heard the first unkind word in that room. You think about what we've decided—life and death, abortion, execution, war and peace, financial ruin, government's relationship with citizens. You name it. We've decided it. And I still have not heard the first *ad hominem* in that room. It is an example of what I would have thought decision making would be at the higher levels of civil government in all parts of our country.

Q: What ensures that decorum?

THOMAS: The human beings on this Court, and people who, in one way or another, one degree or another, understand that it's not about them. It's about the Constitution, our country, and our fellow citizens. They don't take themselves as seriously as they take the work of the Court.

Q: We've learned a lot about the many traditions this Court holds and its processes that are passed down from Court to Court. Some of those happen in the Conference Room, such as the handshake. How important are symbols and traditions to the process that happens here?

THOMAS: I think the handshake, whether you're in sports or church or other activities, it means something. It still means something. We can sense when somebody's phony and they don't mean it. These people, in this room, are genuine. It's warm and professional. There's always a handshake before we go on the bench. When we see each other—it's the first time during the day—we always make sure to shake hands, whether it's in public or in private. There's a sense of courtesy and decency and civility that's a part of it.

On the days that we work, whether we're on the bench or we are in conference, we go to lunch together. In the early years when I first came here, we had that lunch in a small room off the main dining room. Justice O'Connor insisted that we have lunch every day when we were sitting. And she insisted, "Now Clarence, you should come to lunch." She was really sweet, but very persistent. I came to lunch, and it was one of the best things I did. It is hard to be angry or bitter at someone and break bread and look them in the eye. It is a fun lunch; very little work is done there. It's just nine people, eight people—whoever shows up—having a wonderful lunch together. It is wonderful. So the traditions, I think, are important. It's like traditions in our society, in our culture. They developed over time for a reason. And these traditions help sustain us in the other work that we do, I think.

Q: Now, the chief makes the assignment as to who will write the opinion after you've taken your initial round of voting. He told us that he tries to be judicious in handing out the assignments. And do you ever have a sense of "I hope he picks me," or do you indicate to him or lobby that this is one opinion you'd really like to tackle? How does that work?

THOMAS: No, I don't. I think Chief Justice Rehnquist approached me and said years ago that I had not lobbied him for anything and asked if there was anything I wanted. And I said, "Well, there's this Missouri sales tax case I really like, because that's where I started." But I truly believe that the chief justice is fair in what he does. It's his job to make the assignments. If we're on the same side, I write the opinion. And I try to be faithful to the conference in drafting the opinion. But I don't lobby for opinions.

The only time I would ask for assignments is if I have a work imbalance in my chambers. But other than that, I don't lobby. [I don't say,] "I want this opinion because I think I'm the best person to write it." It might be one where the Court is a little bit fractured, and I think I have a way of pulling us together. But that's not an ego thing; that is, "Let's get this done and maybe we can get everybody on board if I try this way." Then if you can't, then at least you've given it the college try. I don't really lobby for it.

Q: Do you intellectually approach the writing of a majority opinion differently than you do a dissent?

THOMAS: Oh yes. You are an agent of the majority when you write the majority opinion; that's the way I approach that. And what you try to do is . . . let's say for example . . . and I'll put it numerically, so it's easier to follow. . . . Let's say I would go the same direction, but I'd go eighty yards. But the majority only wants to go sixty, and sixty would decide this case, too. So, I would write the opinion to go sixty and not say anything about what I would also do to go for the other twenty yards. Now if I were writing a concurrence or dissent on my own, I would write the opinion in a way that reflects that I would go eighty. So we're going the same way. I could not write an opinion that went in a direction that was different from what I actually thought we should go. But you have to make adjustments in the approach to the opinion to reflect the views of the majority. And if you can't do that, then you shouldn't write the opinion.

Q: Do you read the major and longtime reporters who cover the Court? Do you read their work?

THOMAS: I rarely read anything current events [related] about the Court.

Q: I'm wondering what you think about the quality of the reporting about this institution. Do you have an opinion of that?

THOMAS: There's a reason why I don't read it. They are wonderful people out here who do a good job . . . a fantastic job . . . like Jan Greenburg, but I normally do not follow current events. I might look at a few things at the end of the term or things that have been brought to my attention. But I don't want to get distracted. It's like a lot of the really good athletes don't read press clippings. I don't read the ups and downs. My job is to decide cases. People can write what they want to write about it. I think that's up to them, but my job is to decide cases.

Q: So staying out of current events, in the years since you've been appointed, when a new associate justice is up before the Senate for confirmation, do you follow that process at all?

THOMAS: Only what I can't avoid. I did not have a fond experience up there. I just don't wish that on anyone. And also, something Justice White said when I first got here has stuck with me: that it doesn't matter how you got here; it matters what you do after you've gotten here. That has always stuck with me.

The members of the Court, appointed by different presidents, when they walk in this building they become a part of the nine. And we work with them. So, the most important thing is that they're good people who are conscientious and try to do the job in the best way they can consistent with their own [principles]. I respect that. I have to respect that, believe that they will do that. Agreement isn't a consideration. That's why you have elections. They don't have to agree with me. Because I'm certainly not going to agree with them, just to be agreeing with them. . . .

Q: The Court's about to welcome a new associate justice. How long does it take? You talked about walking into conference for the first time. When you've watched new justices come on board since you've arrived, how long does it take before they "get it"?

THOMAS: I don't know. I think we all learn at different paces. But when I came to the Court, I asked that same question, because it was very important to me to figure out when I would get my sea legs. And the common year number was five years.

Q: Five years?

THOMAS: Justice White would often say that it takes about that long to go around the full horn of all the cases, the kinds of cases that we get. That was their number. That may be about right. That doesn't mean you can't do your work. It just means that things are still new for the first five years. You may not have had as many original jurisdiction cases involving water rights or boundaries. You may not have had a lot of admiralty cases. So you get all of that. It was Chief Justice Rehnquist, when I was complaining, "Oh my goodness, what am I doing here?" It was my first year. I would look around me and see people like him who'd been here, at that time, for three decades. I'd see Justice White, who was legendary; Justice O'Connor. And [Justice White] said, "Well, Clarence, in your first five years you wonder how you got here. After that, you wonder how your colleagues got here." I don't know whether that's true, exactly, but it certainly is an indication that that five-year period was fairly well accepted as the break-in period.

Q: What affects the tenor of any particular Court more, the composition of the Court overall—the new justices coming in—or the chief who leads it?

THOMAS: I don't know. I think that they're separate things. The chief is the chief. Chief Justice Rehnquist's style was different from Chief Justice Roberts's style. Chief Justice Roberts is more of a contemporary. Chief Justice Rehnquist could have been my father from a standpoint of age. So there is quite a difference in a lot of things. He was more of, "Let's keep the trains running." Chief Justice Roberts does not push like that.

As far as the composition of the Court, you're bringing in basically, and this word can be overused, you're bringing in a family member. It changes the whole family. It's different. It's different today than it was when I first got here. I have to admit, you grow very fond of the Court that you spent a long time on. There was a period there with Chief Justice Rehnquist and Justice O'Connor when we had a long run together. You get comfortable with that, and then it changes. And now, it's changing again. So, the institution, the nine are different; your reaction is different; you get to learn each other. You have to start all over. The chemistry is different.

Q: You've referenced justices with whom you've served. Are there any throughout history that you find that you refer to frequently as giving you good guidance, good intellectual direction or who were particularly significant on the operation of the Court?

THOMAS: I find the member of the Court that I refer back to is the first Justice Harlan. I find his dissent in *Plessy vs. Ferguson*, where he admits his own biases, but [says] this document, this Constitution knows no caste. [He says,] "I might have a particular view; I might have a bias—but not this document." That, to me, is judging. To admit that you may have a weakness or a problem, but we can't read that into this document. The two are separate.

The members of the Court with whom I've served have been wonderful to me. You learn from people who are around you. And you learn from Justice O'Connor, a wonderful friend. There's no sadder day around here than when a member of this Court leaves. When Justice Souter announced that he was leaving—remember, I've served almost eighteen years with him. He becomes your friend. You don't have to agree, but he's your friend. When you hear one of your colleagues is sick, it's one of your family members who's sick. So much is made of whether we agree or disagree. Can you think of any human being with whom you agree on everything? Large or small, doesn't happen. But there are people you feel a closeness with, people that you've done a job with, people that you've been through difficult decision-making processes with. You feel a closeness and you've done it in a way that you think has been respectful to each other and to the institution and to your fellow citizens.

Q: We've just recently conducted, with the help of a Washington public opinion firm, a survey of a thousand-plus Americans on the Court. We asked just a few questions, but it's interesting that when asked to name any sitting justice a majority of the respondents could not name one. What's your reaction to that? Is that appropriate?

THOMAS: I think that that may be a reflection on the way we teach civics. I don't think that everyone has to know who we are. I would prefer that they know a few of us who are making big decisions that affect their country and their lives. When I was a kid, we took civics and we were required to learn those basic things. But, it may be, it's not the best news. I would prefer that they know a little bit more about their Court.

Q: Does it speak at all to the level of visibility that the Court has as opposed to the teaching of justice?

THOMAS: Well, I don't know how many of those people also knew who their congressman was, their member of Congress was.

Q: Sure. We didn't ask that question, so I can't tell you.

THOMAS: I don't think the Court should necessarily get into every aspect of people's lives. . . . Maybe people shouldn't know who all the federal judges are in their district. Maybe we shouldn't be any more visible than we are. We're not politicians. I don't think we have to be that public. We should do our job. We should be as an institution, the Supreme Court. They're aware of the Supreme Court. Maybe that should be enough. I'm the 106th member of the Court. And I think sometimes that we make too much of who's here now because when you go back it's hard to remember who was here before. Challenge people: name me twenty dead members of the Court. I think they would be hard-pressed, even people who consider themselves Court followers.

Q: To that end, of the minority of the respondents who could name any justices, three were named. You were among the three. When you go out here, outside of this place, are you frequently recognized?

THOMAS: Oh, goodness yes. The anonymity is gone. That is probably, or was probably one of the more difficult things to accept, the lost anonymity, the ability to walk down the Mall unnoticed or to go to the Home Depot unnoticed.

Q: Because of the confirmation hearings?

Clarence Thomas's Senate confirmation hearings, 1991.

THOMAS: No. Those were eighteen years ago.

Q: Right. That's what I was thinking.

THOMAS: But, no it's still, I'm the only black guy up here so I'm easier to recognize—I think like when Justice O'Connor was the only woman—[it's easier] to pick one person out who's different. Maybe that's part of it. I think that I've enjoyed such positive press and notoriety. So, I think that may be a part of it. I have no idea.

Q: When people come up to you, what are the interactions like?

THOMAS: It's always very pleasant. They're very nice people. There are nice people, good people, all over this country. One of the things that happens up here is we tend to be very heavily northeastern in our mentality. Eight of the nine of us are from Ivy League schools. This Court doesn't represent all regions of the country. There's a tendency, there's an easiness to sort of stay, to be almost cliquish in that way, with law clerks, etcetera. I like the idea of getting out to be around the real, the citizens, the other citizens in the country, people who make it all work, people who put out our fires, who build our homes, people who fight our wars. I like being around them. I also like the idea that their kids can come up here and clerk, that they can be a part of all this.

So yeah, I've lost the anonymity and I would prefer to have that back, but that's not going to happen. The good part is to have people, regular people, come up and talk with you. There are some wonderful exchanges. I take my clerks to Gettysburg every year, and a gentleman came up, he was out of breath, and he had a maritime commission case. He was waving it. He had it on this parchment-like paper. He had my opinion. He said, "Would you sign this for me?" I said, "Why, why are you even reading this opinion?" He said, "That's what this is all about." I said, "The maritime commission case?" Or you have someone who comes up and says, "Thanks for writing your opinions in a way that I can understand it." Notice, he didn't say he agreed. But he can understand them. In other words, the Constitution has become accessible to him again. The laws about his Constitution are accessible to him. That's what we try to do, to make sure that those people who come up to you have a part in this institution, and feel a part of this institution. So, it's not all mysterious, as you say the Conference Room is.

Q: So, in the summer and during breaks, you get into that motor coach that you own and go out around the country, that's intentional? To get out. . . .

THOMAS: Oh, yes. Initially, that was one of the reasons I wanted to go. I had never really seen my home state much, and I wanted to ride around it. Someone said the nicest people in the country are in RV parks. I have found nothing, in almost ten years of doing this, I've found nothing to disagree with them about there. They've been nice. They're neighborly. They're friendly. They're good people. . . . We seem to be at each other's throats in this town. In the country, there's still a

Justice Thomas visits the C-SPAN School Bus, 2001.

bunch of people out there who sit down and have a cup of coffee and talk about the game or the weather, how good the country is, problems that we all have, and maybe are a little bit more civil with each other.

Q: Do you think you judge differently as a result of those trips?

THOMAS: I think my focus is more on regular citizens when I judge in these cases, and my fellow citizens. [My focus is] not on who writes about us. It's not about who writes law review articles or teaches con[stitutional] law. It's on the guy who came up to me at Gettysburg, or the man who you run into at Home Depot, or the person who has just returned from a war, or the person who teaches your kid. These are the experiences, in the motor or the RV parks, in the truck stops, the rest stops, the things that stay with you. You ask me about opinions that you are exhilarated about, but what exhilarates me is meeting those people and letting them know that this member of the Court enjoys the same things they enjoy. And this member of the Court is willing to be where you are, in this RV park, enjoying the simple things about this country, and is willing to listen to what you have to say, not about the cases, because that's not what we argue, but about our country and about things that we have a mutual interest in.

Q: Associate Justice Clarence Thomas, thank you so much for the conversation.

THOMAS: Well, thank you.

JUSTICE
RUTH BADER GINSBURG

*R*uth Bader Ginsburg, the 107th justice, had an earlier career as the chief counsel for the ACLU. In 1980, she joined the U.S. Court of Appeals for the DC Circuit. President Bill Clinton appointed her to the Supreme Court in 1993. Justice Ginsburg invited C-SPAN cameras into her chambers for an on-camera tour with Brian Lamb on July 1, 2009.

———————————

LAMB: We're with Justice Ruth Bader Ginsburg in her temporary office, and we're going to take a look at some of the items you have in this office. The first thing I noticed, Justice Ginsburg, was this photograph over here on your bookstand of former Chief Justice Rehnquist. When was that taken?

ASSOCIATE JUSTICE RUTH BADER GINSBURG: That picture was taken in October 1993. It's traditional when a new justice comes on board for the chief to welcome the new justice at the bottom of the stairs. We walked from the door down the stairs together. He greets me and then we go back into the Court together.

Q: What is your philosophy for your office? There are a lot of pictures in here.

GINSBURG: We'll talk first about the paintings that I have—two from the National Gallery, both early Mark Rothkos, and about five from the Museum of American Art from a collection called "The Frost Collection." It's [a collection of] painters all from the United States in the period roughly from 1920 into the 1930s.

Q: Did you pick them yourself?

GINSBURG: Yes.

Q: And which one in here is your favorite?

GINSBURG: My favorite, in fact, is in the outer room. It's called *Infinity*. It looks like a figure eight.

Q: What's the one behind your desk?

GINSBURG: These are the two from the National Gallery; these are the two early Rothkos. Those are my number one favorites of the items from the Museum of American Art. I like Ben Cunningham's *Infinity*.

Q: Talk about these photos over here. Tell us about any one that comes to mind.

GINSBURG: In this photo, Justice Kennedy, Justice Breyer, and I are taking part in the Washington National Opera's production of *Fledermaus*. We were supernumeraries, extras. This is the ball scene from *Die Fledermaus*. The prince welcomes guests of various kinds. So he welcomed the ambassador of Russia, the ambassador of Hungary, and then he greeted the three Supremes and we marched on to the stage and sat on a bank for the rest of that act and watched the show.

Q: What about the gavels?

GINSBURG: The gavels were given to me by various people. They all have inscriptions, and I don't know that any of those are particularly memorable. But there is a photograph there that was taken in 1978. Justice [Thurgood] Marshall and I were judging a moot court at the University of California at Berkeley Law School, and it's one of my fondest remembrances. He was still in very good health then.

Q: When you work in an office like this, what atmosphere do you want? Does it matter to you where you are when you do your writing and thinking and reading?

GINSBURG: I like to be in a quiet place. I like to have my law clerks close at hand. In my regular chambers, all of the law clerks were inside chambers. Now, I have two that are in that office and two down the hall. I'm glad to be overlooking a courtyard and not on the front of the building so I'm not disturbed by demonstrators.

Q: What are these masks right here?

GINSBURG: These masks are from my first trip to China, which was in 1978 when China was barely set up for tourists. Someone gave me this set of masks while I was there.

Q: What about the photos? There's a whole series of them back here.

GINSBURG: Those are also from that 1978 trip to China. I was with the first American Bar Association delegation to visit China at the request of their government. I was most fortunate because I was the only woman on the delegation. China was not well set up for tourists yet, so I had a room of my own throughout the trip. And these pillars of the bar, these distinguished gentlemen, had to double up in a room.

Q: Right next to that is a photograph of Senator [Barbara] Mikulski, it looks like. When was that taken?

GINSBURG: That was taken also in 1993 when I was the new justice. And it's my example of how relative most things are. So if you ask me, am I short? I'd say yes, compared to Chief Justice Rehnquist, but next to Senator Mikulski I'm a giant.

Q: So this desk, is that your personal selection, and where did you get it?

GINSBURG: This desk was made here at the Court. All of the chambers have similar desks. The variation in these chambers is that I have put a granite top on the desk as I have at the worktable.

Q: And what kind of books do you keep on the shelf in front of you?

GINSBURG: Books that I consult most often. I have the books to which I refer in two places, there and also on this cart.

Q: What would be the book that you refer to the most often?

GINSBURG: It would be a toss-up between these two. This one is Hart and Wechsler's *The Federal Courts and the Federal System,* now in the seventh edition. And the *Constitutional Law* casebook now by Kathleen Sullivan. For many, many years Gerald Gunther produced this book by himself until two editions ago when Kathleen Sullivan joined him. And, now, since Professor Gunther's death, she's carrying on the work.

Q: Is this a book that all judges and justices would have in their office?

GINSBURG: They would certainly have some constitutional law reference. I don't know that they would all choose the same one. This is one of the finest casebooks in all of law school. And Gerald Gunther was my teacher at Columbia and my good friend ever after.

Q: What do you remember most about him?

GINSBURG: His brilliance and his humanity.

Q: On the other side of your desk here you have a kind of president's corner. How many presidents have you known?

GINSBURG: We start with Jimmy Carter, who gave me my first good job in this capital city. When Jimmy Carter became president, there was only one woman on a federal appellate bench in the entire country. And Jimmy Carter was determined to change the complexion of the U.S. judiciary. There's a photograph that shows President Carter in October 1980 when he may have sensed that he would lose the election, but he held a reception for women he had appointed to the bench and said that he hoped he would be remembered for changing the face of the U.S. judiciary, for appointing women and members of minority groups in numbers.

He chose people of the very best quality but people who hadn't been looked for before. After he set that pattern, no president ever retreated from it. So President Reagan was determined to be the president who appointed the first woman to this Court, as he did. He made a splendid choice in Justice Sandra Day O'Connor. But it was Jimmy Carter who decided that federal judiciary should draw on the talent of all of the people of the great United States and not just some of them.

Q: What did you do in his administration?

GINSBURG: I was on the U.S. Court of Appeals for the DC circuit, that U.S. courthouse just a few blocks down the road.

Q: So before that, you had not had any government experience?

GINSBURG: Before that, I had been a law teacher for seventeen years and general counsel to the American Civil Liberties Union.

Q: And one of the things that you talk about from time to time is the fact that you were before the Court representing the ACLU.

Justice Ginsburg.

GINSBURG: Yes, representing a client that was supported by the ACLU.

Q: What is the difference between standing in front of the Court and being on the other side?

GINSBURG: The difference is that on the other side you ask the questions and being at counsel's podium, you answer questions.

Q: From your own experience of standing before the Court, have you treated the attorneys any differently because you had that experience originally?

GINSBURG: I think I have a keen understanding of what it's like to be at the receiving end of questions. But I also know that as an attorney I welcomed questions from the bench. I know that some lawyers regard questions as an interruption in an eloquent speech that they are prepared to make. But an advocate wants to know what's on the judge's mind. So she will welcome questions as a way of satisfying the judge on a matter that the judge might not resolve as well without counsel's response.

Q: I've got to ask you about this picture back here.

GINSBURG: That is my husband of fifty-five years, Martin David Ginsburg, professor of law at Georgetown University Law Center. This is a typical Marty pose, relaxing on our patio with a good book.

Q: One of the things you often talk about in speeches is his cooking.

GINSBURG: Yes. He is the master chef in our house. I was phased out of the kitchen by my food-loving children, now thirty years ago.

Q: Does he ever cook for the Court?

GINSBURG: Yes. Martin is much in demand at the quarterly lunches that Supreme Court spouses have. I may be a little biased and prejudiced on this point, but I think he's by far the best cook among all of the spouses.

Q: How do those quarterly lunches work? Are they just for the justices?

GINSBURG: Just for the justices' spouses. For the husband, now the lone husband, and the wives of justices. They also regularly invite the widows of justices, so Cathy Douglas Stone and Annie Stewart and Cissy Marshall are regularly at those lunches.

Q: The wife of William O. Douglas, and the wife of Potter Stewart. Who else do you want to talk about on this table? You have Bill Clinton. George W. Bush. His father. Any remembrances from there?

GINSBURG: And, two more. This was Condoleezza Rice's swearing in as our secretary of state. Condi lived in the building where my husband and I live. She is an accomplished musician. We were fortunate to attend one of her musical evenings. She called me and asked if I would administer the oath of office. I thought that was a great thing to do. It showed a bipartisan spirit. We're all proud to be servants of the

USA. It shouldn't matter that I happen to have been appointed to the bench first by Jimmy Carter and then by President Clinton, both Democrats. So I thought that that was a very nice gesture on her part.

Q: Who else on this table do you want to talk about?

GINSBURG: Well, we might talk about this one. This is my granddaughter, one of three. It was taken in the fall of 1992 when President Clinton was running for office. And his wife, Hillary Clinton, happened that day to be visiting the nursery school attended by my then three-year-old granddaughter. They are doing the toothbrush song together. And this picture was featured in the *New York Post*. When I saw it, I got a copy and sent it to Clara, my granddaughter, then three, now eighteen. I wrote on the bottom, "May you always know where to stand."

Q: Who is this lady right here?

GINSBURG: That's my mother, perhaps the most intelligent person I ever knew. Sadly, she died when I was seventeen.

Q: I read that she died the day before you graduated from high school. What impact did that have on you in those days?

GINSBURG: It was one of the most trying times in my life, but I knew that she wanted me to study hard and get good grades and succeed in life, so that's what I did.

Q: Behind here are some more pictures. I want to ask you about this one over here because this has been published before.

GINSBURG: Yes. That is a photograph of Justice Scalia and me. We are taking an elephant ride at the Rombat Palace. It was the palace of the last maharaja of Rajasthan. It was a very elegant elephant, as you can see, but a rather bumpy ride.

Justices Ginsburg and Scalia at the Rombat Palace. *Collection of the Supreme Court of the United States.*

Q: It's often reported that you and Justice Scalia are good friends.

GINSBURG: Yes, that's true.

Q: And people don't understand how you could be so different in your thinking and still be friends. Can you tell us how that happens?

GINSBURG: I have known Justice Scalia since the days that he was a law professor. I was so taken by his wit and his wonderful sense of humor. I heard a lecture that he gave. I disagreed with most of what he said, but I loved the way he said it. Justice Scalia is a very good writer. He cares about how you say it. And he's a very amusing fellow. When he sat next to me, both on the DC circuit bench and now not this configuration but when Justice O'Connor was with us, I sat next to Justice Scalia. He could say something that was so outrageous or so funny that I had to pinch myself so I wouldn't laugh out loud in the courtroom.

Q: So it's humor.

GINSBURG: It's that, and we both care about family and about each other's families.

Q: So back in here, I know you've got your robes. Tell us how that works on court day.

GINSBURG: On a court day, the robes are kept in the Robing Room, and we all have closets there. We'd enter the Robing Room, and an attendant would help us put on our robe. In this closet is the robe that I use most often in court. This one, the robe is from England. The collar is from Cape Town, South Africa. The standard robe is made for a man because it has a place for the shirt to show and the tie. So Sandra Day O'Connor and I thought it would be appropriate if we included as part of our robe something typical of a woman. So I have many, many collars. This one is one of my favorites. I liked the style. This is a

Justice Ruth Bader Ginsburg and C-SPAN's Brian Lamb in the justice's chambers.

Lord Mayor's robe; in fact, it's not a judge's robe. I saw this in the museum in Cape Town.

Q: What is the importance of the robe for a judge?

GINSBURG: It's a symbol; we are all in the business of impartial judging. In the United States, I think the pattern was set by the great Chief Justice John Marshall who said that judges in the United States should not wear royal robes. They should not wear red robes or maroon robes. They should wear plain black. Every once in a while, not in this Court, but when I judged moot courts at a law school, I would use this robe. This one was a gift to me by the Supreme People's Court in China when I was in China in, I think, it was 1995. I was a guest of their highest court and visited several courts in major cities. When I was in Beijing, I admired the robes that the judges were wearing. By the time I got to Shanghai, they had made up a robe for me and presented it to me as a gift. So this is my Chinese robe.

In Canada, both the lawyers and the judges wear robes. This is the standard French rabat. You can see it in every Daumier print on lawyers. But the women jurists in Quebec thought that they should enhance their rabat with a lovely lace collar.

Q: Tell us about the traditions around the Robing Room before an oral argument begins.

GINSBURG: As we enter the Robing Room, or if we're on the late side, the Conference Room, the first thing we do is we go around the room, each justice shaking hands with every other. And that's a symbol of the work that we do as a collegial body. That is, you may be temporarily miffed because you receive a spicy dissenting opinion from a colleague, but when we go to sit on the bench, we look at each other, shake hands, and it's a way of saying, "We're all in this together." We care about this institution more than our individual egos, and we are all devoted to keeping the Supreme Court in the place that it is, as a co-equal third branch of government and I think a model for the world in the collegiality and independence of judges.

Q: When you're really miffed about some decision and something that somebody says, what do you tell yourself so that you don't take it to the dinner afterward, or whatever? How do you keep it non-personal?

GINSBURG: You think, first, that there's another case ahead. . . . As a great colleague on the DC circuit, Judge Edward Tamm, once told me when I was a new court of appeals judge, when you're working on an appellate bench, where you're never making decisions alone, where you're always having to work with colleagues, you do your best in every case. But when it's over, it's over, and you don't look back. You just go on to the next case and give it your all. That's wonderful advice. Don't worry over what's happened. Just go on to the next case.

Q: You gave a speech in Boston earlier in the year where you talked about the lighter side of the Court, including the musicale. Explain that.

GINSBURG: Justice Harry Blackmun, who spent his summers at Aspen and enjoyed the music festival there, decided that we should have an annual musicale. When the Court's hearings are done, not all its work, because in May and June we're very busy writing opinions, but when we have no more Court hearings, we should take time out for a musical interlude that all of us can enjoy. So he started that in 1988, and initially it was every two years. Then it was once a year; now we have musicales twice a year. When Justice Blackmun retired, he passed the baton to Justice O'Connor, and for the last seven years, I have been attending to the musicale.

Q: Where do they happen in the Court, and how many people can come to them?

GINSBURG: Musicales take place in our beautiful Conference Room, where our lovely Steinway Grand is. We can accommodate, I think, not more than two hundred people. Each justice can invite up to six people and then many people from the Supreme Court Historical Society attend and leaders of the Court's staff, for example, Kathy Arberg, with whom you have worked.

Q: A new justice comes to this Court and they come to you and they sit in your office and say, "Tell me what I should know about this Court that'll make it a better experience." What do you tell them?

GINSBURG: I would say you will be surprised by the high level of collegiality here. This term, I think we divided 5–4 in almost one-third of all the cases. One might get a false impression from that degree of disagreement. Justice Scalia once commented that in his early years on this Court, there was no justice with whom he disagreed more often than Justice Brennan. And yet Justice Scalia considered Justice Brennan his best friend on the Court at that time, and he thought the feeling was reciprocated. The public wouldn't know that from reading an opinion by Brennan, a dissent by Scalia, or the other way around, but these were two men who genuinely liked each other and enjoyed each other's company.

Q: When you're up on the bench, looking out at the Court, what do you see that we don't see, sitting in the Court, looking at you?

GINSBURG: I see our wonderful friezes and the magnificent proportions of that courtroom. Sometimes I say to myself, "Am I really there, or is it all a dream?" It's one of the most beautiful courtrooms in the world.

Q: You have talked about the lunches that you all have after you've been . . . in the Court or at a conference. Where are they held, and what's the atmosphere?

GINSBURG: They are held in the Justices' Dining Room, which is on the second floor. It is a beautiful room, very well-furnished. But the food, as I have said, is not exactly haute cuisine. It comes from the public cafeteria. The justices eat the same things that any visitor to the Court might choose for lunch here.

Q: Do you have to go to that lunch?

GINSBURG: No. It's not obligatory, but we generally do. I try not to miss a post-argument lunch, because you never know what my colleagues will be talking about. They may be talking about the case that we just heard, and I wouldn't want to be absent from that discussion, so I can make my comments about it and listen to my colleagues so I will understand what's in their mind.

Q: Is there any symbolism to the paintings in the room of Marbury and Madison?

GINSBURG: *Marbury v. Madison* is probably the most famous case this Court ever decided, and [the painting] reminds us that we have a responsibility not given to most judges in the world, that is what we call judicial review for constitutionality. We interpret statutes most of the time, but sometimes a question arises under our highest statute, that is the Constitution of the United States. All people who serve government take an oath to support and defend the Constitution, but this Court has the last word on what that Constitution means.

That is not the typical pattern in parliamentary systems, where the legislature will have the last word on what the fundamental instrument of government means. The idea of judicial review for constitutionality, I think, is implicit in the constitutional document. But John Marshall made it explicit in the great case of Marbury against Madison.

Q: Let me just ask you a couple more questions about the conference itself. Explain to us that room and what happens in that conference and who's in there.

GINSBURG: Our Conference Room has a table where we all have a particular seat: the chief justice at one head, the more senior associate

justice at the other, currently Justice John Paul Stevens. When we discuss cases, we go around the room in seniority order, so the chief will
summarize the case and give his tentative view, and then the rest of us
will say what we think about the case, how it should come out and
why. . . .

Q: Is there an argument that ensues?

GINSBURG: Generally there is limited argument. Initially we go around
the table and each justice speaks. Then there will be some, but not a
lot of cross conversation. One justice or another will say, after we've
talked for several minutes . . . "Let's leave it for now . . . it will come
out in the writing." What this Court produces is an opinion of the
Court, so you're not writing just for yourself. You're writing, hopefully, for the entire Court, but if not, at least for the majority of the
members, and you have to take account of what they think.

We don't have any observers in the Conference Room. No one can
enter the room who is not a justice: no secretary, no law clerk, not
even a message-bearer. It would look strangely old-fashioned, I think,
to most people. You will not see a laptop in that room. If notes are
taken, they're taken by each justice individually, by hand. The conferences are not recorded. They're a private conversation among the justices about the case.

What the public will see, eventually, is an opinion with reasons.
The discipline that a judge follows and what makes judges unlike leg-
islators is that we don't just say, "I vote that the petitioner should win"
or "I vote that the respondent should win." We have to give reasons
for every decision we make. Sometimes in the process of stating your
reasons you begin to say, "Am I right? Did I overlook this question or
that question?" And not often, but sometimes, a justice will say, "This
opinion will not write. I was wrong at the conference; I'm going to
take the other position." And that justice will notify the rest of us, and
we will either agree or disagree, and the justice will end up writing for
the majority if we agree, or the dissent if we don't.

So the conferences then, they're what you would see in most appellate courts in the United States, except the typical appellate bench is three and it's easier to have a conversation among three than among nine. So you have to respect that your colleagues are not there to hear a long speech from you. We speak, as I said, in seniority order, so this term I'm number seven. Next term, I'll be number six. It's great to go first because you can tell the rest, in a persuasive statement, what you think of the case. But when you're on the end of that queue, you do have a certain advantage. You know what the others think and you can incorporate what they've said into your own statement about how the case should come out.

Q: Thank you, Justice Ginsburg.

JUSTICE
STEPHEN BREYER

*A*ssociate Justice Stephen Breyer gave C-SPAN's Brian Lamb an on-camera tour of his chambers on June 17, 2009. The 108th justice, Breyer was nominated to the Supreme Court by President Bill Clinton in 1994, after a career that included teaching law and serving on the staff of the U.S. Senate Judiciary Committee and in the Justice Department. He served on the U.S. Court of Appeals for the First District for fourteen years, including four as its chief judge.

LAMB: Justice Breyer, what room is this in your chambers?

ASSOCIATE JUSTICE STEPHEN BREYER: This is where the clerks are, and this is where quite a lot of the work gets done. I have our messenger, Brianne and Aileen and Seth and, they're here for a year. And I have four clerks. The nine of us each have four law clerks. They're invaluable, indeed crucial. They do a lot of work.

Q: Before we talk about some specifics, what does this building mean to you? You're a man that's interested in architecture and art.

BREYER: This is the last neoclassical building built in America. Cass Gilbert built it in the 1920s and '30s, and [William Howard] Taft got the money. Taft was chief justice, and he had been president of the

United States. He went to his friends in Congress and got money for it, and they built this building. It's a very attractive building. It has become the symbol of the Supreme Court. So it's the symbol of justice in America.

Two interesting points. [Willis] Van Devanter, who was one of the justices at the time and did a lot of work on it, didn't want to leave the former chambers, which were in the basement of the Senate. He said, "If we leave these offices in the Senate, no one will ever hear of us again." But he was wrong. [Louis] Brandeis said he wouldn't come in here. . . . He said this building is so elaborate it will go to their heads. And maybe he was right. But it's become over time a symbol of the court system, the third branch of government. And of the need for stability, rule of law, which is what America stands for.

Q: As you know, the public knows very little about how the Court works. What is in this room that you can illuminate on that subject? How does it all work? How do the cases come here?

BREYER: What we actually do? What is it I do every day? First, you have to keep in mind that law in the United States, 90 percent, 95 percent of all law is made in the states. Every state has a system for making law— it has legislature, governor, a court system. When I talk to school children I say, "Where is the law made that affects you?" It's not Washington, DC; it's Sacramento, if you're from California. And I'll say, "Well, over there, you'll see it from my office, the Congress, which is right a block away, they do pass quite a lot of laws. Those are federal laws. But they still make up only a small percentage." There they are. See those are the federal laws, in those books right there. Those are the laws passed by Congress.

Q: How do those books end up on your shelf?

BREYER: We all have copies. Anyone can get one. Anyone in the United States. You could write to the federal government. . . . West Publishing Company puts them out, but this is U.S. Code with cases in it. Here's a

Justice Stephen Breyer in his chambers.

statute book. You can get a copy; it's in every library. This happens to be how you get a request for identifiable records in a patent case. I just turned to it by chance.

But you see there are words in it. Now four hundred years ago the great French philosopher [Michel de] Montaigne pointed out that every word in a statute is a possibility of an argument for lawyers. Does it mean this or does it mean that? So each of these statute books contains thousands of words, and each of those words could produce an argument.

Q: Are these all the laws that have been passed over the years?

BREYER: These are all the federal laws that are still in existence. There they are. And they're even shorter when you take the cases out. That over there is the actual code itself without any cases interpreting them.

That's federal. That's available in every city of the country, every rural district, wherever you want to go. It's available on the Internet. You can find the law of the United States. Anyone can.

Q: How does a case come to you?

BREYER: Remember, there are state laws, and there are federal laws. And you can have a case in a court system that's a state system, in fact, [more than] 95 percent of all the cases in the United States are in state systems. . . . Or you can have a case in the federal system. And the laws for getting which is which are complicated.

Maybe 3 percent or 4 percent are in federal courts, but any of those cases could involve a federal issue of law. An issue of the law, what does it mean? Or what does the Constitution of the United States mean? That's a question that we could decide. We decide just the federal questions, those statute books, and what the Constitution of the United States means in cases where people are disagreeing about it.

There are trials, there are appeals and, finally, by the time you get to the final appeal, maybe there are eighty thousand cases, one hundred thousand cases in the United States that have questions of federal law. What does this word mean? Does it mean this, or does it mean that? What does the word "liberty" in the Fourteenth Amendment mean? How does it apply to someone who wants assisted suicide? That's a case we have. Does he have a constitutional right to it or not? It can be an important case, or it could be the meaning of one of those patent code words.

Now of those eighty thousand cases, eight thousand ask us each year to hear the case. That means about a hundred and fifty a week. A hundred and fifty what? One hundred and fifty requests to hear the case. Here they are for this week, right here [pointing to shelves in his chambers]. . . .

What we do is read through these. We all read all of them. I'm going to qualify this in a minute. We all look at all of them, and then we vote. We meet at conference, and we vote. And if there are four of the nine of us who want to hear any of these cases, we'll hear it. There's one here, a petition, just picked at random. This is a person who can't afford to pay for the printing, so he proceeds *in forma pauperis*. If he's a criminal defendant, the government will pay for this.

Q: Do these petitions have to be a certain length?

BREYER: Yes, it does. Usually it's under fifteen or twenty pages. This one is twenty-one pages. Here's one that they paid for.

Q: And that's in a booklet form?

BREYER: Yes. And this is the lower court; they ask for the petition. See, they say, "Please take our case." Here's the opinion below saying why we should take it. And here's the response saying "please don't take it."

Now, you might wonder how could I read all these in one week. Somebody might wonder that. I'd like to say, "Oh, because I'm so clever," but that isn't the reason. In fact, it would be impossible for one person to read all these every single week. One of the things these wonderful law clerks do is. . . . We have a pool for most of us and, we'll pool our four clerks and—say there are about thirty clerks—those thirty clerks will divide these and each clerk will read five or six. . . . They can do that and, moreover, they can do it very thoroughly. So if I were just to skim through this, maybe I would think this petition— see look, here's somebody's writing here. . . . Maybe [it is] a little scrawled. . . . Maybe he's right. If I had to read 150, I wouldn't necessarily find that. But by reading five or six, [the clerks] are going to find out whether there is a case that we should hear. So what I'll really receive is a pack of memos like this. Now, I go through that pack of memos. I will tell you something; although I say it and all my colleagues say it, almost nobody hears it. It is how we decide what to hear.

Think of these memos like this. I go through that stack in probably a couple of hours. How could I do that? Go through that stack? They're each two to ten pages, sometimes twenty pages. And I'll end up with a small stack like this. Maybe ten or fewer. These are the ones I think we'll hear. Now, how did I get from that big stack to this small stack? Once I tell you the criteria I'm using, you will understand.

Again, Taft, the chief justice, explained it. He said that we are not here to correct mistakes of the lower court. Already every one of these persons has had a trial, they've had one appeal, maybe they've had two appeals, maybe they've had three appeals. We couldn't do it if our job was to look through all these decisions and decide whether it was right or wrong. They are good judges too. Maybe they're right, maybe we're wrong. Who knows? But the primary job is, [according to] Taft, to take the case where there is a need for a nationally uniform decision on the meaning of the particular law. Now suppose all of the lower court judges come to the same conclusion about the meaning of the law—is there a need for us? What do you think?

No. It already is uniform. But suppose they reach different conclusions. Now is there a need for us? Yes, probably. It's not uniform. So the basic rule, it isn't the entire rule, but the basic rule is if they've reached different conclusions, we'll probably hear it. If they've all reached the same conclusion, we probably won't. That isn't 100 percent of it, but that's the basic idea.

Now you see what I'm looking for. Now you can see how I could do this. Now you see how it's possible.

Q: Let me ask you about the atmosphere of your chambers. It seems a lot different than the Capitol where you used to work, over in the Senate.

BREYER: No, [it's not like the Capitol]. It's quiet.

Q: Is it always like this? I mean, you have two clerks in here?

BREYER: I have two upstairs, and they change places in the middle of the year.

Q: And this is basically the atmosphere they work in all the time?

BREYER: Yes. It's quiet. They're reading.

Q: Doesn't get any more exciting than this?

BREYER: Oh, yes. I can rant and rave from time to time. But I try to do it quietly.

Q: But it's a much different atmosphere than when you were, say, working on the Judiciary Committee?

Justices Breyer and Thomas testify before a 2009 House Financial Services Committee.

BREYER: Yes, it is. With the Judiciary Committee, something's happening every minute. Here, what we're doing is we're methodically going, let's say through the *cert*s and then through the cases. . . . We grant about eighty, by the way, during the year. I think that's eighty out of eight thousand who asked us, out of maybe eighty thousand that were possible. Out of say, 8 million in the whole country. We're getting the ones where different judges have disagreed.

Q: Does that mean that there are eighty times that these parties come together in the courtroom that you listen to . . .

BREYER: Eighty different sets of parties. Correct. Eighty times during the year they'll come together in the courtroom. And we'll divide those into two-week sessions. That's the mechanics of it. Two weeks in October, November, December, January. Last two weeks of February, March, April. And roughly, we'll hear between eight to twelve cases during those two week sessions. They each have an hour to argue orally. But before I go into that session, before I've gone into the April sitting. . . . Here we go, here's April. These are the cases that were filed in April. This is what we heard in April. Each one of these boxes is a case.

Q: What's in the box?

BREYER: Let's look at one. Here's a perfectly good case.

Q: You heard this case already?

BREYER: Yes, yes we've heard them all. And by the way, before I go into the oral argument, I have read these booklets. This time I've read them. I've read the whole book. I go through it. And my law clerks go through it. And they write memos analyzing it, which I ask them to do. And we discuss it once or twice.

So I've already read this; here's one. This is an interesting case. This is what we get. This is the blue brief. This is fifty pages or so where the lawyers say why the district court—the courts below—were wrong. All right? Then we have a red brief. That tells us why they're right.

Q: Who writes them?

BREYER: The other side. This case involved a school district; they lost [in lower court], and they want us to reverse. They have a view of what the rule of law in search and seizure is. They say it's our view of the rule of law. . . . And the other side says no, the lower court was right, and they accepted our view of what the law is on search and seizure.

Q: Is there a length that they have to be?

BREYER: Yes. About fifty pages. It's word length, so sometimes they're a little longer.

Q: What if you're poor and can't afford to do this? What do you do then?

BREYER: Well, if your case is granted, and even if you don't have a lawyer, we'll appoint somebody to represent you, and it'll be paid for.

Q: How often do you have people who can't afford to pay for it?

BREYER: Fairly often. That whole docket there, all those white pieces of paper, are all the people who couldn't afford to pay for it. That's why they didn't print those. If their case is granted, then they'll get the money to print it.

Q: What is your feeling about those numbers, eight thousand and eighty?

BREYER: What we're looking for are the legal issues where people have disagreed below. And maybe a few others. I'm not saying that if a court below holds a statute of Congress unconstitutional, we'll hear that case. Maybe you could have Guantanamo, you know, some huge issue for the country. The key to what they have in common is that four of us [justices], at least, think there is a need in this case to have a uniform rule of federal law in the country. Therefore, we need to decide it because we're the court that can do that.

Q: In that box, what else is in there?

BREYER: This is a reply brief.

Q: What does that mean?

BREYER: That means after this side filed a blue brief, read everything else, he filed a reply.

Q: And they have to be those colors?

BREYER: Yes. It helps us. The government is always gray [covers on their filings] . . .

Q: Is there a reason for that?

BREYER: I don't know; you have to ask them. They're supporting the petitioners here. So then there are these briefs, *amicus curiae* briefs, that any group can file. That's what's called a friend of the court. Any group can file a brief. . . .

Q: And they're always [filed in covers that are] light green?

BREYER: The light green is on the side of the petitioner. The dark green is on the side of the respondent. And this is the record below. The opinions below are in here.

What I will do is, as I say, I'll go read these twelve sets of briefs. Look at the number of *amicus* briefs here. As I discover that they get repetitive, I might not read them quite as thoroughly. But I'll look at them all. And I'll be sure that I've seen what's in each one.

Q: Does it ever feel like there's too much?

BREYER: We're reading continuously. If I'm flying somewhere, I'll have briefs in my bag. I read them on the airplane. I read them at home. Briefs follow me around during the year. . . .

Q: What about security in an office like this, in a building like this where you're worried about computers that people could hack . . .

BREYER: It's pretty secure; they can't hack in. We have a very secure computer system. It's really impossible. They can't.

Q: So you all communicate among your offices . . . the different justices?

BREYER: We can. But with judges, normally it's better to communicate in writing. If, for example, I'm talking about this case. They're complicated, these cases. If I want to talk to you about it, we might not even think we're even talking about the same case. But if I have to put it in writing, I have to be very clear. And then you know just what I mean. So writing is a good way to communicate. Though that's not the only way. We also talk to each other.

Q: After you read all this and you've talked to your clerks . . . how often do you change your mind sitting up on the bench?

BREYER: Well, it depends. If you say how often, when I hear the oral argument, do I think differently about the case? Quite often. Forty percent is probably a little high. Thirty percent could be in the ballpark. If you say how often do I come in thinking this side wins, now I think the other side wins, I'd say it's a much smaller number. But 5 percent maybe, 10 percent, somewhere in there. I do change my mind.

Q: So the oral argument does matter?

BREYER: It does matter. Law clerks think it doesn't. Ask them. I think it does because it helps me characterize the case. And I see what my colleagues are thinking very often. I listen to their questions.

Once we hear the oral argument, we go to the Conference Room that week and we sit around the table and we talk about it. No one else is in the room. And then we vote. The vote is tentative, but it's always becoming firmer. And on the basis of that vote, it's pretty apparent how it's going to come out. Maybe about 40 percent [of cases] are unanimous. Five to four perhaps 25 percent of the time, 20 percent of the time. Not always the same five and four.

People don't usually understand [this]. Look at this; this is a case involving the tonnage clause. That's not going to be in the newspaper. But it's important to the parties and to many people in business who own ships and who want to tax ships. So many of these cases are quite significant, but the press isn't going to write about them and so people won't know about them. But they will write about those very controversial issues where maybe we might divide 5–4. So I think the impression of division is greater than it really is.

q: The next room is what?

BREYER: This is where my office is. I have two assistants, and they are kept pretty busy. Amy's job here is primarily to keep all of these papers in order, to keep lots and lots of pieces of paper flowing around. Each case as it comes up . . . people begin to decide it, then they begin to write opinions, circulate opinions. Toni keeps track of the rest of the world coming in here, which in my case is quite a lot—the people who want me to give a talk, or friends or my family might call, or other judges, or who knows? She's the face to the world.

q: One of the things I noticed just standing where you are, you can hear the noise—I don't mean to call it noise—but the tourists that are visiting the Court down the hallway.

BREYER: Yes, that's true.

q: But you get a sense that not many people ever get back here.

BREYER: They don't because it's a secure area. Unfortunately there are fewer people who come to the building now. But when I was first appointed, there were about a million people a year who came through the building, which was a wonderful thing, a wonderful thing, and now I think it's dropped somewhat. But that's not who comes to these offices. The offices are in this area, which is kept secure.

q: Let me ask you a question; if I'm an attorney and I'm representing a client, and they're going to be before the Supreme Court, can I call you up and come visit with you in the office?

BREYER: No.

Q: Why not?

BREYER: Because the basic rule of our court system is that—that's what's called an *ex parte* communication. If you have two people in a case and they're suing each other, or it's the government against one, these two parties are represented by lawyers, and the judge shouldn't have anything to do with the lawyers without the other one being present. We have a really very formal system for making presentations.

Q: Do you ever have to say to a friend or an acquaintance, "I'm sorry you've gone too far in asking me questions?"

BREYER: It would be unusual that I would be talking in a context to . . . it could happen, but it'd be very unusual to talk to somebody who's representing somebody in a case. If we're just at dinner and you start talking about a case, I usually say that you can ask what you want, but I am very restricted in what I can answer. That usually ends the conversation on that subject.

Q: Up on the bookcases in this office are a lot of photographs.

BREYER: These are my law clerks. We had a law clerk reunion. I was a judge for thirteen years in Boston, on the court of appeals there, and I've been here fifteen years. We had a reunion of my clerks. I've had 111 law clerks, and 87 of them came to the reunion a couple of weeks ago. [It was] absolutely wonderful. It's like having this marvelous family, and they're married and they have children, so I feel like a grandparent of one thousand children. It's really nice.

Q: What's the job of the law clerk?

BREYER: First of all, they're going through all of the *cert* petitions. Then, when we hear the case, they'll read those briefs, too. I'll talk to them about it, and I'll ask them to do research, and they'll write memos. Then, when we've decided the case, the next step is to write an opinion, and that's divided among the judges. So in a particular case, if it's my job to write the opinion, I'll first get the law clerk to produce a long memo, maybe forty pages or a draft, or whatever they would like to call it. I'll then take that memo and I'll take the briefs, which you saw, and I will read them. So we're now over here. So this is where this goes on. So what I do is I read them . . . then having done that—see these are the [computer] systems. I go over here. See we have two. This is the computer going to the outside world, and if I want the secure system—which I'd use for that—I just push that button and it's totally separate.

I sit here, and I write a draft. A lot of my day is spent writing a draft. I'll write a draft of the opinion, and I give it back to my law clerks. They look at it and they think, "medium." And then they will write a draft based on my draft. I'll get their draft. I'll do it again. And this goes back and forth. I usually discover its personal style. But I usually have to write two or three drafts pretty much from scratch before I'm reasonably satisfied that we're going somewhere. And then we edit them back and forth. After they're edited back and forth, I circulate it, and I hope four other judges join. If four other judges join, I have the Court. I'd like nine to join.

Q: Who decided in the first place that you'd write the . . .

BREYER: The chief justice, if he's in the majority. He's constrained because he has to have the same number of opinions for everybody over the years. So everybody's first assigned one . . . then two, then three, and so forth. But it'll be up to him if he's in the majority, same side I'm on.

If he's not in the majority then whoever's senior—could be John Stevens, for example—they'll make that decision. It balances out over the year.

Q: Let me ask you about your office. These are some very old-looking books.

BREYER: They are. They're my uncle's. He liked to collect books. I don't know if they're very valuable, but some are nice. He was a philosophy professor, and he spent a long time collecting different books.

Q: Where was he a philosopher?

BREYER: In Cambridge. He was at Johns Hopkins and then he went to Harvard. Then he started working the library, and he spent most of his life working in the library. He didn't have a lot of money, but he loved these books. I have some here, and I have some up in Cambridge.

Q: Did you clerk?

BREYER: Yes, I did. There's the man I clerked for.

Q: Arthur Goldberg from New York.

BREYER: Yes. Well, he was from Chicago.

Q: And what year did you clerk?

BREYER: In 1964 or '65.

Q: What did that do to you, that experience?

BREYER: It was wonderful. I loved Arthur Goldberg. His clerks loved him. It was great fun working for him. I learned a lot about the Court, and I learned a lot about the law.

Q: How were you picked for that?

BREYER: I think I was recommended by faculty people at Harvard, and then he interviewed me.

Q: How do you pick your hundred and how many clerks?

Justice Breyer at DC's Bell Multicultural High School as a part of C-SPAN's *Students and Leaders* program in 2003.

BREYER: Each year we have four. I have a committee of former clerks that acts as a screening committee. And then other judges call me on the court of appeals and say, "I have a wonderful clerk for you who would be very good." We get maybe several hundred applications. Between the screening committee and the calls from the different court of appeals judges, I might interview ten or fifteen and then pick four from that.

Q: Normally, when I see you, certainly in the courtroom, you've got robes on and otherwise. Do you normally work without a coat on?

BREYER: Yes. This is what I normally wear around.

Q: And what kind of an atmosphere have you created for yourself in this room?

BREYER: It's pleasant. I like the pictures. I like the books. People give me odd things. This is an Indian tribe's talking stick. Somebody gave me that. I think that's sort of fun. And it's supposed to be that when you hold it up, people will listen to you. It doesn't work, but I can pretend it might.

Q: What about this piece of art right here behind you?

BREYER: We have the privilege, as many government appointees do, of going to the museums here and seeing if there are paintings they're not displaying. And if not, they'll lend them to us for the office. I went to the Museum of American Art, and they had some pictures they were not displaying. So I borrowed them. And here they are. They can take them back.

That's New England, and those are some designs in the courthouse in Wisconsin, which I like. And that's a nice one. I think that's a woman by Gilbert Stuart. They're all nice, but that's a famous artist.

Q: What's your favorite thing in this office? Anything in particular?

BREYER: I like this baseball. This was a great thing for me because I got an invitation from the Red Sox to throw out the baseball. Now, that's not so easy to do; I'm not the world's greatest thrower. And the Boston Red Sox fans are not great at forgiving people who can't throw the ball. So I practiced, then we worked it out; see, if you look very carefully, here's how we did this: We got Clara, who is my four-year-old granddaughter. Clara went out there, and she threw the ball to grandpa. Then grandpa threw the ball to Joanna, my wife, who is a very good athlete, and Joanna threw the ball right over the plate. She works at Dana-Farber, which is a cancer hospital in Boston, and the Red Sox do a lot for Dana-Farber. So the announcer said I was throwing the ball, but that Joanna was going to do this for the children at Dana-Farber. Perfect. She got a lot of applause for that. So, I like this very much.

Q: What do people not know about this Court that you want them to know? For the average person who's not a lawyer and doesn't understand it, where does it fit in?

BREYER: I think two things. One is, the job of the Court is much more a straight legal job than people think. What they think is that we just decide what we like. That isn't true. I feel I never decide what I like. The reason that there's division is very often that these questions are hard and the law is not clear.

The Fourteenth Amendment says no person shall be deprived of life, liberty, or property without due process of law. Does that mean you cannot be deprived of a right to ask a doctor—if you're at the end of life and you're seriously ill—to commit suicide? Do you have that constitutional right, or not? You can look at that word "liberty" fifty times, and it's not going to tell you the answer. So there are ways of finding out that have nothing to do with my preferences, but it isn't surprising that people divide on such questions. It's hard. And that doesn't mean that they're just deciding according to their preferences. That's one thing.

But there's a more important thing, I think, and I'm looking here for a copy of my Constitution. . . . Look at this document. It's a very, very thin document. But it has been in existence for two hundred years.

Now, what I see every day in my job, which amazed me the first day and continues to amaze me, sitting up on the bench, I see in front of me people of every race, every religion, every nationality, every point of view imaginable. We have 300 million people; probably 900 million points of view; people in this country don't agree about a lot of things. And despite enormous disagreement, they've decided to resolve their differences under law. I see that every day. We're seeing countries on the television non-stop where they don't have that tradition, and what happens is they shoot each other. Here, we don't. We decided that, even when people think that this document is being misinterpreted by the Court, they'll still follow what the Court says. That hasn't always been true. Think, we had to fight a civil war for that. We had eighty years of racial segregation. A lot of bad things have happened in the country. But over time people have come to the realization that it's better to follow the law, including interpretations that you don't agree with, than it is to take to the streets. Now that's a tremendous treasure for the United States of America. People have agreed to follow that document, and we're entrusted with its interpretation.

Q: Let me ask you about the proximity of this building. As you referred to earlier, the Court used to be over inside the Capitol.

BREYER: Yes, there it is. If you look out the window, you will see the Capitol.

Q: You worked over there in the Senate. You can look at this building in two ways. It's either surrounded by the Congress or the Congress is looking up at the Supreme Court.

BREYER: I think the overall impression that I had working in Congress is that's where the power is. We're a democracy, and power flows up from the people. You cannot work there without thinking every minute that we are responsible directly to the people. I can remember one day—I had a small office over there—and I came into my office and there was someone looking through my law books. So I said, "Excuse me, can I help you?" I think it was probably a student. She said, "Well, I had a question and I just thought I'd come in and look at these books." So I thought, "Shall I be a little annoyed?" No. Maybe she's a constituent.

Do you see? That is the thinking that people have when they're elected. And they should because they are representing the people.

But over here what we're doing with this document, the Constitution, is not telling them over there what they can and cannot do. We're looking at this as the ground rules. These are the ground rules. What they say in this document is that, [number] one, we'll have a democratic process. We will have a democracy. Basic rules are here.

It's a certain kind of democracy. It insists on a degree of equality. It insists on protection for fundamental rights. It insists on separating powers into pockets—state, federal and executive, legislative, judicial—so no group becomes too powerful. And it insists upon a rule of law. Those things don't say how to live in society. They tell you the ground rules as to how to live in society. We apply those ground rules to what people themselves, through democratic processes, decide to do. They're the ones who have to figure out what kinds of cities, towns, counties they want. But they have to follow these rules.

Our job is a very different one. It's to take the product of what others, like Congress, have done, look at it carefully where lower court judges have disagreed about what it means about whether it's constitutional, and spend time—we'll probably spend two, three, maybe four months on a case—look into it with care, and then come up with a conclusion about what it means or whether it's consistent with the Constitution.

Most importantly here is the end product: When we're finally finished and everybody's written the dissent or everybody's written a majority or everybody's joined the majority or everybody's written anything he wants to say, the next argument day—there's no strategizing or anything—the next argument day that opinion is released, and here it is in the books.

All these cases are a little essay. Here's an essay [a written opinion by the Court] I'm just taking at random, something called *Jones v. the United States*. I don't know what that was about, but here's a dissent by Justice Brennan so I guess there were some people in the majority and there were some people dissenting. There were three people dissenting, and I guess six in the majority. And it's about, twenty, thirty pages—twenty-five pages. And that's it.

Now, the key to that document is that the judges in those opinions are giving their real reasons—not some made-up reasons—they're giving their real reasons as to why they think the law is the way they've written.

It's very different from Congress because Congress isn't supposed to tell you why the statute is on the book. The statute just tells you what to do. Of course, there's an inside story because it doesn't tell you why Congress decided to have you do it. [Whereas] these documents tell you why the judge came to the conclusion. And the upshot is, the inside story of the court is, there isn't one. Not much of one.

Q: So often you'll see concurring opinions and dissenting opinions. Do those have any impact on the decisions?

BREYER: I think yes. I would say yes because the part you haven't seen is the first time I write an opinion and you write a dissent. I read what you say and I think, "Did I really say that? Oh dear. He has a good point. I better rewrite what I did. I better be certain that my argument is as good as I thought it was the first time." The impact of your dissent will be, at the least, to make me write a better decision.

Q: So you get the dissents before you write the final decisions?

BREYER: Absolutely. And then when I revise my decision, you'll read what I wrote. And then you'll revise your dissent. And then, ultimately—and it doesn't always work this way but most of the time it does—we narrow our differences to the point where I think an objective person would have to say, most of the time, that these differences are within the range of reason. Nobody has made a mistake here. It's simply different people reaching reasonable conclusions for somewhat different reasons, but I can understand how people can differ.

Q: Let's just say that nine members of the Court, they all concur, they all agree. Who decides when it's the final word typed and you say, okay, we have an opinion that we can now announce?

BREYER: At the conference—remember the conference where we were going to have the four votes to grant, the conference where we were going to discuss how people tentatively thought about the case—the first order of business of that conference is always a list of opinions that are circulating. The chief justice always says—and he knows because he keeps track, as do we all—"Is everyone in on this?" That means, "Has everyone written what he has or joined?" And when everyone has joined and everyone agrees, "I have nothing more to say," that's when it comes out.

Q: What if you can't get to that point?

BREYER: We get to it. It doesn't happen that we can't get to it. The job is to get to it. We're not here . . . to spin out theories. We're not here producing works that are never going to see the light of day. We're here to decide things. The job is to decide. We decide.

Q: You've been on the Court fifteen years. What is the longest time period you can remember from the moment you accepted a case, granted it *cert*, to the moment you announced the decision on the bench?

BREYER: I won't have to remember; I know the longest that it can be possible and that would be that we'd hear argument in the week of October and we wouldn't get it out until the end of June. That's the longest it could take.

Q: It can't go over to the next June?

BREYER: No. Now, I'm being slightly more absolute than is warranted; that is, it can happen. We have the power to hold the case over for the next term. I don't think that's happened since I've been here. If you were to find a counterexample, fine. But I don't think it's happened since I've been here. It's rare.

Q: What is your favorite place in this building?

BREYER: I like this office, to tell you the truth. I've become a homebody. I'd say the job is reading and writing. I told my son this. I've used this joke a hundred times, but it's true. If you do your homework really well, then you'll get a job where you can do homework for the rest of your life. I'm reading and I'm writing. This is a very, very pleasant room to work in. I like it. I occasionally go out; every two weeks I'm hearing oral argument. Sitting in the courtroom is always an impressive experience, and I very much like that, too. I can't say I really like the exercise room the most. It's the hardest work. There is a Nordic Track down there. But this is comfortable. I like it in the winter, and I like it in the summer. It's a very nice view. It's a very great privilege to be here.

Q: You often read that there are nine different law offices, basically, among the Court. Is that the way it works from your perspective?

BREYER: To a degree. It's somewhat of an overstatement because the suggestion there is that we don't talk to each other or try to figure out what the others are thinking. That's an overstatement. We do talk to each other. We have ways of finding out—mostly by memo but sometimes directly—what other judges are thinking. But it's an individual law office in the sense that when I'm writing an opinion, as I'm doing, I'll have my draft. I have my law clerks. They will do the research necessary. If I want to know something, they'll look it up. The library here is fabulous. It is connected to the Library of Congress, to the whole world. If I want to know what the French statute of limitations is in some kind of commercial action, I can ask them, and the next day it will be on my desk. They're very, very good.

Q: How often do you find yourself on a point that you can't resolve and you get out of your chair and you walk down the hallway to another justice's office?

BREYER: Sometimes.

Q: So there is that kind of back-and-forth?

BREYER: Yes, sometimes. The first thing I want to know from my law clerks is, what's the answer? There are two different kinds of questions. I might say, "Well, gee, what is the statute saying on this? What are the cases?" I'll go ask the clerks, or I'll go ask the library. But sometimes I've got all that, and I say, "My God, I wonder how I should factor that in or how does that—I'm having a problem here." I might go ask someone else and say, "What are you thinking?" You can't do it all the time or you couldn't get the work done. To just say you never do it would be an exaggeration.

Q: When you were back in Boston on the circuit court, you had something to do with the courthouse. . . . You were involved in the architecture.

BREYER: Well, we got the money to build a new courthouse. We needed one. Two of us, Judge [Douglas] Woodlock on the district court and I in the court of appeals, were the judges in charge. We spent a long time trying to get a decent building built. . . . I think it is a nice building. Ellsworth Kelly produced this, and he was the artist. This was a kind of award because they liked the design of the building.

He put his paintings in, and Harry Cobb was selecting that architect. Finding the painter and the decoration, we probably spent, my guess would be an afternoon a week for three or four years. It required meeting after meeting after meeting after meeting because you're working—government architecture is not easy. Harry was fabulous in getting the money and getting it built. I hope you look at it sometime because the theme of it is that it's a public building, judges are part of the community, and that building should be used for community activity. We want to bring people into it. So there is, in fact, a staff there that really does nothing other than try to get the lawyers to bring high school classes in or to bring public school students so they learn something about the court. Also, it's used for all kinds of community activities. Private people can rent out part of it. It has a very pretty view. The jury room is used for meetings of all different kinds. It needn't be legal.

Q: What's the difference in the feel that you have in that courthouse in Boston and the one here at the Supreme Court?

BREYER: That's a district court, trial court, and court of appeals. Go to London and look at the courthouse on the Strand, and that's the feeling we wanted; the feeling that there's business going on. The public's business is being conducted. It is not a procession to a throne where the judge sits. Rather it is a marketplace—or has an architectural feeling—of the lawyers who are going back and forth and carrying on the business of their clients. The judge is there, in a sense, as part of the furniture.

Here, there is not quite that feeling. This is a different court. This is more processional. But it's viewed as symbolic. It's a very important building. If you say, do I like the activity more? Well, I worked at the Senate, but this is a different job.

Q: What about this building; if you had to do it over again, would you do it the same way?

BREYER: I might have it a little bit more open. But I'm not an architect. The person who did design this building, Cass Gilbert, was a very good architect. I was happier when there were a million people a year visiting us than I am with five hundred thousand.

Q: Why has that number gone down?

BREYER: I think it's because of the general concern in Washington and also because we're redoing it. This building has been under construction for the last I don't know how many years. And slowly, bit by bit, they're redoing the heating system and the air-conditioning system, the electricity system. It was built in the '30s, and apparently everything wore out. So the appearance won't change, but the insides will change.

Q: So you're going to move out of this office, and they're going to work on it for a year or so. Are you going to come back? And if you are, why?

BREYER: I'm going to come back. I like this office.

Q: Was there any other office you'd want in the building?

BREYER: No. I was very lucky to have this office. It was Harry Blackmun's office. He was my predecessor here. It's a lovely office. I think the year before Ruth Ginsburg was appointed, everybody moved because you gain offices by seniority, really. I was the most junior. But when I was appointed, no one wanted to move. I said, "That's fine with me." I was lucky. . . .

Q: [Before we close, can you talk about Court traditions?]

BREYER: Before we go into the oral argument, in the weeks we have oral arguments—usually between 10 a.m. and 12 p.m.—we gather at five minutes to ten. You'll see the room; it's a dressing room where our robes are hanging up. We put [our robes] on. We walk into the Conference Room in back of the Court, and we all shake hands with each other.

When we have conference, we always shake hands with each other before the conference. I was the most junior member of this Court for eleven years. And always when we had our conferences—since no one else was in the room—I had the special job of opening the door in case somebody knocked. . . . Usually somebody forgot a paper. Once they had coffee for Justice Scalia. I said, "Well, I've been doing this for ten years," and I said, "I think I've gotten pretty good at it." And he said, "Well, I'm not sure."

We get on very well. The nine of us get on very well.

Q: Do you have lunch every week together?

BREYER: We have lunch—not everyone comes to every lunch—but when we're in session, when we're hearing oral argument, or when we have a conference, we usually have a lunch together in the dining room.

Q: Let me ask you one more question on the conference itself. There are no staff in there?

BREYER: No.

Q: Is there any recording device?

BREYER: No.

Q: Are there any notes taken?

BREYER: Yes. Each of us takes notes about what everybody else says. And that's necessary. There are two very good customs and rules I'll mention. First, everybody takes notes because if I'm writing the opinion, I better know what you think. If I don't know what you think, you're not going to join my opinion. So that helps produce the consensus.

And we keep track of everyone's tentative vote because there's a little section where I'll put down the essence of what you're saying. Now, one of the best rules—and I think it's true for any group—the rule of that conference is that no one speaks twice until everyone has spoken once. Of course, I was the most junior so it helped me, but I think it's a very good rule. It produces very good feeling because everyone feels that he's been heard.

And the other rule which is absolute is what I call "Tomorrow is another day." You and I, we're the greatest allies in the world on this case. We think, "We are 100 percent right, and those who disagree with us are completely wrong." And we are going to convince them; so we are complete allies.

Now the case is over. On the next case, we're on totally opposite sides. The fact that you were my ally in case one has nothing to do with how I will decide or how you will decide case two. There is no linkage as there is sometimes in the political system.

That's good, too. It also produces good human relations because when you disagree, you know that tomorrow you may agree.

Q: Thank you, sir.

JUSTICE
SAMUEL ALITO

*J*ustice Samuel Alito was interviewed in the Court's West Conference
Room on September 2, 2009, by C-SPAN's Brian Lamb. The 110th justice, a New Jersey native and Yale Law School graduate, spent more than
fifteen years as a judge for the U.S. Court of Appeals for the Third Circuit
before being nominated to the Supreme Court by President George W.
Bush.

———————————

LAMB: Justice Samuel Alito, can you remember what it was like the
first day you came to this Court?

ASSOCIATE JUSTICE SAMUEL ALITO: I will never forget it. It was right in
the middle of the Court term because former Chief Justice Rehnquist
had died during the fall, creating the vacancy. So this was on January
31, 2006. I watched the [Senate] vote over in the Old Executive Office
Building and immediately was brought over here to the Court and
was sworn in by the chief justice. Then they showed me to my office. I
think that very day I received a very difficult application for a stay of
execution in a capital case, so I was thrown right into the heart of the
Court's work.

Q: What happens when you get something like that? Do you have to
operate on your own in that case?

Chief Justice John Roberts swears in Samuel Alito, January 2006. *Collection of the Supreme Court of the United States.*

ALITO: I was operating entirely on my own. I didn't even have a staff here at the time.

Q: So what do you do in those cases?

ALITO: I did what I had been doing for fifteen years as a court of appeals judge. I studied the case and came to my conclusion about what I thought we should do in that particular instance.

Q: So, first day and forward, what goes on then?

ALITO: I think it's different, depending on whether you start in the middle of the term like I did or whether you start at the beginning of the term, which is usually what happens when the replacement is due to a planned retirement.

For me, I just was plunged right into the work. I immediately got the briefs on the cases that were coming up for argument in two weeks and started reading those briefs. I had the benefit of having the assistance of two of Justice O'Connor's law clerks who stayed over and helped me, and they were familiar with the Court's internal operating procedures. But it was sort of baptism by fire.

Q: Does anybody give you a briefing on what to expect, on what you can do and can't do, and on what the traditions and customs are?

ALITO: A little bit about the traditions and customs, but I don't remember any formal training. It was learn as you go, but it may have been just because it was hectic right in the middle of the term.

Q: We've heard often in our discussions with the justices that the junior justice has special privileges and responsibilities in the conference. Can you explain how that works?

ALITO: I don't think the junior justice has any special privileges, but the junior justice has two duties. The first and the less onerous is to open the door in the Conference Room. We meet in the conference, and there are no staff members present. Occasionally someone will knock on the door, and it's the job of the junior justice to get up and answer the door, and usually it's somebody's glasses or a memo or something like that.

The other duty is to keep the official vote of grants of *cert* or a decision to hold a case. When we have a conference, we'll go through a long list of cases and we'll vote on whether we're going to take the case or deny it or do something else. It's the junior justice's responsibility again, since there are no staff present, to keep the official vote.

Q: And what about the way justices speak in conference? I understand you speak in order of seniority, ending with the most junior. Is that an advantage or disadvantage?

ALITO: Well, I think it's a disadvantage to the junior justice, because by the time he or she speaks everybody else has spoken and voted. When I was the junior, which has been up until now, by the time they got to me I was either irrelevant or I was very important, depending on how the vote had come out.

Q: You mentioned that you got a couple of clerks who had served as clerks for other justices, and I noticed in your background you were a clerk for the third circuit court and you served on the third circuit. What's that experience like?

ALITO: It's an advantage if you've clerked on the court where you're serving. You know the internal operating rules and practices of the court. In any court there are a lot of things that go on internally— some important, some not so important—that people on the outside, even practitioners who argue cases before the court, are not familiar with. So it's an advantage in that sense.

When I served on the third circuit, some of the judges who had been on the court when I was a law clerk were still serving. So that was an interesting change of roles. I sat with the judge for whom I clerked shortly after I joined the court, and that was different. I think he sort of expected me to write bench memos for him in the cases.

Q: I got on the Web and found the twenty clerks you've had so far, and you have four a term?

ALITO: Four, that's right.

Q: I noticed that nine of the twenty you've had clerk for you before on the third circuit. Explain how that works. What's that advantage to you?

ALITO: They were absolutely known quantities to me. I think I have a very good relationship with my clerks. We work closely together. Those were people who had done a great job for me, and I knew exactly how they would perform as a clerk, so that was a big advantage. I'm pretty much running out of former clerks now, but they have served me very well.

Q: What do they do, and how important are they to a justice?

ALITO: They're very important. They do two main things: They help me decide how I'm going to vote, and they help me prepare to make the decision on how to vote. And they help in the process of drafting opinions. So those are the two main things. Now, they don't make the decisions for me, and they don't decide the substance of what goes in any opinion that I write. But they provide a lot of help with research. And this is especially important: They give me the opportunity to discuss the case and the strengths and weaknesses of the arguments that are made before going into the oral argument and before voting at conference.

Q: Is it apocryphal or true that when you interviewed with Justice Byron White about becoming his clerk that he mostly talked about football?

ALITO: It's apocryphal.

Q: What was it like when you interviewed with Justice Byron White?

ALITO: I don't remember too many of the details. I don't think he said anything about football. I think I saw a football in his chambers. He was very gracious and substantive, and he asked me about the things that I had done, things of that nature.

Q: How do you pick your clerks? What are your criteria?

ALITO: I look for people who can do the two things that I mentioned: help me analyze cases, analyze difficult legal issues, and help in the process of writing the opinions. Now, it's not easy for me to identify the people who are best able to help me with those two duties. Here we have—and this was true as well in the court of appeals—an enormous number of tremendously qualified applications. So it's really hard to go wrong, and I feel very disappointed every year that I have to decline the applications of so many people who I'm sure would do a fantastic job.

Q: Right now you're getting a new colleague, and you're not going to be junior any longer. Have you talked to Justice Sotomayor? And if you have, or haven't, what would you advise her about being a new justice?

ALITO: I have spoken to her a little bit, and I think we'll have a chance to talk a little bit more about these two big junior justice duties before she actually has to take them on. I remember when Justice Breyer, who had been the junior justice for almost a record length of time, I think eleven years before I started, took me aside and briefed me. It took him a while to adjust to not being the junior justice. I remember very distinctly at the first conference there was a knock at the door, and I was processing this: "Someone is knocking at the door; it's my job now to get up and answer the door." And before I could even start to get out of the chair, Justice Breyer was out of his chair and headed for the door. The chief justice had to say, "Steve, sit down, that's not your job anymore." I haven't been in that role quite as long, but I bet I'll feel the same way.

Q: What about the supposed practice that a new justice writes his or her first opinion after it's been a unanimous decision on a particular case?

ALITO: I think that's something the Court has tried to do. They did that with me. My first opinion was an opinion in which we were unanimous. I think it's a good practice. I remember when I sent it around, and I had gotten back approvals from everybody with a few changes. Somebody said, "Don't think it's going to be this easy all the time in the future," and that certainly has proven to be the case.

I distinctly remember drafting that opinion. Before I came here, I had been a court of appeals judge for fifteen years. I had written hundreds of opinions, and I thought I had done my best on all of those. But when I drafted that first opinion, realizing where I was now, I went back over it, and over it, and over it. I have never revised an opinion as many times as I did before I sent that out.

Q: How much of it do you remember writing yourself, and how much did the clerks do on that first opinion?

ALITO: They always do a draft for me, and most of the time what finally emerges is not very similar to what I get originally from the clerk. But it provides a good starting point. I'm a very fussy editor and a fussy writer. So I like to say things in a particular way.

Q: Who taught you how to write?

ALITO: Mostly my father. He was a former English teacher, among other things. I remember when I had a paper for school, I would write it and then we would sit down and painstakingly go over it, word for word, sentence by sentence, and he would suggest better ways of saying things. Any writing ability that I have was mostly the result of that laborious process. I think writing well is very difficult. It takes a lot of intensive, one-on-one instruction, and I had that opportunity with him.

Q: Are there one or two rules you have that you use in writing?

ALITO: There are rules. I like very clear organization; that's probably the most important thing. I like everything to go in its place and in the proper place. And I like the old rules about writing a topic sentence for each paragraph. I don't put anything in that's superfluous, and I don't put anything in that's unclear.

My father used to say, "If you're having problems saying it, you're probably having a problem with the thought." If the thought is clear, then you can translate it into understandable prose. I think that's mostly true.

Q: You suggested that things got a little tougher after that first opinion that you wrote. Can you explain what changed after you got into votes that may have been not so unanimous?

ALITO: When it's not unanimous, then obviously you have to be ready to respond to the dissent, and the dissents here are very rigorous. They don't pull punches. So I think it ultimately improves the quality of the majority opinion, but it's something you have to anticipate. And then, if the Court is not entirely of one mind, not just on the results but on the reasoning, there is the problem if you're drafting a majority opinion, of writing something that will get five votes, six votes, seven votes, whatever the number is. There may be certain things that you can't say and certain things that you have to put in a particular way. You have to think about not just what you would like to say if you were writing just for yourself, but what the majority as a group wants to say.

Q: Did I read correctly that you argued before the Court when you worked for Rex Lee, solicitor general, twelve times?

ALITO: That's right. Yes.

Q: What's the difference between standing in front of the Court and arguing for the government or whomever and being on the other side of the bench?

ALITO: It's a lot easier to ask questions than it is to answer them. That's the biggest thing. And when you're a judge or a justice, you can anticipate what you're going to say, what you're interested in asking about. When you argue a case it's hard sometimes to anticipate, as much as you may try to anticipate, what the justices or judges will be interested in.

Justice Samuel Alito sits for his interview with C-SPAN, September 2009.

Q: I read the transcript of the argument of the unanimous decision that you wrote your [first] opinion on, and I was trying to track when justices jumped in and asked questions. For a long time, it was the new justice all the way, and then it mixed up. Is there a rule among your colleagues that everybody gets a chance to ask a question before the next one starts in?

ALITO: No, there is no rule like that. I learned when I got here that it's a lot harder to get in a question on a bench of nine than it is on a bench of three. It had been my practice on the court of appeals to try to wait for the end of the lawyer's paragraph before interrupting with a question. Here I learned that if, in a hot case, if you wait until the end of the sentence, you will never get a question in. You have to interrupt to make your voice heard.

Q: What would you tell a lawyer if they came to you—and I know they can't—and asked for advice on arguing before the Court? What would you tell them about what you expect of them?

ALITO: The most important things are the things that everybody knows but tends to forget in the course of an argument. The best advocates understand exactly where they want to go and have in mind alternative routes to get there. And they can evaluate based on the questions whether route A is going to work and if it isn't then they will be open to talking about route B, route C, route D. They're not rigid, and they certainly know where they want to go.

Less experienced advocates don't pick up the signals that they get from the questions, less skillful advocates. They are much more rigid in their approach, and I think they lose opportunities by doing that.

Q: What has been your sense after, what, sixteen years on the circuit court . . .

ALITO: Fifteen, yes.

Q: And you've been here about three years, three and a half years . . .

ALITO: Yes.

Q: What's your sense of oral arguments' importance? Have you ever changed your mind after an oral argument?

ALITO: Oh yes, certainly. Less frequently about the bottom line, affirm or reverse, than about other things, about how the case should be decided, but sometimes on the bottom line [my mind] will change.

We do an awful lot of preparation before we go into the oral argument. I will have read hundreds of pages of briefs and opinions and other materials before the argument begins. So I've thought about the case pretty thoroughly. But here particularly, I find [oral argument] helpful because every case that gets here, even the ones that end up being nine to nothing, is a case in which there's a good argument on both sides. So if you have a case like that where there are good arguments on both sides and you have skillful lawyers—and we really do have a very high level of advocacy here—I find it a very

The Supreme Court's official 2009 "class photo."
Top row, left to right: Justice Samuel Alito, Justice Ruth Bader Ginsburg, Justice Stephen Breyer, and Justice Sonia Sotomayor.
Front row, left to right: Justice Anthony Kennedy, Justice John Paul Stevens, Chief Justice John Roberts, Justice Antonin Scalia, and Justice Clarence Thomas.
Steve Petteway, collection of the Supreme Court of the United States

The Supreme Court met in two main locations in the U.S. Capitol until 1935. Pictured at left is the Old Supreme Court Chamber, designed by Benjamin Latrobe, located on the ground floor of the Capitol building and used by the Court from 1810 to 1860. Its vaulted ceiling is considered architecturally significant. From 1860 until 1935, the Court moved upstairs in the Capitol to the Old Senate Chamber (**above photo**), depicted here in a 1904 photograph. *Collection of the Supreme Court of the United States.*

April 2, 1932. The Supreme Court construction site, viewed from the east, showing the building's proximity to the Capitol.

All photographs these pages: collection of the Supreme Court of the United States.

August 1, 1932. Steel girders in place demonstrate the essential framework of the building.

September 1, 1932. With the steel frame nearly complete, work begins on the exterior.

December 1, 1932. A view of the east portico showing progress on the marble exterior.

February 1, 1933. This view from the north shows the near completion of the exterior.

May 2, 1934. Interior view of the Great Hall under construction.

Above: The ceremonial Bronze Doors at the west entrance. The eight panels depict the evolution of western law. **Inset, top,** King John putting his seal on the Magna Carta; **inset, middle,** Chief Justice John Marshall and Justice Joseph Story in *Marbury v. Madison;* and **inset, bottom,** "Praetor's Edict," symbolizing development of common law during the Roman Republic. **Below:** One of the Court's two marble and bronze spiral staircases, standing five stories tall and supported only by their overlapping steps anchored into the walls. Justice John Paul Stevens calls the staircase "one of the most interesting places in the Court."

Above: The library, located on the third floor, is reserved for the use of the Supreme Court as well as members of its bar. Among its collection are all the volumes of state and federal law, most of which are now available digitally. Justice Souter called it "a breathtakingly beautiful room" that "[anybody] hardly sees today." **Below:** The Robing Room is located just behind the Supreme Court chamber. Here, justices gather approximately ten minutes before each session to put on their robes, shake hands by tradition, and begin a procession into the courtroom by order of sen-

The West Plaza of the Supreme Court represents the purpose of the building to visitors through architectural symbols and statuary. The large statues at either side of the entrance are titled *Contemplation of Justice* and *Authority of Law*. The plaza is the site where demonstrators frequently gather when court is in session.

helpful last step in the decision-making process. It tends to crystallize things for me.

Q: As you watch an attorney in front of you, is there any way to describe what you as a justice like and dislike in the way they perform—the approach they take, the volume they use, all those little things that people practice?

ALITO: Yes, there's a big difference between arguing a case in an appellate court and arguing a case to a jury. We don't get many lawyers here who think they're arguing to juries, but sometimes on the court of appeals we would get that. Every court has its own style. I think it's a mistake for any advocate to argue before a court without having seen arguments there because the style is different and what's expected is different.

Q: In your lead-up to being a member of the Supreme Court, you did everything from argue before it and work for the solicitor general, work in the Justice Department, circuit court judge, U.S. attorney, assistant U.S. attorney . . . go down the list. Were you editor of the law review at Yale?

ALITO: I was an editor, one of the editors, yes.

Q: So, of all those experiences what prepared you the most for the job?

ALITO: I think they all helped me. The working in the solicitor general's office was most directly related to it. And it was a tremendous experience for me, a tremendous learning experience.

Q: Explain it. What does the solicitor general do?

ALITO: The solicitor general handles all of the U.S. government's litigation in the Supreme Court and also must authorize any appeal that is taken by the government in any of the lower courts, or any request for rehearing *en banque*. So while I was there I had the opportunity to brief many cases here and argue twelve, as you mentioned, and it was a tremendous learning experience for me.

Q: I saw a quote of yours that supposedly ended up in your Princeton yearbook, and you can explain this one, was that you hoped to eventually "warm a seat on the Supreme Court."

ALITO: I did write that. But that was really a joke. It was like saying my ambition is to be the quarterback in the Super Bowl or the winning pitcher in the World Series. It was a dream that I never thought I would come close to realizing.

Q: When did you first know that you had a good chance of being on the Court?

ALITO: I knew I was a possibility—I wouldn't even term it a good chance—when I was first called down for an interview with the White House in 2001. After that point, I knew that they were interviewing many other people, but at least I was among that group.

Q: How long was it from the first interview until it was made public?

ALITO: It was a long time because they interviewed me in 2001 in anticipation of the possibility of a resignation, which did not take place. I was not interviewed again until 2005.

Q: Was that hard on you? Knowing that they were interested?

ALITO: Yes, in a way. In a way it was. Because I told myself that it was very unlikely that it would happen and that I loved my job on the court of appeals and so I should continue to do my best there, enjoy that with the expectation that that's where I would serve out my career. If something else developed, that would be great, but I didn't want to put myself in a position of thinking that it would happen and feeling disappointed if it didn't.

Samuel Alito's confirmation hearings.

Q: And you came here in January of 2006, three and a half years later. How long did it take for you to feel comfortable?

ALITO: I felt pretty comfortable with the substance of the work pretty quickly. It takes awhile to learn the rules of the Court; if you're not familiar with those, the internal practices of the Court, there are a lot of little things about it. [It takes awhile] to get a feel for the dynamics of a nine-person group rather than the three-judge panel on the court of appeals, to get a feel for the difference in the docket. Our docket is almost entirely discretionary. We choose almost all of our cases. There are a few where the party has a right to an appeal, but for the most part we choose our cases. On the court of appeals, it's exactly the opposite. Almost all the cases are cases that parties have a right to take to the court of appeals; very few are chosen. So it takes a little while to get used to that.

But I think every single year is a learning process. I've now been a judge for nineteen years, and I think I've learned something every year, and I hope I will continue.

Q: What's the major difference between being a circuit court judge and being a Supreme Court justice?

ALITO: The biggest thing is the difference in the docket—the number of cases, the nature of the cases. On the court of appeals you have a huge number of cases; we had a little under three hundred a year per judge. On some courts of appeals they are up to almost five hundred a year. Here we have around eighty merits cases. But the cases here are much harder. On the court of appeals they're messy, many issues. Here, generally [they are on] one narrowly focused legal issue. But here they're all difficult issues. . . . That's why we take them.

Q: Now, since you've been on the Court, has your relationship with people outside that you knew changed? And what do they, in general, think you're doing here?

ALITO: I don't think [those relationships have] changed much. Obviously, I don't see my old court of appeals colleagues the way I used to, and we've moved from New Jersey to the Washington area. But other than that, I don't think my relationships with the people I knew before have changed. A lot of people are very knowledgeable about what we do. Although even people who are on the outside who are very knowledgeable don't appreciate some of the ineffable aspects of this job.

Q: What role does this institution play in the overall American society?

ALITO: The simplest answer—and I think it's an accurate answer—is the answer that I saw on the Web site where they have sample questions that are given to people who are taking the naturalization test. It said, "What is the role of the Supreme Court?" And they had a nice short answer, which if I remember correctly, was to interpret and apply the Constitution and laws of the United States, and that's it. Now, in truth it's not simple. It's not a mechanical process. No computer could take over what we do. But that is what we do. We have the Constitution and the laws, and I think they mean something. They don't necessarily mean what I want them to mean in every instance. They mean something, and I think the people of the United States trust us to interpret and apply those laws fairly and even handedly and objectively. That's the great responsibility that we have.

Q: What about this building? How does it feel in your life? In other words, what do you think of it? Is it what it should be for the Supreme Court of the United States?

ALITO: It is. It's a great building. I think we're indebted to Chief Justice Taft, whose portrait is behind you. He had been president, and he became chief justice, and he was, in my understanding, a moving force in constructing a separate building for the Supreme Court. It's very impressive to visitors, to the lawyers who argue here, to people who come to hear the arguments, and it's impressive to me.

I experience the building in two ways. Most of the time, it's the place where I'm going to work. I drive to work, I drive into the garage, and it's like the other places where I've worked on a day-to-day basis. But often, when I go home at night, the building is vacant and it's dark, and I walk through the Great Hall on my way to the elevator, and I look around at the pillars. The building impresses upon me the importance of the work that we're doing. As many times as I've walked through that hall, it never ceases to have that impression on me.

Q: What about this job is not what you expected it to be?

ALITO: It's a much more public job than my old job on the court of appeals. I don't think I had thought about that. Now, we're not like politicians. We're not out in public, conferring with constituents the way they do, but still there's a lot more public attention focused on what we do than I was used to in my previous position.

q: Often you read about the Court and it's portrayed as right versus left, conservative versus liberal, Republican versus Democrat. What does it feel like inside?

ALITO: Republican versus Democrat, no. Many of the cases do not break down along the so-called conservative/liberal lines. I think the public and the media tend to, understandably, focus very heavily on the most controversial cases, but those are just one part of our docket. Most of our cases, for example, don't involve interpretation of the Constitution, and most of them don't involve hot button issues. There are plenty of instances, even when the Court's divided, in which the makeup of the majority and the dissent is not what anybody would have expected if they thought along the lines that you mentioned.

q: Do you have a pet peeve about how this institution is portrayed by outsiders?

ALITO: It would be exactly what I just mentioned. It's understandable, but I think that people don't appreciate the full breadth of what we do. And unfortunately a lot of people think that we are deciding what the rules should be in cases. I talk to a lot of school groups, high school kids, college kids, some elementary school kids, middle school kids. They usually think of questions before they come in. And very often, particularly high school kids will ask me, "What do you think about this?" or "What do you think about that?" [They raise] all the most controversial issues, as if that's what I'm doing. I think there's confusion in the minds of a lot of people between what we do and what the elected branches of the government do.

q: Justice Alito, thank you for your time.

ALITO: Thank you.

JUSTICE
SONIA SOTOMAYOR

*S*onia Sotomayor was President Barack Obama's first Supreme Court *appointment, the Court's third female justice, and its first Hispanic American. A New Yorker, Sonia Sotomayor served previously on the U.S. District Court and on the U.S. Court of Appeals for the Second Circuit. Appointed to fill the seat of retiring Justice David Souter, Justice Sotomayor spoke to C-SPAN's Susan Swain at the Court on September 16, 2009, just a short time after her swearing-in.*

SWAIN: Justice Sotomayor, more than twenty years later, Justice O'-Connor could remember vividly the details of her first oral argument, telling us stories about what it was like in the courtroom. What are the impressions you're going to take away from yours?

ASSOCIATE JUSTICE SONIA SOTOMAYOR: The moment that I sat down and was able to look out and see all of the people in the audience, that's probably the moment I will most intensely remember because there were lawyers whom I've known for years sitting at the table in front of us ready to argue. Watching the intensity of everyone's face, I'd forgotten how much people believe—believe and know—that they're affected by the Court's decisions. You see the anticipation. I can't actually say that it's pleasurable. You note in people's faces their concerns. Clearly, I knew the sides some parties in the audience were on, and I forget how important it is to people, sometimes. When you're in your office reading the briefs you understand the voices that they're giving you, but when you see their faces, it just reinforces that importance in a way nothing else can.

What's the other emotion? Absolute fear. You don't know what it's like to sit with eight other colleagues. I sat *en banque* when I was on the circuit court, but to sit on the Supreme Court and listen to the questions of your colleagues is somewhat humbling. Completely humbling.

So, yes, just like Justice O'Connor I will always remember that day.

Q: You had to have the awareness that everyone in that room was waiting for your first question.

SOTOMAYOR: Yes. I had gone in prepared with any number of questions, and most of them except the two I asked were asked by other justices. And so, yes, I was aware, but I didn't know what the first question would actually be because I didn't know what direction my colleagues were going to go with their questions and what would be left for me to ask. The questions I eventually did ask were a product of the flow of the conversation.

Q: So it felt natural? It wasn't as if you had to say to yourself, "Okay, now dive in"?

SOTOMAYOR: Something most people will learn about me is that I get so intensely engaged in argument that it's never fake. Every question I ask has a purpose; it has some importance to something that is troubling me or that I'm curious about. So no, it wasn't fake.

Q: What was that recent week like for you with the investiture ceremony, your family coming here to be with you for that, and all of the media coverage that you got? Are you able to process all of this?

SOTOMAYOR: I haven't connected physically with my mind and body yet. I'm still somewhere out here looking down and saying, "Wow, is this really happening to me?" That's what that felt like.

Justice Sotomayor
during her September
2009 investiture.
*Collection of the
Supreme Court of
the United States.*

One question that you probably wouldn't know to ask is, What was the most symbolically meaningful moment for me during my public investiture? It was sitting in Justice Marshall's chair and taking the oath with my hand on Justice Harlan's bible. It was like history coursing through me and—it's an interesting admission to make—I don't think any person can be assured that they're up to the task. I don't know that. Those moments are at one point incredibly meaningful and in a different way, incredibly frightening. It's hard to convey the coursing of emotions that goes through one at a moment like that.

Q: Describe what you think your role and largely the role of this Court is in our society.

SOTOMAYOR: It always thrills me, amazes me, and gives me faith in our country to know how much people trust the courts. Despite the skepticism with which some decisions are received, in the end, I think the American people and the world have confidence that the nine justices are rendering decisions based on their best ability to arrive at a fair answer under the law; fair being defined as, What does the law say? That to me is the most meaningful part of the role we serve among the three branches of government. The public looks at [the Court] and says, "Ah, there is an objective viewpoint; there are people who are not a part of a party, who are not part of an executive branch agenda. They are there to look at this subjectively in a neutral way and help us come to a resolution about whatever dispute there may be in an objective way." It's a real testimony to our founding fathers that they created our branch in this way.

Q: And, going back to the sense of responsibility, it's the court of last appeal.

SOTOMAYOR: It is. Very much so. And isn't it wonderful that we also have the ability to rethink issues over time? We have the ability to look at them, and think about them, and review them and consider whether the answers we've given should be revisited at any point. It shouldn't be done lightly and it never is, but it is a gift to America that we can do that.

Q: I believe this might be the first time that you sat down with television since your appointment was announced. Would you mind, for history, telling us the story of when you got the telephone call?

SOTOMAYOR: I had been told all weekend that the president would be making his decision sometime on Monday, and I had been sitting in my office from 8 o'clock that morning waiting for a phone call. The phone calls I got instead were from my family telling me, or asking me, what was happening. I was getting the calls almost hourly. Every hour I would say, "I don't know." Two o'clock was arriving, and my family had been told that they would have to start moving to the airport shortly. So they were more and more anxious about whether they should be going to the airport or not and my response was, "I don't know."

Finally, at about 5 p.m., they're at the airports, and they're still calling asking me whether they should get on the planes. And my response was, "I still don't know. If they haven't pulled you back, I guess you should." My brother calls me from, I think it was Baltimore. He had to make a stop at Baltimore and then take a shuttle over to Washington and he said, "Should I keep going?" I said, "If they haven't told you to stop, you should." It's now nearly 7 o'clock in the evening, and I call the White House and say, "Well you're getting my family to Washington, have any of you given any thought about how I'm going to get there?" They stopped and said, "Oh, I guess we should figure that out, shouldn't we?" Literally, that was the response. What I was told was that the president had gotten distracted with some important other business that was going on at the time, and that he would call me at about 8 p.m. but that I should go home and pack to come to Washington, and that they would prefer that I didn't take a plane.

So I rushed out of my office, went home, put a suitcase on top of my bed, and with my assistant, Theresa, who had come home with me, started packing a suitcase. I called a friend to ask him to drive me to Washington. He came, or was on his way, and at 8:10 p.m. I received a call on my cell phone. The White House operator tells you that the president is on the line.

Q: You were somewhere on the road at this point?

SOTOMAYOR: Nope, I was still at home, still packing. I stood by my balcony doors, and I had my cell phone in my right hand, and I had my left hand over my chest trying to calm my beating heart, literally. The president got on the phone and said to me, "Judge, I would like to announce you as my selection to be the next associate justice of the United States Supreme Court."

I caught my breath and started to cry and said, "Thank you, Mr. President." That was what the moment was like.

President Obama announces the Sotomayor appointment, May 26, 2009. *Courtesy of the White House.*

He asked me to make him two promises. The first was to remain the person I was, and the second was to stay connected to my community. I said to him that those were two easy promises to make, because those two things I could not change. And he then said we would see each other in the morning, which we did.

Q: And did you, in fact, drive? What was that drive like?

SOTOMAYOR: It went very quickly, in part because I was working the entire time on my speech for the next day. They had told me to anticipate making a speech, so I had a draft, but I was still working on it.

Q: It's about four hours plus from New York to Washington?

SOTOMAYOR: It took us a little longer because a torrential rain started on the drive, and it knocked out our GPS. We got lost, and all of sudden I'm in Virginia. I'm looking up because I had been scribbling on a piece of paper, making changes, and all of a sudden I look up and I look at my friend and say, "Tom, we're not going into Washington, we're going away from Washington, we'd better stop." We pulled over on a road, and I called up a friend and said, "Please get on the computer and figure out how we get back to where we have to go." I had a law clerk—my law clerks and my staff and my assistant and everybody had been driving down in separate cars—and he was from Washington and he talked us back onto the road and to the hotel.

So it was a very busy five and a half, close to six hours. Between the rain and getting lost, it was a very eventful night.

Q: It sounds like not much sleep before the next day.

SOTOMAYOR: No, we arrived in Washington at 2:30 a.m. I practiced my speech for an hour. The last thing I did before I went to bed was reread it and try to commit it again to memory. Three hours later when I got up, the first thing I did was give the speech without the papers in front of me. When I was able to do that I said, "I got it." Then I was able to shower and get dressed comfortably.

Q: You mentioned your clerks; can you talk to us a bit about how you're setting up your office here?

SOTOMAYOR: I have a colleague who is like a brother on the second cir- cuit. When this process was going on, I was getting applications for clerkships and I didn't want to jinx the process by becoming involved in thinking about picking clerks. So I asked him to look over all the applications and review them and pick a handful of people that he thought would be suitable for me. Suitability was measured by two things. I want smart people, but I want people who are good people, too. They have to be kind and caring and really smart.

Q: How did he do?

SOTOMAYOR: He batted one hundred. I have four people I'm absolutely delighted with. I interviewed them shortly after the hearings concluded, and I had pretty much made up my mind. The day that I was sworn in I was able to call them. Two of them started that Monday and two the Monday after.

Q: You're one of the few associate justices who have served in all three levels of the federal court system, which means you've gotten to go through the nomination and confirmation process three times. What are your perspectives on how it works for our society today?

SOTOMAYOR: Interestingly enough, within a couple of months of my hearings I had moderated a panel for the Federalist Society at Yale Law School. On the panel were a couple of professors and a couple of people involved in the [nomination and confirmation] process, and each of them had a different perspective on the meaning of the process and fair statement criticisms about the process. My very last question to the panelists was, "What would you do instead of what we do?" They all had some minor tinkering fixes, as I call them, except for one.

One of the panelists looked up and said that the purpose of the nomination process and the confirmation hearing process today is to introduce a prospective justice to the America people so they can get to know that justice, because once the selection is made most Americans will never again have an opportunity to hear the justice talk or to learn anything about them until the end of their service. It gives the American people that chance. I think that's what I learned, that he was right. That may be the most important purpose of the confirmation hearings.

Questions even over three days are not going to tell you much about a prospective judge; you have to look at their life's work. That will be a clearer reflection of who they are and how they think and what they will do.

In the end, though, getting to know the person is very hard from an artificial setting like a hearing. But I think over three days that you get some sense of what the person is and that must—and it does—have value.

Q: The White House said that you ended up visiting eighty-nine United States senators.

SOTOMAYOR: Ninety-two. I interviewed with three others after the hearing, but before the hearing it was eighty-nine.

Q: What was that like? What is necessary? Do you look back on that and say that was time well invested?

SOTOMAYOR: I think I am the first justice who has met with that many senators . . . certainly among the more recent justices. Necessary? I don't know that I can answer that question. I think it was helpful. With many senators I had very meaningful conversations, and I think that it is important, just like it is for the American people to see a potential nominee. I think it's helpful for the senators to look someone in the eye, to borrow a phrase that one of them used, and to sit with them and chat personally and talk openly.

Obviously when one speaks about "openly," there are lots of topics that they would like to cover that I can't talk about for the very reasons that I explained during the hearing. You can't comment on current issues. It would be totally inappropriate to speak about my personal views on questions because that's not how I decide a case. I decide a case in the ways I described during the hearing, which is based on the arguments that are presented, what the Constitution or a statute says, and what precedent teaches us about those things.

But there is still something about the informality of a personal meeting that gives both they and me an opportunity to talk and I think talk is important in people's decision-making processes.

Q: Do you suspect it changed any minds?

SOTOMAYOR: Actually, I do. I'm smiling. There were six unexpected votes.

Q: You said that the confirmation process is the last time that the American public sees people after they are sworn in and take their seats on the Court. In fact, throughout your career, most observers of you have noted that you've made a special effort—you mentioned that panel session that you were involved in—to be visible, to be out talking about the role of the courts. Is that something you intend to continue here?

SOTOMAYOR: Yes, and it was part of the president's request of me, to stay committed to my community.

My community is not defined in any one way; it is everyone who's interested in the court system. I think it is important for justices to help people understand our system better, and there's no way of doing that unless you're a part of the process of talking with them. I fully expect to stay involved in all of the activities I did before and, I fear, more now. I say "fear" because given the number of invitations that I'm receiving, I think I have a wider audience now.

Q: Are you intending to make your primary home in Washington or stay in New York?

SOTOMAYOR: Right now, like many other Americans, it would not be wise for me to sell my home because the market is so low. So I'm going to keep my home in New York. I think I am going to be like many other people: have two homes, one in New York and one in Washington.

Q: Americans did hear a great deal about your biography as you went through the confirmation process, and you talk about the invitations you've gotten. Has anyone approached you yet to write a memoir? Your life story?

SOTOMAYOR: Many people have.

Q: Do you intend to do it?

SOTOMAYOR: Eventually, yes.

Justice Sonia Sotomayor, meeting the C-SPAN crew prior to her September 2009 interview.

Q: Many of the justices that we've talked to in this process have told us that it takes years to be comfortable in this Court. Do you anticipate, given your service on the federal bench, that it will take you years to feel comfortable here?

SOTOMAYOR: Yes.

Q: Why?

SOTOMAYOR: When I started on the district court, I don't think that any start would have that same amount of anxiety, new learning, a need for reaching deep within yourself to absorb new information. In giving a speech during my first year on the district court, near the end of the first year, I said, "I have finally understood why the mind is a muscle." There were days on the district court at the end of which—after I had spent a day in conferences where I would be dealing with twenty-five, thirty different subject areas of litigation, twenty-five and thirty and sometimes sixty to one hundred different legal questions that parties were asking me to rule on.

I didn't have a headache, I had a brain ache. It was as if I had stretched the muscles of my brain to their outer limits, and they would throb with the amount of information that I was asking my brain to absorb. I don't think I'll ever experience that again, but with each type of judging—process of judging—there is new information to learn. Even in this last month as I've been reviewing *cert* petitions, there are areas of controversy that I wasn't aware existed. And I, as a circuit court judge, thought that I knew about what all of the areas of legal contention were. That's not true. There are so many new areas of law that I will have to become involved in, new processes that the Court's involved in that I'll have to become aware of. So I have no reason to doubt that it will take years to feel some degree of comfort in this process.

Q: In the process of getting acclimated, are you finding that you have any particular mentors?

SOTOMAYOR: All of the justices. All of my colleagues have been extraordinarily warm and welcoming. Each one of them has offered advice; each one of them has invited me to call them with questions. I don't know if I can identify any one in particular that I've been turning to. It depends a great deal on whether I'm meeting them in the hall because there's always a question on my mind, and when I meet them in the hall I just go up to them and say, "Can you?" or "Would you?" They've each been delightfully generous in giving me time to walk me through whatever it is that I'm asking about. And so not just one person yet, but they've been all wonderful.

Q: Do you have any sense as to whether or not the workload might actually be lighter than what you experienced at the appellate level?

SOTOMAYOR: I found when I was on the court of appeals that most district court judges had no real idea about the workload of court of appeals judges. I'm finding that most people outside the Court have very little understanding of the burdens of the Court. Reviewing *cert* petitions of which the numbers have been growing exponentially each year is an extraordinarily time-consuming process. I obviously have only had an occasion to work on one case so far, but reading the briefs and the *amicus* briefs that came in was also quite time consuming. It's too early in my tenure to really talk about that yet; I don't have enough experience with it, but I don't anticipate that it's as light as the public perceives it to be.

q: What can your colleagues expect from you in the opinion writing process?

SOTOMAYOR: I welcome the views of my colleagues on every draft that I do, and I share with my colleagues my views of ways in which to ensure that each issue we're addressing and each draft that we're issuing is addressing the important points that the parties are making. And so, what they could expect from me is a very interactive colleague both in welcoming their suggestions and incorporating them into drafts and sharing with them my own views as well.

q: Do you anticipate doing that here? Do you intend to work in chambers, or do you think better in your own environment?

SOTOMAYOR: I think better in chambers. I also draft on the computer, and so I like being at my desk and having everything around me. I also like being able to call out to my law clerks with an idea or pop out of my desk and run in to them and say, "How about this?" [I like] engaging them with the idea. But I do like working at my desk.

q: You've only experienced one conference and certainly it was a shortened one, but when that door closes, what is that experience like? What was it like for you?

SOTOMAYOR: There's a real gift in the practice of the Court of letting all of the other justices speak in turn. I didn't expect any less, but I had my expectation pleasantly confirmed that the justices are very thoughtful about what they're doing. Each one was very thoughtful about giving their reasons for their vote. As I said, I didn't expect any less, but I was very pleased that my expectation was confirmed.

Q: As the junior justice, you will be last in line in the first go-around to make the arguments in the case. How do you intend to use that to your advantage?

SOTOMAYOR: I don't have a preset intent. My sense is that if you go in with a plan it's likely to go awry. When I was a lawyer, I always knew that you had to plan everything to the last detail, but the best lawyer was the one who went in and just did what was right at the moment. That's how I think I will approach everything I do in my judging process.

Q: Justice Alito has the chance to turn over to you the responsibilities of the junior-most justice. Did he brief you on how to handle the traditional things, such as answering the door in conference?

SOTOMAYOR: That I don't think he had to brief me on. We spoke about that, but on my first day of conference, at the end of conference, I brought cookies from an Italian bakery in Brooklyn. I was having the coffee and cookies come in, and the court personnel who was helping us with that wanted to open the door as the justices were leaving and I said to him, "No you can't take my job; I just got here." And I jumped ahead to open the door.

I haven't sat down with [Justice Alito] yet on recording the Court's decisions. That process we're going to do in the next couple of weeks, before the first conference day.

Q: With regard to being the junior justice, people watch that role so carefully, where you sit in the Court and the like. What about the traditions that go with that role? Why are they important to an institution such as this?

SOTOMAYOR: Why are traditions important to families? I've often thought about that because tradition is very important to me—what I do on holidays, who I spend them with, the roles that each person plays. I think it's because those traditions anchor us in a process that's greater than ourselves. They remind us that the role that we're playing is not a personal role and not a role that should have a personal agenda, but one that has an institutional importance and that that institutional importance is bigger than us. I think that that is an important role for tradition, to underscore that for us. And so yes, where you sit, what order you sit in, how you vote, all of those traditions, all of those practices remind us of our institutional importance, not our individual importance. I like them. I like traditions. I think that they measure our history, and they give us history to pass on to others. That is what has kept us alive as a nation for over two hundred years. It's rare in the history of mankind that any form of government has lasted as peacefully as we have for as long.

Q: You referenced the sense of history streaming through you as you took the oath and knew that you were about to get this job. Do you have touchstones as you've studied the history of the Court, of certain justices who you return to, who inspire you for the way they approached their jobs?

SOTOMAYOR: I'm smiling only because when you do that—when you select a justice—there is a perception that you're selecting a judicial philosophy, a way of reaching decisions. I think there's some danger in that perception because the history of the Court is not one individual justice; the history of the Court is how each of the justices of the Court has contributed a view, a way of writing, a way of thinking, a way of approaching one topic or another. Each justice has made valuable contributions, but no justice has defined the Court as a whole, and I think that's the beauty of this Court and of the fact that decisions are not made by just three judges, but by nine now. So no, I won't select one justice as setting a definition of that history. I would say that it is the combined body of work that I draw from and that we all draw from in coming to decisions in each new case that comes before us.

Q: I'll close with a biographical question because we heard when meeting you as a nation about characters in contemporary culture like Perry Mason, who were important to you as a young child in leading you in this career direction. What would you say to young people in America in 2009 or 2010 contemplating a career in the law?

SOTOMAYOR: I hadn't anticipated that question, but what I tell young people in selecting careers at all is, pick the career that every day gives you some joy in the task that you're doing. That sounds simple, but it's very, very hard. If you like working with your hands, then find a career that lets you do that because that will give you joy. If you like figuring out puzzles and things of that nature, you might like computers because that will give you a moment of joy each day.

If you like thinking about problems that people are having and you like reading in a way to solve those problems, as opposed to actually sitting in the room and working them out with the person, then you might like to be a lawyer because you can do both as a lawyer. You can sit in a room and help people talk through their problems and give them a framework to do that in. Or you could be a judge like I am and read about their problems and listen to their problems and go back to books and try to figure out how to answer their problem. In the end what advice I give most young people is that the law will let you be a part of everyone's lives because the law affects every part of our society. As a lawyer or as a judge, you will get to learn about what other people do and you will help them figure out how to do it better because we help solve their problems. That to me is the fascination of law. I get to review cases that involve every facet of our society. As a judge, I don't have a voice in resolving those problems because those are decided by the law, but I have a part in that process of deciding their issues. So I would tell young people, if you want to follow a career in law, figure out if that will give you joy. And if it will, then follow your heart's dream.

Q: In these very early days of your tenure in the Supreme Court we thank you for spending time with us.

SOTOMAYOR: Thank you.

JUSTICE SANDRA DAY O'CONNOR (RETIRED)

Sandra Day O'Connor made history as the first woman nominated to the Supreme Court when she was chosen by President Ronald Reagan in 1981. The 102nd justice had been an Arizona elected official and, later, a judge in the Arizona court system. She retired from the Court in 2006, but continues to work on behalf of the federal judicial system. This interview with Susan Swain took place on June 25, 2009, in the Supreme Court's West Conference Room.

SWAIN: Justice O'Connor, we're talking in the Conference Room at the Supreme Court on a very busy day just before the end of session, with many opinions being delivered. I'm wondering how often you come back to the Court since you've retired?

FORMER JUSTICE SANDRA DAY O'CONNOR: My calendar has been rather haphazard since my retirement. I've not tried to set a specific schedule saying that, for instance, I'll be in Washington, DC, one month and then in Arizona another. I've instead accepted various specific engagements and have adjusted my calendar accordingly. In an ideal world, I think I would do it a little differently, but it hasn't settled down yet. I hope it will.

I've been involved, as perhaps you know, with some projects concerning educating America a little bit about what the Framers of our

Constitution had in mind when they established an independent judicial branch at the federal level. I think people have lost sight of that over time. When our states first formed, they all followed the pattern set by the federal government with gubernatorial appointments of state judges and then with confirmation, typically by a state legislative action, either by the state senate or some larger action.

It was President Andrew Jackson who persuaded states to take a different approach. He was what we call a populist. It was his thinking that states should elect their judges in popular elections. What happened was that Georgia was the first state to say yes, that's a good idea, and they changed to popular election of judges. Many other states followed suit, and we can talk more about that later, but it hasn't been a wonderful development over time.

Q: In preparation for our interview today, I referred back to the book that you wrote in 2002, I believe, *The Majesty of the Law*. . . . Early on in the book, you talk about the work of art in the Supreme Court courtroom, called the *Majesty of the Law,* an allegorical work, and how it always had an important symbolism for you. Would you talk about that symbolism?

O'CONNOR: It's just the symbolism that the Supreme Court itself has as the court in our country whose opinions are binding on all of the lower courts, whether they're state or federal. Of course, the Supreme Court is only responsible for deciding issues of federal law, whether it's statutory or constitutional. The Court does not get involved in trying to interpret and apply state law. That's up to the states.

But the symbolism is that this is the highest court in the land, and the Framers created it after studying the great lawgivers in history, and after taking a look at what they thought worldwide was important for the judicial branch to do and how it should be structured.

As you know, the courtroom contains representative figures of great lawgivers in the past, and that concept was carried forward by the architects, with the knowledge that the Framers had also considered contributions from the great lawgivers of history. And so we have

Justice O'Connor was sworn in by Chief Justice Warren Burger on September 25, 1981, as her husband, John J. O'Connor, looked on. *Collection of the Supreme Court of the United States.*

a very majestic courtroom representing the majesty of the law in the process of governance.

Q: You write in the book that the first time you really experienced an oral argument was as a brand-new sitting justice. . . . Do you still have strong memories of that day, and if so, can you tell me about them?

O'CONNOR: My first day on the Court? It was such a remarkable feeling to have been sworn in as a justice of the Court, a position I never anticipated holding. I never aspired to that. I didn't think it was a realistic aspiration, and I never spent time thinking about it.

And all of a sudden out of the blue, here came inquiries about my availability to talk about a position on the Court. That was a shock. I didn't believe that it would occur because, in the first place, already serving on the Court was one of my classmates from law school,

William Rehnquist. He had been a good friend. He lived in Arizona. I knew his wife as an undergraduate at Stanford. Nan and Bill Rehnquist were personal friends of my husband and mine, and it just was inconceivable to me that we would be asked to serve on the Court at the same time. There are many states that to this day have never had anyone serve on this Court, and so for the small state of Arizona to all of a sudden have two at the same time was unimaginable to me.

When I was interviewed by William French Smith and some of the cabinet members in the Reagan administration, I didn't believe for a minute that I would be asked to serve. I went back to Arizona after those interviews and said to my husband how interesting it was to visit Washington, DC, to meet the people around the president, and indeed to meet the president himself and talk to him. But I said, "Thank goodness, I don't have to go do that job." I didn't want it. And I wasn't sure that I could do the job well enough to justify trying. I've often said it's wonderful to be the first to do something, but I didn't want to be the last. If I didn't do a good job, it might have been the last. And indeed, when I retired, I was not replaced then by a woman, which gives one pause to think, "Oh, what did I do wrong that led to this?"

But I'm sure that the future will show that we have other women serving on the Court. It's hard to be the only woman on the Court, which I experienced for about ten years or so, and in a population which these days produces at least 50 percent of law school graduates being women, it's realistic to think in terms of a number of women on the Court, not just one.

Q: Back to that initial oral argument, having not come from the federal court system, sitting there and going through that process, fast-paced as it can be, for the first time—what was it like?

O'CONNOR: It had a sense of unreality about it for me because I still didn't believe that I was the person asked to serve on the Court. It just didn't seem real. The arguments of the Court are not long. There's only an hour allotted for a case, normally, unless extended time is granted. A half an hour goes very quickly for each side, particularly if the lawyers are asked a number of questions.

I discovered that indeed we did have members of the Court who liked to ask a number of questions. So the time at the oral argument went by very quickly. I was somewhat hesitant to ask questions at first because of my lack of experience in the courtroom at this level, and my lack of knowledge about how my new colleagues acted in that setting, and to learn how often they felt it was appropriate to ask questions and to learn how they asked questions, and how the whole process unfolded. I had a high learning curve at first. I had to see how the cases unfolded in the courtroom at oral argument and what was appropriate and what wasn't.

Q: When you are sitting on the bench and watching the lawyers before you, are you cognizant of the public in the back? Are you conscious of all that's going on in the room or are you just focused on the lawyers making the case?

O'CONNOR: Normally, the focus would be just on the lawyers making the case. There were a couple of times in the years I served when someone created a bit of a disturbance in the courtroom. Though that was quickly resolved, of course, it would divert your attention.

For the most part, people in the audience are very quiet, and the staff at the Court escorts them in quietly and seats them and explains that they should try to be very quiet while in the courtroom. They're told not to even sit there taking notes. The focus is on the lawyers and what they have to say. And some focus is on your colleagues. If they're asking questions, you're interested in what it is that's troubling your colleagues. They can lead you into a new area of inquiry that perhaps you didn't have yourself.

Q: Again, to your early days on the Court, everything you did was wrought with symbolism and creating new traditions. We talked with Justice Scalia about the fact that the members of the judiciary continue to wear robes. How did you make the choice about what your robe would look like as the first female justice?

O'CONNOR: I didn't make much of a choice. There were very few robes available. I didn't know anybody who made robes for women justices, and I think most of what was available was something like a choir robe or an academic robe—often used for academic processions and graduations from universities. I think that was all that was available. I just got whatever was available, and put it on.

A harder choice for a woman [concerned] a judicial collar. I remember that when I first sat on the Court, I had a plain black robe that I'd used in Arizona in the courtroom, and I brought that robe with me. It was very simple. I did not have a judicial collar in those days in Arizona. I just put it on over whatever I was wearing. I was given a note that had been written by someone sitting in the audience one day in the courtroom, and it said, "Dear Justice O'Connor, I've been in the audience watching the court today, and I noticed that you did not have a judicial collar. Now, all your colleagues were wearing white shirt collars, and they showed under the robe, and you just looked like a washed-out justice to me. What's happening here?" I took that note to heart. I thought that maybe I should try to find some kind of a white judicial collar that I could wear because I didn't always have a white shirt under the robe. It was hard to find. Nobody in those days made judicial white collars for women. I discovered that the only places you could get them were in England or France. I did manage to get a collar or two from France, and there was a woman who had been the first female judge in the state of Delaware. She was older at that time, and I had met her. She gave me her judicial collar, which was a lace thing that she had acquired somewhere down the line, and that was pretty elegant, so I used that as well. But finding an appropriate judicial collar for a woman turned out to be quite a task.

Q: Our cameras have visited the Robing Room, though obviously not when justices are there. Can you tell us what the procedure is like in the Robing Room on a day when argument is being heard?

O'CONNOR: First of all, on days of oral argument, a bell or buzzer is sounded in each chambers of a justice about ten minutes ahead, reminding you that in ten minutes you're supposed to be on the bench. At that point, you need to go down to the Robing Room to get your robe on and be ready to go into the courtroom at the appointed hour. Chief justices don't like to be late, as you can imagine, into the courtroom. The Robing Room just has a number of narrow little sections of a larger cabinet in which the justices' robe or robes are hung. Your judicial collar, if you have one, can be on the shelf. There are attendants there, and you can pick out the robe that you're going to put on that day, if you have more than one, and they'll help you into the robe. You get it fastened in front, and in my case, then worry about getting the judicial collar on right, which can be a challenge. Then all the justices walk, as they are finished with that, into the Conference Room where we sit around a table and confer on the cases.

There it's the custom, happily so, that every justice shakes every other justice's hand before going in the courtroom. I think that's a great custom. Not all courts do that. I think it's wonderful. If you take someone's hand and shake it, you're much less likely, I think, to hold a grudge. There's something about human contact that matters.

And when all nine are there and accounted for, the chief justice says it's time to go, and people line up in order of seniority. They are seated on the bench, and so they line up, cross the hallway to enter the back of the courtroom and divide—three justices on the left, three in the middle, and three on the right, depending on where you're seated or where you're going to be seated.

When the chief justice gives the signal to some member of the staff, then the gavel drops in the courtroom by the marshal and people enter. The justices go up the two steps and stand behind their chairs until the formal introduction of the Court is made by the clerk of the Court.

Q: Is it always a very solemn process?

O'CONNOR: Well, yes, it is. You don't go in there making a joke. You're not laughing. You're not talking. The last gavel sounds and you're seated—someone behind the chair helps you get your chair seated—

and the chief justice will normally call for the lawyers who are going to introduce and propose admission to the bar of some new member of the bar. That usually occurs first, and then the chief justice will call upon the lawyer for the petitioner in the first case, and will call them by name, and they come and proceed.

There are lights at the podium for the lawyer who's making the argument, and when the lawyer has only five minutes remaining, a yellow light goes on. When the time is all up, a red light goes on, and depending on the chief justice, that can be closely observed or somewhat relaxed. When Bill Rehnquist was chief justice, he made them adhere to the time limits very strictly.

Q: You mentioned that you line up in order of seniority. We've learned that seniority is important in the traditions throughout the operation of the Supreme Court. As the years progressed and you were able to move along in seniority, does that make a difference in the way you approach the argument?

O'CONNOR: It makes a difference in what part of the line you're in when we're all lined up. You change your position. It doesn't change anything about the argument or what you do. You're still what you are, one of the justices, and some like to ask questions and some don't. We have justices who seldom ask questions, and we have justices who always ask questions. So that doesn't seem to change from whatever position they're in.

Q: And what was your own approach to asking questions as the years progressed?

O'CONNOR: I asked what I thought I needed to know. We all read the briefs before the oral argument. We spend a lot of time in advance of the oral argument preparing. We read the briefs filed by the parties to the case. And this Court, unlike most courts around the world, allows the filing of Friend of the Court briefs by other interested groups or parties, not parties to this case, who want to weigh in on the issue.

Justice Sandra Day O'Connor before her June 2009 interview with C-SPAN's Mark Farkas at left.

They can file an application asking leave to file a Friend of the Court brief, and if it's a timely request and there's no objection, it's granted.

So we typically have a number of Friend of the Court briefs in addition to the ones filed by the parties. That means you've done a great deal of reading before ever coming into the courtroom, and the justices are thoroughly familiar with the arguments that are going to be made. I'm sure that most of the justices, as did I, had a tentative opinion on every case before the argument began, how it should be resolved. We'd done our homework, and you can't do that and not form some views about the particular case, the facts, and the law.

So when you go into the courtroom, you have tentatively concluded one thing or another about the case. But oftentimes, you still have questions. You'd like to know about some factual background or some legal position that's being urged and you have what-if kinds of questions: What if the facts were so and so instead of what they are in this case, how would it come out? There are lots of things you can ask.

Q: You talked about justices having a tentative opinion before oral argument is heard. In other interviews we've learned about the initial vote that happens in conference after the cases have been heard, a tentative understanding of which direction the final outcome might be. But we've not gotten to the final stage of the process. How do you arrive at the final vote tally on any case? Take us from that Conference Room and the assignment of the writing of opinions to the final outcome.

O'CONNOR: First of all, let me go back just a moment to the conference discussion on the merits of the case, because that's very important. That discussion does not take place until later in the week during which the oral arguments are heard. The nine justices get together around the table in the Conference Room and talk about the merits of the case. Normally, there's only one discussion that takes place, and it's that discussion. Sometimes there are cases where there isn't a clear consensus, and there has to be a second discussion. That's the exception not the rule.

So normally it's the one discussion that occurs in that Conference Room in the week of the oral argument. And as you've heard, it starts with the chief justice and goes down the line to the junior justice.

Those discussions lead the justices to conclude tentatively to affirm or reverse in a particular case. That vote is not cast in concrete. You are not walking on wet concrete yet. You can change your mind.

Occasionally a justice will do that, but a writing assignment is made based on that first conference discussion. And if the chief justice is in the majority on the case, the chief justice makes a writing assignment to someone in the majority or [keeps it himself].

Now, the dissenting view is also typically assigned by the most senior justice on the dissenting side if there's going to be a dissent. Sometimes the Court is unanimous. That's a happy circumstance, but that's a minority of cases. I don't know what it is at present, but normally it runs about 15 or 20 percent of the cases being unanimous.

Now, once the person assigned to write for the majority opinion circulates an opinion draft, then the other eight have a chance to weigh in. Normally, they start acting within a day or two. They'll read it and say, "Dear Sandra, I join," or, "Dear Sandra, I'll wait for the dissent," or "Dear Sandra, I want to give a little more thought to this before I act," or "Dear Sandra, if you will change A, B, C and D to E, F, G and H, I would be able to join."

Now if there is a dissenting opinion to be written, often people will wait and look at the dissent before casting their vote. Once the dissent circulates, it could be so powerful that is causes someone who tentatively had been with the majority to change their view to some extent.

So all of this, the details are worked out not around the conference table. It's in the writing of the opinions that the persuasion takes place. And that's appropriate because when you're sitting around having an oral discussion, it's too general, you can't be specific. When you have the words in front of you on a printed page and you read them exactly, then you can get specific . . . about what it is that you might find some question about. [The discussion] really occurs in the writing.

Q: Did you enjoy the intellectualism of the job? It seems as though there's much that challenges one intellectually.

O'CONNOR: Yes, there is a lot. Deciding your view of the case itself is terribly challenging. Some of the issues are really tough. Some are not. Some are clear-cut, but some are enormously challenging. And some cause you to want to wait yourself until you see other views expressed before being firm in your own view, and it is a help to see it in writing. It's a help when you have to put it down in words rather than just think it through. It's a real challenge, and it's exciting.

Q: Were there any particular types of cases that you were most attracted to?

O'CONNOR: No, I don't think so at all. Even a case on a subject that you think of as boring can turn out to be enormously challenging at the end of the day. It could be anything, so I don't think subject matter determines the extent of your interest in it. It's the challenge of solving this particular question of law and making it work. It could be on any subject.

Q: The dissents or commentary written in the opinions, sometimes when you read them, they can be quite sharp, and sometimes they sound a bit personal. Did you ever take them that way?

O'CONNOR: Yes, and if I thought it was too unfortunate, I would go to the justice and say, "I wonder if you really want to say that that way. Wouldn't it be a help if you removed this sentence or that sentence and said something a little more gentle?" I was not averse to making that request on occasion.

Q: You write in *The Majesty of the Law* about the warm acceptance by the other justices of your arrival. As a whole, is this Court much like a family? Are the justices friends outside of the building as well as working in the hallways here?

O'CONNOR: Yes, by and large it is a very collegial group. I was very blessed for twenty-five years here to be at a Court where that was the case. It was not always that way. Historically, there have been times when certain members of the Court had strong antipathy to someone else on the bench. That wouldn't be a happy time to be here. I was very grateful that during my years here people got along pretty well.

Q: About the building itself, you've gotten a bit of a distance and you come back now to a place where you spent a quarter century of your life. What are your thoughts about this complex, and this building in particular, and its effectiveness as a symbol of the judicial process?

O'CONNOR: The building is beautiful. The architect, Cass Gilbert, thought he had done such a great job that the U.S. Capitol should be moved so that people would have a better view of the Court, did you know that? I think he did create a beautiful building, but there's no way the Capitol's going to be moved to provide a better view. It's built in the overall theme of a Greek temple, and it has the beautiful steps up in front. It's marble from different places in the United States. You

Justice O'Connor with Gonzaga College High School students, in DC, during C-SPAN's *Students and Leaders* program in 2003.

walk through the marble hallway from the main entrance and into the courtroom, which is much like the Greek temple design. And it is an inspiring area. It's smaller than you might think if you hadn't been here before. It's not a huge courtroom. There are court of appeals courtrooms that are larger than this one.

And the offices of the justices are not large. There are many circuit court judges and even some district court judges in federal court-houses around the land that have larger chambers than those of a justice on this Court. So it isn't size that makes the grandeur or the specialness of the place. It's what it symbolizes and what goes on here that makes it special, and it is.

Q: Do you have any favorite places inside this building that you retreat to?

O'CONNOR: There's no place to retreat. You retreat to your own chambers if you want to get anything done. We have a beautiful library upstairs, a reading room. There are tables up there. There have been a few times when I had to use material from so many cases that we occupied two or three of those tables, leaving the books out so that the law clerks and I could go up there and sit up in the reading room and refer to all those passages in the preparation of an opinion. But that's not often. Normally we can put the books on a cart and get them downstairs to use them downstairs. In these times, you can find [most of the material you need] on a computer screen, so you're more apt to use a computer screen.

When I first came to the Court, we had massive computers that were hard to use. They were called Atex machines. They were not simple, and you were not at all tempted to go to your computer. Today they tend to be small and agile and much easier to use.

Q: You said at the outset that you've been spending a great deal of time hoping to educate people about the role of the Court. Will you reflect on the role of the Supreme Court in society and what you think people's opinions are that they should perhaps be educated about?

O'CONNOR: The Supreme Court, in general, has been respected by the American people. I think it's been one of the institutions of government that is most respected. Obviously the legislative branch creates a mixed impression among citizens because you have members from both political parties offering very different views of things. And the president himself can be criticized by some groups and admired by others. But the Court, in general, has had the respect and admiration of the people. I hope we can keep it that way.

There have been more criticisms of judges in general that I've heard in the last twenty-five years than has been typical in previous years with a few exceptions, and that distresses me. I think it is time that Americans wake up to what it is the Framers had in mind when they tried to create an independent federal judicial branch.

They had a clear vision in mind and that was that the federal courts would be deciding issues of federal law—constitutional and statutory. And the view was that those judgments would be binding on all courts—state and federal.

That was the Framers' concept, and they provided no term of years for the service. [The Constitution] says that federal judges will serve for good behavior. The Framers provided that the salary of a federal judge could not be reduced during that term of service of a federal judge. They very much did not want the other branches of government imposing sanctions on federal judges by virtue of some decision with which they disagreed, and that was a remarkable concept.

Q: You told us at the outset that when you came home from the interview with William French Smith, this was a job you didn't think you wanted. Now that you've had the job and look back, can you ever imagine if you had said no, what life would have been like?

O'CONNOR: My life would have been fine, thank you. But I have been very privileged to be here. It was a great privilege, and it enabled me to see from inside just what a wonderful institution the Supreme Court of the United States really is.

Q: Thank you for your time.

O'CONNOR: Thank you.

PART TWO

SUPREME COURT EXPERTS

JOAN BISKUPIC

Reporter, *USA Today*

*J*oan Biskupic has been reporting about the Supreme Court since 1989, first for Congressional Quarterly, *later the* Washington Post, *and since 2000 for* USA Today. *A graduate of Georgetown Law School, she is a biographer of Justice O'Connor and, most recently, Antonin Scalia. Ms. Biskupic was interviewed by C-SPAN's Mark Farkas on July 13, 2009.*

FARKAS: We're going to have a change on the Court coming in the fall. What is the potential for change that a new justice brings to the Court that you've seen over the years?

JOAN BISKUPIC: A new justice does a couple different things for the Court. Obviously on the law—that's what matters, this is a court that sets the law of the land—a new justice can change things, can tip the ideological balance, can change the votes in a case. That's the most substantive thing that a new justice can do. But a justice also changes the personal dynamic among the nine. You've probably heard from many people the old adage of Byron White that with a new justice you get a new Court. They all start shifting a little bit. Imagine any kind of group that you've been part of, a group of nine where a new person comes in and everyone rearranges slightly to accommodate that person's personality, that person's approach to the law, and how that person does business.

Q: In your experience in watching these folks and talking with them over the years, how long does it take for them to hit their stride?

BISKUPIC: It varies among justices how they hit their stride when they come onto the Court. For several of these members, it's seamless because they have been lower court judges, they were on the federal bench, they were close followers of the Supreme Court. For other new members it can take up to five years. Justice David Souter who came from only a few months on a federal court before he was appointed to the Supreme Court in 1990 always talked about how hard it was to get up to speed and how it would take several years. In fact, I think one of the reasons that he announced earlier in the recent session that he'd be leaving was to get a new justice in place for the start of the term on the first Monday in October. He got a little bit of a late start because he succeeded Justice William Brennan who retired late in the summer of 1990.

Q: What happens at the Court when a new justice comes in?

BISKUPIC: There are all sorts of changes at the Supreme Court when a new member comes on. First of all, they rearrange themselves at the bench. Everything is done by seniority, alternating seniority as they sit at the bench. So you would come in and see them in different positions. The chief justice will retain his position, but the others will change their positions based on seniority. The newest justice would now be over at one end, and then they'd alternate as they narrowed toward the middle. The prime seating is at the middle of the Court on the two sides of the chief justice.

Q: It seems like a place of traditions that unless you cover the Court, unless you're there, people don't really know about. Can you talk about some of those traditions and what the new justices have to do to get up to speed on them?

BISKUPIC: The Supreme Court is imbued with great tradition. In fact, we sometimes kid that the quill pens that they give to the oral advocates are exactly how they'd write their opinions. There are some justices who still write out their opinions in longhand on a legal pad rather than type at a computer the way most people would do today. The whole thing is set by tradition. For example, oral arguments go for a specific hour. Each side gets thirty minutes. A white light comes on when there's only five minutes more left in the argument then a red light pipes on. There are certain days that they have their meetings. The Court runs in its own rhythms. It has its own rhythms and its own orbit, and Chief Justice Rehnquist, especially, didn't like to have any of those disturbed.

Newer Chief Justice John Roberts who came on in 2005 is a little bit more flexible on things and will let oral arguments go a little bit longer. But his predecessor Chief Justice Rehnquist would often interrupt someone speaking at the lectern right when the red light went on, even in mid-syllable.

Q: How much does a chief justice impact the Court?

BISKUPIC: The chief justice sets a tone in a couple different ways. The most important power the chief justice has is to assign opinions. When the chief justice is on the winning side, he determines who writes that opinion for the Court. That's a very important role because that opinion will speak for at least five justices, a majority. It will also guide lower courts and the public in terms of what the law of the land is. So that's the most important role. The chief justice also has a ceremonial position. He sets the tone. He's the one who runs the private conferences with the other justices. He's the member of other boards in town. It's both representative and substantive. But when it comes to the actual law of the land, his vote counts as much as the newest justice.

Q: Backtrack for one second, because the Supreme Court seems to be, in a lot of people's minds, the most mysterious or least understood of the three branches of government. Can you tell us why you think that is or if you think that is? Demystify it for us if you can.

BISKUPIC: I think the Supreme Court is the most mysterious branch to the public. Most of the justices are not well-known to the public. They do their work in a marble building where cameras aren't allowed. They are not recognizable generally to the average person on the street. Their pictures are not displayed in any real, regular way. You'll see them on front pages of newspapers at a time of big rulings. They just are not known. They speak to the public through their opinions. So in some ways they're very public because anything that they do that will matter in your life will be down in black and white in a court opinion. But yet they themselves will not be publicly announcing that before a camera. So there is a real mystery to the Supreme Court.

Also, face it. It's the law. And the law can be complicated to many people. And so that gives it an element of, "Exactly what are they doing up there?" Everything is based on precedent; their current rulings are based on rulings from years, decades, even centuries ago. I think that gives it a more mysterious aura than the two other branches of government.

Q: How does that impact your job? What's the most difficult part of your job in covering the Court?

BISKUPIC: The mysterious nature of the Supreme Court is one of the more challenging parts of my job, especially for me writing for a very mainstream audience. *USA Today* has more readers than any other newspaper, but it also has people who are coming to it as very general interest readers of a paper that offers many things. It's not specialized. People don't come to it looking for special politics or the law. So I really have to bring what the justices do down to an everyman level. And that can be challenging in a very good way. It can also be frustrating sometimes because I know that these opinions are very nuanced, and I have to avoid some of that to explain it to our readers.

Q: You have been covering the Court for a long time for a number of different publications. You have written a couple different books now. What's a favorite part of covering the Court for you?

BISKUPIC: I really like a lot of the elements of covering the Court. I love oral arguments. I love to see the justices up there, see the give and take and how they respond to each other as well as the advocate who stands at the lectern before them. I always describe it as one of the [best] field trips in Washington, DC. It's a lot of fun, especially since it's not televised. People don't know what's going to go on.

It's very ceremonial. The whole room is beautiful. It's this deep crimson velvet and white marble with two beautiful American flags that flank the bench. The justices come in in their robes, and they really like to mix it up. We have a very active bench these days so there's a lot of give and take, and that's very intriguing to watch. Sometimes you can get clues from the oral argument as to how they might rule, and sometimes they surprise you when they finally issue an opinion. It's not where they appeared to be headed when they were on the bench.

Q: Do you ever have a time in the Court where you soak in the history and think of what's happened in that room?

BISKUPIC: I'm aware of the fact that the building opened in the 1930s, and I've gone back and read about some of the oral arguments that were held in those early days and about how many hundreds of people rotated through to see those arguments. Think of when that building opened. We were in the middle of Franklin Delano Roosevelt's New Deal Plan, and so many of these New Deal initiatives were challenged at the Supreme Court. Lots of people would come to watch these cases.

So in reading the history and thinking of all the hundreds of people that would come in, even in the early days of the Supreme Court, you do get a sense of history. You get a sense of the men and women who occupied the bench but also the thousands, millions of people who came in to watch these arguments.

Q: Again, because people know very little about it, they don't know who these people are, is there a human aspect of things that happen between those justices inside the building that the people should know about?

BISKUPIC: Oh, yes. There's a very human aspect. In fact, two of the closest justices would be the ones that you would think might not be so close: Antonin Scalia, very much of a conservative, and Ruth Bader Ginsburg, very much of a liberal. Justice Ruth Bader Ginsburg and Antonin Scalia are very close friends. Their friendship developed when they were both on a lower court together in Washington, DC, and they are quite opposites on the law. They have very different manners from the bench. Justice Scalia is incredibly aggressive and right out there in an advocate's face. Justice Ruth Bader Ginsburg, who asks lots of questions, tends to pride herself in a certain tone of civility. They are very close pals. They go to the opera together. They celebrate New Year's Eve dinners together. They have deep respect for each other. When they were lower court judges on the U.S. Court of Appeals for the DC Circuit, they would swap opinions sometimes and ask each other for advice on some of the language in their opinions. They're pals.

Other justices have formed bridge clubs. They've traveled together. It's a very human institution. Remember, they're appointed for life, so there is an incentive for them to get along.

Q: Justice Ginsburg mentioned in an interview with us that when she was sitting next to Scalia on the bench sometimes she had to pinch herself so she wouldn't laugh when Justice Scalia was saying something outrageous. Did you pick up any of that when you were attending the oral arguments?

BISKUPIC: Justice Ginsburg finds Justice Scalia to be a very funny man. I understand what you're saying about how she would have to pinch herself to make sure she didn't laugh at his statements. His statements can be humorous to her, they can be outrageous to her, and they can be infuriating to her. As I said, they come to the law from very different points of view, and she does not engage in the kind of hyperbole that he engages in regularly.

Q: What type of interaction do the journalists covering the Court have with the justices?

BISKUPIC: I go up and interview the justices regularly. I would never consider myself a social friend of any of the justices. I'm friendly with the justices, but I don't socialize as a matter of course with them. I will go to receptions that they're attending, and I feel like I have good access to talk to them about either my work for the newspaper or my work for the books.

Q: I was over there one day, and Justice Breyer was taking you all out to lunch. What goes on at those lunches, and how do they help you in terms of informing you about what you're going to write about the Court?

BISKUPIC: Those lunches that the individual justices will do with reporters are very helpful in terms of our getting to know the justices as people rather than just as folks who interpret the law. They're also helpful as a give and take. We let these individual justices know what our jobs are all about, what our constraints are, what we're trying to do for our readers, and what sort of dictates we might be under from our editors. It's a very nice casual thing to do, especially since Supreme Court justices are appointed for life and some people might believe that journalists come to the beat for life. I have been covering the Court for more than twenty years, and I am by far not among the most senior reporters. People come to this beat and they never leave it.

Q: Why is that?

BISKUPIC: I think it draws a certain kind of reporter. We're all in it, of course, for the chase and for information, but we tend as a group to be a little bit more of a bookish crowd. We all carry yellow highlighters with us. We love to read opinions and look back at precedent. I think all of us appreciate the law, enjoy it, and I think it draws a different kind of reporter that way. The Court's on a school year cycle. It draws a lot of us who've gone to graduate school, gone to law school. We somehow don't want to break out of the school year cycle.

Q: We have been at the Court for several opinion release days. Describe what goes on during these days.

BISKUPIC: As soon as an opinion comes down from the bench—and I personally do go up and want to hear the opinion announced from the bench. I like the pageantry of that. I like to hear the justice himself or herself announce what's in the opinion and also to potentially hear a dissenting justice explain why he or she does not like that majority opinion. Then I race down the stairs to the Court press area where we all have our laptops set up. I write a first version of that story so that it can get on our Internet site. This is much different than how it was when I first started covering the Court, when you would essentially take all day to digest an opinion, call people, get their reaction, and then file a story around 6 or 7 p.m. that would appear in the next day's newspaper. Now, readers want to know as soon as possible what the Court ruled and potentially what that might mean.

Q: Are you doing that for every opinion that they announce or just the big ones?

BISKUPIC: I will write an immediate quick hit story for our Web site in the important cases, in the important oral arguments. I want to be able to do that for our readers, but I don't want to do that all the time because some cases just don't rise to that level where I know that our readers will be signing on looking for information as it happens. This is a much different approach to the way we used to cover the Court. We used to take much more time to read the opinion, to think about it before we even wrote one word for readers. Now what I'll do is essen-

Joan Biskupic in the Supreme Court Press Room.

tially two or three stories during the course of the day. I'll do a quick hit of what the justices decided, just so that we can get it on record. Then I'll take a more careful read of the opinion, talk to some of my sources, try to figure out what I would like to say about this opinion for the next day's paper. Even with the mass readership of *USA Today*, many of those readers will have already known how the Court ruled, so I have to give them something extra in the next day's paper. Maybe a new take on it. Maybe what the consequence will be in certain states. Maybe what the consequence will be for members of Congress who might want to try to counter the opinion in some way.

So at every stop now in covering the Court you have to have a plus factor. You have to be ready and flexible to turn around and write a different type of story out of the same opinion.

Q: Have the new media made your job more difficult?

BISKUPIC: It has made it more challenging, and it's also made it more exciting. If we don't do it this way, no one will be reading us. If I wrote for the next day's paper simply that the Court ruled 5–4 in a certain way, who would care? Everyone would know it by the time they woke up the next morning and got their newspaper. What they want to know at essentially 10:30 or 11 on the day of the ruling is how the justices ruled. And then, what they want the next day is something that's more analytical that goes further in terms of reaction from others to the opinion.

Q: Do you ever spend some time outside watching the protesters? Does it say anything about the symbolism of what this judicial branch and this building means to the country that people can stand out there and voice their opinions?

BISKUPIC: I often will interview people who've come to either protest or who have lined up for seats in the courtroom because you want to get a sense of what they expect from the Court and why they're there. Hundreds of people rotate through the courtroom each week, and people come to protest outside. They want media coverage, and they want attention. I do talk to those people to figure out what their beef is, why they're there. If they're there just for a one-shot deal, [I try to figure out] what prompted them to come from wherever they live to try to make their point before the highest court in the land.

Q: Take a moment or two to reflect on that west plaza, the building, its symbolism, and its purpose.

BISKUPIC: The West Plaza really is beautiful, isn't it? You walk up and it's so grand, and you have that terrific engraving, "Equal Justice Under Law," and the beautiful statues and all the motifs. The building is just filled with all sorts of motifs that signify justice and equality and the integrity of the building. I don't know if you've noticed, but it's a very bright plaza. The police officers out there wear sunglasses, and you can't cut through there without your sunglasses on because it's so illuminated, the white marble is very bright. It's quite stunning. Especially on big court days when an exciting oral argument is about to be held, all sorts of people are lining up. Then right beyond the plaza you'll have all sorts of protesters and cameras. It's an exciting place, and it's a place where, even though cameras are not allowed inside, you can really get a feel for the business of the nation's highest court by being there.

Q: What is your opinion about cameras in the courtroom?

BISKUPIC: I think being able to see the advocates for each side argue a case and being able to see the justices ask the questions and interact with each other is a wonderful way to get a clue for how the nation's highest court operates. . . . These people are there for life. It's a wonderful window into how they operate and do their business. I think it is a wonderful opportunity for those who can come to see it and those who can also hear the justices speak when they actually leave the marble walls.

Q: Do you sometimes get the feeling that the justices are having a conversation between themselves through the attorneys?

BISKUPIC: During oral arguments the justices are definitely having a conversation among themselves and not just asking questions of the advocate at the lectern. They're telegraphing their own interest in the case. They're trying to make arguments to each other. That's for a couple different reasons. First of all, when they hear oral arguments, it's one of the rare times during a week that they are all nine sitting together, so they have an opportunity to essentially speak and argue to each other then. Also, during their private conferences where they vote on cases, in some ways many of the justices have already made up their minds. The discussion can be quite brief and not a real vigorous give-and-take on many of the cases. So oral arguments give the individual justices a chance to actually make their case, so to speak, before they all go into the private conference to vote on something.

Q: We talked with Justice Kennedy, and he said that for him, when he goes in the conference, he's a lawyer again. He's getting his adrenaline up. He's got to make his case again. You know the backgrounds of a lot of these folks. Do they change when they come on the Court, or do they stay the same? There's still that lawyer inside them.

BISKUPIC: That's a good question about how an individual changes when he or she comes on the Court. Remember most of them come on the Court mid- or late-career. They're going to be in their fifties or sixties. So their personalities are pretty set. But they all came up as different kinds of lawyers so they have that natural "my side, your side" approach to things. . . . Most of them feel a stake in the case. They want to persuade their colleagues to where they're coming from. So I can see how somebody like Justice Kennedy might feel revved up when he argues his point of view.

Q: Do you have any favorite places inside the building?

BISKUPIC: Wow, well you've seen that wonderful spiral staircase, right? You've got that. The courtroom's beautiful. Have you been up to the gym yet? In that gym that is fondly called the "nation's highest basketball court," there's all sorts of old Nautilus equipment. The gym itself actually has quite a history just like the courtroom. It was the site for quite an athlete, Byron White, to play regular basketball games just as Sandra Day O'Connor, when she came to the Court, started a women's-only aerobics class. It's where the clerks go to work off steam between working on cases. That's a wonderful spot. All sorts of nooks and crannies of the Court building have neat history. There was a seamstress, a woodworking shop down in the basement; there used to be a barber. A little world existed in that building.

Q: How much outside of the press room and the courtroom itself do you get access to? Are you able to go in the chambers? The courtyards? The library?

BISKUPIC: I can go up to the library at any point. In fact, the sad thing is very few people use the library anymore because they use their computers to look up electronic databases. The library is beautiful.

USA Today's Joan Biskupic in her July 2009 C-SPAN interview.

That's a gorgeous room. I like to go up and use the library on occasion. I can go to chambers, but I cannot go to chambers unannounced. You must be accompanied, and the justice must have arranged that you can come and interview him or her for whatever you're doing, either for the newspaper or a book.

Q: Describe a typical justice's chamber for us.

BISKUPIC: They're different. Most have basic clubby black leather furniture. Each justice picks out his or her own artwork. Justice Ginsburg has added a very modern touch to her chamber. There are a lot of beiges and grays, and she lightened it up a lot compared to some of the clubby male chambers that exist on the floor below hers. The chambers all have a little bit of their signatures. Justice John Paul Stevens, who's a golfer, has something that commemorates his first hole in one. They all have a little bit of their personality in their chamber as well as different artwork that they've selected.

Q: Let me go back to the traditions of the Court. How relevant do you think they still are?

BISKUPIC: They take tradition very seriously at the Supreme Court. As fancy as it gets is when former Chief Justice William Rehnquist put those four gold stripes on each of his sleeves or when Justices O'Connor or Ginsburg wore a fancy collar with their black robes. That was daring. This is a place that's imbued with tradition. They don't like to break the decorum or what was done in the past. I think they feel that they have inherited a certain trust and way of doing things from the prior justices, from the prior generation, and it's very hard for them to think about doing things differently. That said, I do have to note that over the years, Chief Justice John Roberts has made the Court more accessible in ways, for example, making oral argument transcripts available to reporters and to the public on the same day. But those steps have come slowly. I think that all of the justices feel that one thing that makes the Court work and one thing that brings the Court the respect it has is the tradition in the building.

Q: You've written a book on Sandra Day O'Connor, first woman Supreme Court justice, who was later joined by Ruth Bader Ginsburg. Did two women on the Court change anything inside that building?

BISKUPIC: The two women came to the Court and were very careful in how they entered it. Both of them were very wise and understood that there was a lot of tradition here. They didn't want to challenge too much. Justice Sandra Day O'Connor came to the Court at a time when there was only a men's bathroom near the Conference Room. There were all sorts of things that were male dominated. When she started her aerobics class up on the top floor gym, everyone drew back a touch. But she was wise about how she handled things as was Ruth Bader Ginsburg. Both of them had broken gender barriers earlier in their lives so they were accustomed to being the only woman. Justice Sandra Day O'Connor was the only woman on the Court from 1981 to 1993, and when Justice Ruth Bader Ginsburg came on in 1993 [Justice O'Connor] expressed so much glee at that. Justice Ginsburg herself said that it was so much easier for the two of them to be there together rather than be only one.

Then in 2006 when Justice Sandra Day O'Connor stepped down, in January of that year, it was really quite a shock to Justice Ginsburg at how male it suddenly felt and how much she missed the presence of Justice O'Connor, personally, but also Justice O'Connor as a woman.

Q: We've got nine individuals, but how important is collegiality in the Supreme Court?

BISKUPIC: There are nine individuals, and all nine very much value collegiality. They're appointed for life. They know they have to work with each other. No matter their differences on the law they want to get along. I think they were most challenged in 2000 after *Bush v. Gore,* which decided the presidential election between George W. Bush and Al Gore. That was probably the biggest challenge in recent years. They have their differences, and those emerge in very strong statements in their written opinions and sometimes statements from the bench given orally. . . . Many of these justices come and stay for twenty years, thirty years, and I think there's an incentive to appreciate each other's company no matter how much they differ on the law. Actually, in recent years most of the justices who've been appointed have been easy-going-enough types that a tone was set that encouraged collegiality rather than undercut it.

Q: A number of the justices have talked about the idea of getting together in the justices' dining room for lunch after oral argument where it's a rule they may talk about an attorney, but they don't talk about the case.

BISKUPIC: This is a tradition, eating lunch together, that was really pushed by Justice O'Connor when she was on the Court, and it stuck. The justices go into their dining room after an oral argument. They might talk a little bit about the oral argument, some stylistic things, but they don't really talk about the law. They talk about movies. They talk about their children. They talk about the weather. They talk about things that you would talk about. They enjoy each other's company. They talk about upcoming plans. This is quite a traveling group of justices; they go to far-flung locales, and they'll talk about those, too. That's another way that they can maintain collegiality, set aside their differences on the law, and try to work together.

Q: Why is that important?

BISKUPIC: It's important for any group of nine—any group that's going to be with each other day in and day out to be able to work together. At least that's their sentiment, and I think it makes sense. If you're going to spend the bulk of your days with these other, folks, why not try to get along? Again, that does not mean they're not going to have very sharp differences on the law, very sharp differences on how they might approach a case. But it's a human institution, a very human institution. The nine have an incentive to get along as they decide the law of the land and to try to make their days as pleasant as possible. I think for the most part they do.

Q: History's about to be made again as potentially another female justice will come on the Court: Justice Sotomayor. How do you think that will change the dynamic? Having not just a new justice, but another female?

BISKUPIC: A new justice who brings another female voice and who happens to be Hispanic will bring great diversity to that bench. When a visitor walks into the courtroom now, it looks quite male and quite white. There's only one African American justice right now. Adding a Hispanic justice will certainly increase the diversity there, and adding a second female voice certainly will do that, too. When you think of how America is—half male, half female—to have nine justices with only one female certainly appears quite lopsided from the reality of most visitors' lives. Even two out of the nine won't be representative of America, but it will be more representative than it is now.

Q: What happens inside that building when a new justice is confirmed?

BISKUPIC: When a new justice comes on to the Court, a new chair is made for him or her, a black leather chair that will be pulled up to the mahogany bench will be made for the new justice. There will be a ceremonial swearing in at the Court. And then the justices will get right down to business. In fact, the ceremony will fade rather quickly as a new justice has to consider all the pending petitions from the summer, all the cases that are ready to be heard in the fall sitting. So there will be some pageantry and there will be some beautiful pictures taken of the chief justice walking down those grand marble steps outside the west front of the Court. But right after that, the new justice will be in chambers going through cases and trying to figure out what are the key issues that will have to be tested at oral argument . . . and then resolved in private conference.

Q: What challenges does a new justice coming onto the Court pose for you as a journalist?

BISKUPIC: When a new justice comes onto the Court, a journalist wants to know how will he or she be as an individual. What will that personality be like? How will he or she decide the law? But also what will that individual do to the other eight justices? Will she end up being someone whom other justices play off of? Will she play off of some of those existing justices? New Justice Sotomayor happens to be from the Bronx. We have a couple of other New Yorkers and people from New Jersey up there who can give it out pretty strong. Ruth Bader Ginsburg is from Brooklyn; Antonin Scalia is from Queens; Samuel Alito is from Trenton, New Jersey. You just wonder if we're going to have a little East Coast thing, a little more mixing it up from the bench with the addition of Justice Sotomayor.

Q: Speaking of mixing it up, you're coming out with a book. Why did you choose Justice Scalia as your subject at this time?

BISKUPIC: Justice Scalia is the Court's most fascinating justice. He is a man who came onto this Court with a different approach to the law tied to the original intentions of the men who drafted and ratified the

Justices Ginsburg and Scalia in the Washington National Opera's production of *Ariadne auf Naxos*, 2009. *Karin Cooper—Washington National Opera.*

Constitution. For many years, he was alone in his view, mostly speaking to people beyond the marble walls. Now he has nearly a majority on the Court supporting his approach to the law. Meanwhile, he's such an interesting figure. He's larger than life between his duck hunting with Dick Cheney and his opera watching with Ruth Bader Ginsburg; he's someone that I've found that people really want to know more about. He's very much out there. He's out there during oral arguments; he'll say very bold, blunt things. He'll say very candid things when he's out speaking to student groups. I thought it would be interesting to show how Scalia became Scalia.

Q: Have you been inside the justices' Conference Room itself?

BISKUPIC: Yes.

Q: Talk to us about that. I know you're not in there for the conference itself.

BISKUPIC: Don't I wish.

Q: From what you understand of what goes on, could you demystify that a little bit for us?

BISKUPIC: For their private conference, the Justices sit around a rectangular table. They go around, by order of seniority, after the chief justice has set up the case, and then they start casting votes, starting with the chief justice. If someone isn't quite ready to cast the vote, he or she can wait, but typically it's up to the final ninth justice to have his say. Then once every justice has been able to speak, they might have some give and take among the others. That's what they do for every case that has been argued earlier in the week. Also they go through on seniority if there's discussion to be had for a case that might be up there on a petition or an appeal, and they have to decide whether they're going to take the case and schedule it for oral argument.

Even though it's a very serious business that goes on there, no secretaries, no law clerks are allowed in the room. It's just the nine justices. Before they start, they do a couple things. They start with a little coffee and pastries. They have a little till that they keep that supplies them with the coffee and pastries, just to foster some collegiality. They all shake hands, all around; they do that before they go on the bench, and they do that before they hold their conference. Justice O'Connor used to say that she just loved the idea of shaking hands with a colleague and having that human contact before they were about to disagree vigorously.

After they meet in conference, they all go back to their respective chambers, and just about every conversation that they have from here on out is done in writing with the document that then is carried by messenger from chamber to chamber. If a justice wants to make amendments in a draft opinion or write a note to a fellow justice about [something] he or she might be prepared to rule or changes suggested in language, the justice writes that down, types it up, either through the computer or has a secretary type it up, and then it is hand delivered to another chamber. There will be occasion when a justice will pick up the phone and talk to another justice or a justice will go into another justice's chamber, but that is rare. They communicate by messenger. They do things the old fashioned way.

Why do they communicate via hand deliveries, throughout that whole building, when they're only a few feet from each other, and when the rest of the world is now communicating via e-mail? It's because they're still an old-fashioned crowd, and not all of them use e-mail. Some of them are very adept at computers and have their own personal laptops. I've been in Justice Breyer's chambers, talking to him about something, and he'll say, "Wait, let me Google that." And he'll leap up and go check it on his computer. But there are others who write everything out in longhand. They have a secretary keyboard it or an assistant, a law clerk handles the keyboarding. The law clerks themselves are connected through an e-mail system, but the justices themselves are not all on it, so the way they communicate is to have a document delivered to their chamber via messenger.

Q: As you look toward the future of the Supreme Court, it could be twenty-five, fifty years from now, when do you think they'll catch up or the technology will mesh? Or do you see it being the same type of place in the future?

BISKUPIC: In the future, I think the Supreme Court might be in pace with the country on the law, maybe even ahead of the country on the law, as it has been at different times, but in terms of technology, in terms of those old quill pens, they'll probably always be a little bit behind the rest of us.

Q: As you leave work, do you ever consider that building; do you think about this place as a sort of temple to the law?

BISKUPIC: There's not a day that goes by that I'm not aware of the symbolism throughout that building. The "Equal Justice Under Law" engraved in the front façade, and then in the building, ancient lawgivers in history, Hammurabi, Moses; all throughout the courtroom, the gold rosette ceiling—everything is an echo of the law, of the idea of precedent, of the integrity of the law. Everything has a stillness in that room. It's amazing when you walk in how fixed in time it is. Even the two American flags that flank the mahogany bench hang perfectly still. If any spectator comes in and starts whispering, they are immediately hushed. The lawyers in the bar section, in those first rows of seats that you see when you come into the courtroom, sit with their knees together and their hands on their lap, and if any one of them dares to drape an arm over an adjacent chair, a police officer comes by and says, "Don't do that." It is a room filled with ritual and decorum, and only once in my many, many years of covering the Court did I hear a cell phone go off, and that was a big mistake.

Q: Joan, thank you, again, very much.

BISKUPIC: Thanks.

DREW DAYS III

Former Solicitor General

*D*rew Days served as solicitor general of the United States from 1993 to 1996, under President Bill Clinton. A graduate of Yale Law School, where he is a longtime faculty member, Mr. Days was a staff member of the NAACP Legal Defense Fund and served as assistant attorney general for civil rights during the Carter administration. He was interviewed by C-SPAN's Mark Farkas on June 18, 2009.

FARKAS: I want to start out with a larger question about the Supreme Court building itself. When you look at it, what does it represent to you; what does it symbolize to you?

DREW DAYS III: It's a monument that reminds us of our core values in our society, reminds us that any democratic representative government has to be committed to equal justice under law, the rule of law, and without that it's hard to imagine that any society can hold together and treat people fairly.

Q: With your involvement with the NAACP legal defense fund back in the late sixties and with the civil rights movement, my assumption is that at some point you've played a part in some type of protest out in front of that Court.

DAYS: My protests have been mostly in court. I let other people protest outside the Court. My sense is that I have access and they don't. Because of my profession, I can make arguments to the Court through lawsuits and make my mark that way.

Q: Does it say something about our system though and our democracy that people come outside the Court and try to be heard?

DAYS: Absolutely. The area outside of the Court, that plaza, is really a tribute to free speech and the exercise of people's First Amendment rights. One is reminded of that every time there is an argument when one sees people lined up to go into the Court, but also those who are protesting, those who are disagreeing with certain decisions of the Court. One example is people who are wearing masks, wearing things covering their mouths because they feel that their speech has not been properly recognized by the Court.

Q: It says on the pediment "Equal Justice Under Law." What does that mean or symbolize to you?

DAYS: "Equal Justice Under Law" is really a statement of the fact that judges ought to be independent, that the law ought to be blind in certain respects and not recognize any differences in terms of people's rights based upon their race or their color or their religion or their background. And the sense that communicates is that one can stand before the Court and expect to be treated fairly.

It also has to do with our statutes. The statutes are supposed to recognize differences among groups, but ultimately they have to be fair; they have to be laws that don't single out particularly vulnerable groups or individuals in our society and make them scapegoats or penalize them in one way or the other criminally or economically, but treat them fairly.

Q: Have you ever walked up the plaza, up those steps? And if you have, describe the feeling of the place you are going into and the import of it.

Protesters outside the Supreme Court during the *University of Michigan* case in 2003.

DAYS: The experience, I suppose, is one of walking up the stairs and seeking judgment from, to a certain extent, a higher authority. There is the sense of that elevation, and I think that carries over to the status of the Supreme Court and our judicial system. I think it also represents the fact that one has that last chance to be heard and to get a decision that's going to be fair and unbiased.

Q: What were your experiences at the Court before you were solicitor general? Had you argued cases in front of the Court before that time?

DAYS: I had. I was in the Carter administration. I was head of the civil rights division, so I argued civil rights cases. It was the time when the Supreme Court was taking many more cases than it does now, anywhere between 125 and 150 cases, and the solicitor general then felt that he could share some of the wealth in terms of oral arguments, so I argued five cases in that capacity. It was a marvelous experience. I was a little shaky the first time around, but I got accustomed to it pretty quickly.

Q: Describe that first experience; you were a little shaky. Can it be an intimidating experience?

DAYS: I don't know whether you call it intimidating. It can create a certain nervousness in people who appear before the Court. My recollection is that I argued a voting rights case before the Court, and my opponent was not a particularly skilled or well-prepared advocate. So I got the sense that the Court was reaching out to help him and I wanted to know, "Why not me?" But ultimately, I won the case.

One of the things that I remember about that period was the different rhythm of oral arguments when Chief Justice Burger headed the Court. They were fairly relaxed. One had the full thirty minutes. Justices held off on their questioning for a while, at least let you get in maybe five or so minutes of your argument, and then the questions began to fly. When I argued under Chief Justice Rehnquist's tenure, the rhythm was quite different. He ran it in a military way, where you got thirty minutes. When you got to the end of your time, if you were mid-syllable, he would say, "Thank you, General Days," and that was the end of the story. I had to get accustomed to that difference in rhythm.

Now, under Chief Justice Roberts, we're back to a more relaxed sense in the Court, I think largely because Chief Justice Roberts was an advocate before the Court a number of times. I think to the extent that he's allowed, he identifies with those who are standing up and arguing cases, and thinks that maybe they should be allowed to finish their sentences before they are told to sit down.

Q: Describe the process, even before the oral argument begins. Describe it for someone who has never been there.

DAYS: The lawyers who are appearing before the Court and arguing cases meet with the clerk early on, perhaps an hour before the Court actually begins, and he gives a lecture to them. It's actually a recitation of a "Guide to Counsel" that he's prepared. Basically, it's designed to calm lawyers down who are doing their arguments for the first time to make certain that there are not *faux pas,* that they don't attempt to tell jokes during their oral arguments or don't refer to their familiarity with one of the justices. And that indeed, they will survive the experience and they ought to see it as a place where they can make their best case and the Court will hear them and they will get a fair decision.

Then a little later, the lawyers are escorted into the courtroom, and they are shown to the tables where they are going to sit. There are two tables on either side of the lectern and there are usually two or three chairs. There will be the person arguing, and he or she will have back-ups there who are usually carrying the extra books and notes. There is a process. It doesn't happen every session, but people are sworn in as members of the Court, and this gives friends and sometimes political officials an opportunity to make an argument before the Court. It's a very short argument. It basically says, "I move the admission of so and so, I am confident or I am satisfied that he or she possesses the necessary qualifications." The joke is that there are some lawyers who are so bad, they actually lose that motion. They are not persuasive advocates even then . . . it's a joke. Then the people who are sworn in rise, and they are sworn in by the clerk, and they usually get really good seats for the argument. One of the tricks is to be sworn in on a day when there is a major case and the courtroom is likely to be packed. You'll have a seat if you are one of the people being sworn in. Of course, before that the justices have come in and the chief justice is there and he welcomes people to the bar of the Court and his officers to the Court.

The curtain is pulled aside and the justices come out and they go to their respective seats. There are pages who usually turn their chairs around, so they can sit down, and they have goblets on the desk with water in it, I presume, and they may begin sipping. They may come in with a stack of briefs that they want to consult during oral arguments.

And after the swearing in, the chief justice calls for the first case, calls it by its number and calls the name. The lawyer who is going to be arguing for the petitioner will stand up, and the chief justice will say, "Mr. so and so" or "Ms. so and so, you may begin." There ensues arguably thirty minutes of presentation by the lawyer, but it is rarely that way. As I said, under Chief Justice Roberts who's just a little more, shall we say, responsive and sympathetic, you are allowed to get in a few of your best lines.

Then the questioning begins, and it takes various forms. There are some questions that are real questions. Justices want to know the answer to the question, something that's been playing on their minds. Other times they are talking to a fellow justice through you. You are kind of a ventriloquist dummy. The justices have already gotten to know something about their fellow justices' views on the issue. Then there will be back and forth, and you will be pushed. One of the things that the justices do is take your argument and move it to the next level and the next level after that, because the Court is concerned with resolving not only the case before it, but thinking about how their decision will affect similar cases or related cases down the road. What will be the impact of precedent? And so, one of the answers that is often given—though is not helpful to the Court—but you just can't restrain yourself from saying, "But that's not this case." And usually one of the justices will say, "We know that; that's why we asked the question." Sometimes it's not so blunt as that. The argument goes on for a while. One of the bad signs of an oral argument is when the questions stop. It means that you know you've either not persuaded them or they've figured it out already and there is nothing more you can add. Under the best of circumstances, it means that you've been so persuasive that they don't need to hear any further from you. Then you sit down and the respondent's lawyer gets up. He or she has the job of setting out that argument but also trying to poke holes in the argument that was made by the petitioner. That's thirty minutes. After that, there can be a rebuttal by the petitioner. One of the challenges for the petitioner's lawyer is trying to determine whether he or she should make a further argument. There is a risk to getting up and opening up issues that were resolved in the main argument; there is some peril associated with that.

While all this is going on, there are lights on the lectern and . . . when you get to twenty-five minutes, a light goes on, a white light. Then when you've gotten to thirty minutes, a red light goes on, and that's when you are supposed to sit down. . . .

The justices are very different in their questioning. There are some who are very active on the bench, and there are some who are not. Justice O'Connor always liked to ask the first question. I don't know whether they work this out in conference, but she would ask a very probing question . . . and then it goes back and forth. Justice Scalia is a very active questioner, and I think Chief Justice Roberts is more engaged than Chief Justice Rehnquist was in asking questions that are lawyer questions, reflective of his experience as an advocate. He wants to get to the heart of the matter as quickly as possible.

Q: Have you ever gotten to the point where that light goes off, and you think, "Oh no, I'm not nearly done?"

DAYS: Oh, yes. On a number of occasions. As solicitor general, I got a little latitude and became perhaps a little bit more courageous toward the end of my tenure. I actually asked, in a couple of occasions, the chief justice whether I could finish my sentence. He would say, "Go ahead," and I thought that was a very kind thing.

Q: Do you go into a case knowing that a certain justice might be that swing vote and try to either sway that particular justice or make eye contact? Do you gear your argument toward that one or two that you think might be the key?

DAYS: Talking about whether one focuses on a particular justice, I think all really skilled advocates before the Court, and even novices, understand that they ought to be familiar with the views of the respective justices based upon what they've done in related cases, and be prepared to recognize questions that are the result of the set of positions that a justice has taken. But I think it's not a very smart approach as an oral advocate to seem to ignore the other justices and focus physically on another justice, who may well be the pivotal justice. I don't think the justices like that very much. They are not thin skinned . . . but I think it's probably not a good idea.

Very surprising things happen during oral argument. I remember a case, one of the early cases I argued. I was convinced that Justice Stevens was with me every step of the way. He was asking great questions, and he was looking, I thought, benignly at me as I argued. I even thought there was a nod somewhere. When the opinion came out, it was 7–2, and he was one of the dissenters. I wrote a law review article about the issue that I was addressing in the lawsuit. It said, "Don't take people for granted on this issue." Justice Stevens wrote a dissent that is kind of a roadmap of how legislation and how administrative actions ought to be taken just to steer clear some of the problems that he saw in the federal statute that I was defending.

Q: Justice Souter described the courtroom and oral argument as a very intimate experience. Would you agree with that? He said you can almost lean out over the bench and touch the attorneys.

DAYS: It's absolutely the case. At a point in the argument, and usually very early on, my experience is that there are nine people up there, and I am with them and we are talking. This is a conversation. I really have no awareness of the courtroom, the people in the courtroom, any physical movements that may be going on. It's quite remarkable. There is this physical closeness, proximity, and there is also something about the [audio] system in the Court, which is very, very sensitive. The justices, if they whispered, one could hear their questions.

Some lawyers have a real problem [with oral argument in the Court]. Even pros every once in a while look down at their notes or are inattentive for a moment; they forget where the question is coming from, because it could be coming from any place. When Justice Ginsburg came on, so there were two women, the sense was the question was from a female justice and the person would turn and say, "No, Justice Ginsburg," and it would have been a question from Justice O'Connor. When Justice O'Connor left, there was a party, and they gave out T-shirts that said, "No, I am not Sandra, I am Ruth," and the other one said, "I am not Ruth, I am Sandra," just to remind some of the lawyers of mistakes that had been made during oral argument.

Q: Did you have any type of process you went through before you went in there, whether it's superstition or a routine right before an oral argument?

DAYS: A rabbit's foot?

Q: Is there something that you did almost every time?

DAYS: Deep breathing. You try to keep focused and try to remember where you are going. It's a very challenging situation. You may get there with a set piece that is not the greatest idea, and you'll be disrupted fairly early on in your argument, and the question is how to get back to your main argument. . . . I would go swimming in the morning, or go running, to get physically in shape, to get my blood flowing. And before that of course, usually there are moot courts in which one is grilled by other lawyers on one's staff or by partners to prepare you. My sense has been that rarely do they ask the questions that the justices ask. I think that's in part true because the justices are not focused on one area of the law. They are thinking about the entire body of the law that they have to interpret, and only they really know that. An example would be a situation where the issue was intent. Intent is a matter or a principle that flows throughout the entire body of law. And so one day, the justices in oral argument may be thinking about intent in a labor law context; a couple of days later, it's intent in a criminal law context. I had an experience sitting in the Court when I probably watched three hundred oral arguments, and I turned to one of my assistants and I said, "That question is going to come up in my argument." I had a criminal case on a Wednesday; the case we were watching argued was on a Monday. But it's clear that the justices were struggling with this notion of how do we define intent and under what circumstances, and what are the exceptions. It was really quite sobering. I think it also suggests why the solicitor general's office, in particular, is effective beyond expectations before the Court, because somebody from the SG's office is in court just about every day that there is oral argument. That wisdom is incorporated into the thinking of the office and the lawyers who appear for the United States.

Q: Speaking of the solicitor general, what is the definition of that job?

DAYS: The original definition was somebody who could assist the attorney general for many years. Attorneys general suffered not in silence asking for assistants. It was not until 1870 that the Office of Solicitor General was created, and it was defined as providing an assistant to the attorney general.

At that time, attorneys general argued cases before the Court. Private lawyers were retained by the government to argue cases—Daniel Webster and so forth. But over the years, principally in the early part of the 1900s, the job of the attorney general began to be so complex that gradually the responsibility for handling cases before the Court, arguing cases and writing briefs fell to the solicitor general. It has been that way ever since.

The attorney general can overrule the solicitor general. He or she can decide to argue cases. But there was a legal opinion written in about 1977 during the Carter administration that suggested that the president and the attorney general ought to leave the solicitor general alone for the most part. There might be circumstances where they would have to intercede, but the notion was that the solicitor general is supposed to be learned in the law. One of my predecessors said, "If you are not learned in the law, when you become SG, you are by the time you leave." I think that's right. Attorneys general have all kinds of responsibilities because of the political dimension of their roles. It's really good to have someone who reads law all the time and is attuned to where the Supreme Court [stands] on any particular question of law.

Q: How did you as solicitor general decide which cases you wanted to argue in front of the Court, and which ones you would delegate? Did a case have to measure up to a certain level?

DAYS: I learned very early on that I was not the decider, to quote someone else. The senior staff basically said, "This is a case that you are going to argue; it's an SG case." They tended to be major cases where in particular the administration's position was at issue before the Court.

Drew Days.

In one instance, I really pushed back in a big way. There was a case having to do with the constitutionality of the courts-martial system of the United States. I was a Peace Corps volunteer. I turned to my staff and said, "I can't argue this, I have not been in the military; I really don't know anything about the courts-martial." They said, "No. This is the type of case that comes around only once a decade and this is your case, this is your decade."

I was really intimidated by that, but on the way home, I stopped by a local video store in my neighborhood and took out a tape. I put it in the—this obviously dates me— I put it in the machine, and watched it and took notes with my yellow pad. The next day when I got to my office I got a call from an admiral, the head of a Naval Yard. He said, "General"—I got to be called general, as solicitor general. He said, "General, I understand you're going to be arguing one of our cases." And I said, "Yes, Admiral, and I want you to know that I'm on the job. I've been working ever since last night. The moment I knew I was going to have to do this, I sat and watched very carefully and took notes of *A Few Good Men*." There was silence on the other end of the line for about twenty seconds, and then the voice came back and it said, "General, what are you doing tomorrow at 8 a.m.?" I said, "Well, I don't think I have anything." He said, "A car will pick you up, and you'll be taken to the Navy Yard, so you could observe a courts-martial." That's what I did for an entire day, which was very educational in all kinds of ways, and it helped me prepare for the oral argument.

Q: How did the case turn out?

DAYS: It turned out well. I knew shortly after the argument began, when Justice Blackmun looked down at my opponent and he said, "Counsel, can you explain to the Court why this is the first time in two hundred years this issue has been presented to the Court?" I thought that was moving in the right direction, and I was successful in that argument.

I had learned a lot about all the experience in the military by the justices of the Supreme Court. I learned that Chief Justice Rehnquist had been a meteorological expert in Europe during the Second World War. So I was ready for any question about the weather.

Q: We did an interview with the clerk of the Court a couple of days ago, and we saw him in this morning coat. Are there similar traditions for the solicitor general?

DAYS: Yes, the tradition is to wear striped pants, a cutaway, a dark gray vest, and you don't have to wear a wig or a bowler, but that's been the tradition. There was a time when all lawyers appearing before the Court, I'm told, dressed accordingly. For a long time, women were not permitted to argue before the Court. . . . And when I became solicitor general, I was told that there was a woman who argued before the Court who had designed her own outfit, which was a striped skirt and a cutaway, and a dark gray vest. I decided to call her directly. She is a lawyer in Chicago. I said, "Is this correct?" And she said, "Yes." And she said, "You know, the truth of it all was that was the most interesting thing about my argument." Apparently, it didn't turn out well for her. But there are now women. I hired several women, and at least one of the women decided that she was going to wear striped pants and a cutaway. She looks very smart that way.

Q: The robes, are they anachronistic? Are they outdated, or do they add something to it, do you think?

DAYS: I love pomp and circumstance and ceremonies, so I am probably not the right person to ask about that. I think [the tradition of the robes] lends a sense of seriousness and importance to the way the Court carries out its business. I don't think it has to be there. I appeared before many courts in the federal system and the state system. But when Chief Justice Rehnquist came out with his new stripes from a Gilbert and Sullivan operetta, and Justice O'Connor and Justice Ginsburg began to wear these lacy collars, I thought it was fine. I don't think that it detracts from the very weighty responsibilities that the justices have and the important role that the Court plays in our society.

Q: The solicitor general has an office there at the Supreme Court. Could you describe that office? Where is it, and do you utilize it very often?

DAYS: It's not very far from the main courtroom. It's something that confounds anybody who took ninth grade civics—you know, separation of powers, three branches, and so forth—because an officer of the executive branch has an office in the building of the judicial branch, and the judicial branch pays for the office. This is very dicey. Indeed, I joked one time with General Suter, I was half serious, and he responded very nicely to it. [I joked] "This couch here; it looks pretty grubby; I'd like another couch." Sure enough, I got another couch, and I probably violated some law down the road.

Solicitors general use that room differently. Seth Waxman who succeeded me as solicitor general actually went up there to work because it's very quiet, particularly when there are no oral arguments and there are no telephones that can come after you. I used it from time to time, but mostly before arguments or after arguments. It's a very serene place. It's right off the Lawyers' Lounge. It has period furniture, and it has portraits of the worthies there. Sitting there, one gets a sense of continuity, and of where one fits into the historical picture. There is a plaque there, so you can look and see after you leave, "There I am. I've become part of history." It's a very moving experience, quite frankly.

Q: Right outside the solicitor general's office is the Lawyers' Lounge. As solicitor general, did you partake in the tradition there where the clerk talks with the lawyer beforehand?

DAYS: Yes. I didn't have to do it as solicitor general. The clerk might say, "This is not for you." But you do go there because you hand out cards, and he does other things that are important to get into the courtroom.

Q: Now opposing attorneys, are they in the room at the same time? Do they talk to each other?

DAYS: Yes, very often. These are people we've known over the years; and so, it's natural that we'd speak and relive old times. The competitive juices are flowing by that time, and so once the argument takes place, it's quite likely that there will be conversations after the argument about how it went. I had an argument very recently, in fact, when one of my associates made the unhelpful point that I was going to be arguing before my third chief justice. I told him that observation was not really helpful and that we ought to go back to the merits of the case. Anyhow, the other fellow on the other side was someone I know very well, and after that argument, we chatted after the case and decided that we were never going to get involved in another case that had to do with this very complex economic investment situation.

Q: You have argued cases about congressional redistricting and term limits and Indian gaming, things that really have a huge impact on this country. Do you get a sense of whether there's a heightened national interest in the case you are about to argue? Does that make any difference to you at all, or is every case in front of that Court just as important?

DAYS: They're all important. But I think one naturally responds to cases that have a higher profile. It doesn't mean that you're necessarily going to do anything differently, but you probably breathe a little bit harder, getting ready to argue the case.

There was one that had to do with the census. It was a very important case and debated in the Congress and in the media and a variety of other places—that question of whether sampling was a reliable technique in determining the existence of certain minority populations. There were allegations of manipulation by the prior administration, and indeed, the critic of the prior administration and its secretary of commerce became the secretary of commerce in the Clinton administration.

So, one of the things I had to do was convince the secretary that he was no longer a critic of the administration. He was the guy, and so he ought to be concerned about, not only the protection of his authority, but the protection of those who follow him. So there was an institutional interest that was fairly profound. I sensed that as I was preparing for the argument and making the argument.

There was another case that had to do with a challenge to the way in which federal prosecutors handled certain types of cases, and it had a racial component to it. The question was, "Was the United States attorney in a jurisdiction intentionally working with the local prosecutor to ensure that people charged with certain drug offenses appeared before federal judges as opposed to state judges, federal judges having much heavier sentences to mete out?" Was there a racial bias in the charging process? And as an African American, this is something that I felt. But I also became absolutely convinced, having gone through the entire record, that there was no problem in that respect. I thought it was important to protect the discretion of federal prosecutors to decide how they want to handle certain types of matters that could have been prosecuted in either federal or state courts.

Those are just a couple of examples, but there are many others where I think I felt the tension. In another case there was what I called a $4 billion misunderstanding, involving a United States bank—indeed, an international bank—in the state of California. It was a case that had drawn the interest of all our trading partners. And so, I had to be careful not to say certain things during the oral argument that would perhaps create further tension between the United States and these other countries.

Q: Have you had a favorite experience in the courtroom during oral argument?

DAYS: There have been some fairly humorous moments that I'm not sure were entirely viewed as humor when I was arguing. I argued a case during the time that *Bakke* had been previously decided, and there were some other affirmative action cases coming before the Court. I had prepared myself to point to a concurrence that Justice Powell had written in the *Bakke* case. It's very well known. And so, as they say in the law, there came a point in the argument when I said, "But Justice Powell, you said in *Bakke*," and I read him back to himself. He said, "I did say that, but no one else on the Court agreed with me." That was the end of that stroke of genius on my part. I thought that was pretty funny.

There was another time, maybe during the same argument, when Justice Rehnquist asked me why Aleuts and Eskimos had been included in this affirmative action provision. He wanted to know how much research had been done in the treatment of Aleuts and Eskimos in Alaska. And I told him I was confident that Congress had done its job. He let me go.

Q: Have you had moments in that courtroom, maybe when you're in there alone, when you feel the history of what happened there?

DAYS: Yes, that's the sense that one gets just walking into the courtroom and watching the ceremony unfold leading up to the oral argument.

When the Court comes in and people rise, and the Court is announced and people are told to draw nigh if they have matters before the Court. And they sit down and you're called to stand before the lectern. It's a very powerful experience. I think everyone feels it. Even people who have been before the Court many, many times still get a rush when that happens. In fact, I went to one of the lawyers on my staff, quite a good lawyer, when I was fairly new in the office, and I said, "How do you feel when you argue? Do you have butterflies?" He said, "I do, but,"—and this is a big, hulking guy—he said, "but I've decided it's like playing ball." And I said, "What do you mean?" He said, "You're nervous until the first hit. After that, it's fine."

There's the first question and you respond, and then the rest kind of flows the way it's going to flow. But a guy named Larry Wallace, who holds the record for the number of arguments before the Supreme Court that I think will never be surpassed, was nervous before the Court. He used to wear what we used to call moccasins. He would be in his cutaway and striped pants, and he would take his shoes off. He would actually be standing before the Court in his stocking feet because he'd knock the moccasins off as he was arguing. He'd make a point, and he'd move his shoe and the moccasin would come off. I've rarely seen someone who seemed to be so self-possessed that he wasn't [anxious], at least at the start.

Q: Have you been in a courtroom when there's no one else in there?

DAYS: Yes, I have.

Q: What goes through your mind?

DAYS: I relive my arguments, among other things. I see justices before me who are no longer around. I see the frieze around the ceiling of the courtroom with all of the lawgivers—that's very moving—to the left side, the one facing the Court where the press sits. And I remember a lot of people who were there over the years, looking at the family section on the right-hand side where various people have come in, including the widows of justices. I remember Justice White would come in, after he retired from the Court, and he'd sit there, his long lanky self, wearing loafers and kind of stretched out. He'd probably have a sports jacket or something like that, watching the events unfold on the Court during the oral argument.

Q: Do you get a sense sometimes during an oral argument that you're going to win or you're going to lose?

DAYS: I think it's hard when you're in the moment to do that. But other people can discern some direction of the Court. Some political scientists have done studies, and the one who gets the most questions is most likely to lose. But some cases are very close, and the dynamics can shift during the oral argument. There are justices who seem to be following and moving along in your direction, and then something happens during the oral argument. There's a button that's pushed or a word that's used by the lawyer that changes that dynamic. Sometimes that's perceptible. It's very interesting to watch.

Q: Have you ever had the feeling that you've got this, you're going to win, and then the decision comes out and you were wrong?

DAYS: No, I haven't. I know when things are not going very well, and I knew when things were going pretty well. In that example, with respect to Justice Stevens, I thought he was with me, and he turned out not to be with me. But, in general, I seem to be moving in the right direction. The justices were a little bit closer to the vest when Chief Justice Burger headed the Court. They would not let on in many instances what they really thought. In more recent years, the justices have been pretty outspoken. They will say, "I understand your argument, but I'm not buying that. Do you have anything better to offer?" There are justices who actually begin their questions saying, "My problem is such-and-so." That's very helpful to lawyers who would prefer not to be dealing with a black box. And the justices will then duel verbally with one another on certain things. There will be justices that will try to help one through the argument. One of the things that novices usually don't know is that most of the time, the questions are designed to help. They're not trick questions. And so, the sense is, this is too good to be true; there must be a hook somewhere that the justices want to be able to grab on to. But this is the time they're trying to argue with one another through you. And so, take the help.

Q: Does it matter to you whether you win a case 5–4 or 9–0 or 8–1?

DAYS: I think a win is a win, but looking down the road, the question is, What precedential value is the case going to have? Does it simply leave for another day the same issue where you have a very closely divided court? There are issues that one wanted to have really nailed down but don't get nailed down. But I think, as one of my colleagues said, you'd rather lose 9–zip because if it's 5–4 you'll always think, "What could I have done to push one justice into my column?" I think those are the ends: 9–zip, nothing could have been done, a hopeless case; 5–4, there was a point where you might have been able to shift one vote.

Q: There are quill pens on the table in the courtroom. There's a little placard that says who all the justices are. Could you describe what those are and what they're there for?

DAYS: It's symbolism; the quills are given to the people who argue before the Court, and they're great to give to friends or family. They actually work. You can write with them; there are inkblots there so you could do that if you wanted to. But they're there to communicate that what you are engaging in is a tradition that's been around for a very long time, and you have a responsibility in caring for the Court. It's an honor. It's a burden that is imposed by that tradition.

My sense has been that, even when I was unhappy with the Court's decisions and had for a moment that "I was robbed" sense, that the Supreme Court is so impressive to visitors—particularly to people from other countries, but also American citizens—when they walk

Quill pens in the courtroom.

into that Court, I think they get the sense that these are very serious people who understand the weight on their shoulders who are trying to do the best that they can. I love to take people from other countries into the Court and have them watch smart people asking probing questions and trying to find helpful answers to the issues that are before them.

When you get to this time in which we find ourselves, when a vacancy is going to be filled, [public opinion about the Court goes] up and down. But I think the Supreme Court is generally viewed by the American people as an institution that is worthy of their respect and trust. We have things like *Bush v. Gore* where there are fissures, but all in all, they tend to pass.

Q: Do you know the justices socially, outside the courtroom?

DAYS: I've seen them from time to time, and when I was solicitor general, I saw them fairly often. There were receptions and dinners at the Court. But I think there is no truth to the claim that there's some special relationship between the solicitor general and the justices. Indeed, we know each other, and I think we understand that there's some kind of symbiotic relationship. The justices tend to read what we call the gray brief first in a case because they look to it as the straightest story that can be told about the case. It says what the issues are, it's easier to read, it's well-written, and so forth. I think that's one of the challenges that one has as solicitor general or as a person on the solicitor general's staff: We are repeat players. If you are arguing your one and only case before the Court, you may make certain errors, you may miss certain cases, and do things that might be understandable under the circumstances. But the solicitor general really is expected to get it right, and in some cases, provide the Court with a middle way when the parties are contending over an issue that seems intractable. It's a very good feeling to go in and say, "We think this is the way the Court ought to resolve this issue." It opens some other areas that don't need to be resolved here, resolves this case; it solves some other things, and the Court can wait for another case to perhaps work things out.

There's a very strange procedure, at least to the uninitiated, and that is something called "calling for the views of the solicitor general"— CVSG. I talked about that problem with civics lessons when you see the solicitor general's office in the Supreme Court, but this is problematic even for lawyers. Imagine a petition filed by a private lawyer against a private party also represented by a private lawyer pending before the Supreme Court, and the Supreme Court is trying to decide whether it's going to accept that case for review or oral argument and decision. In some of those cases, the Court asks for the views of the solicitor general: "What do you think about this, General Days? Is this the type of case you think we should take? Is it important enough for us to spend our very limited resources on?" And the solicitor general is expected to answer within sixty days or soon thereafter. That is largely because the solicitor general can draw upon the entire executive branch to bring a context to bear with respect to that particular issue. Cases are filed that appear to be of interest, but they may not be represented by sophisticated counsel. The justices have a sense that there's something there, and it's attractive, it's interesting, but they'd like another set of eyes to take a look at it.

Q: When the building opened in 1935, some justices didn't want to move into it; they thought it was too grand. Do you have an opinion on that when you look at that building?

DAYS: Hamilton called it the least dangerous branch. But I liked the fact that, looking out on the Capitol and at the congressional buildings and the Library of Congress right next door, it is very clear that the Court is an important part of our democratic system of our federal government. The success of our society depends upon those branches ultimately working together, finding accommodations; the executive branch and the legislative branch ultimately have to accept the notion that there has to be an arbiter of disputes, and that arbiter has to be independent, nonpartisan, objective, and sharing in the transcendent values that mark our society.

Q: You train attorneys to practice in front of the court. What are the important things for them to know before they go up there that first time?

DAYS: Overall, my message to young lawyers is, remember that it's not your argument; it's their argument. You are there to help them solve their problems, not the other way around. Often lawyers think, "I've got to convince them of this or that" and "I've got to get this argument in." No, that's not really it. The [justices] have problems. They're going to have to make a decision, and you ought to be there to help them in that process of decision making.

Q: Do you ever see a first-time lawyer who's about to argue his or her first case in front of the Court in that Lawyers' Lounge just completely . . .

DAYS: No, I must say, I've seen some really wonderful arguments made by first-timers. I won't mention the case, but I saw a case last term, a major case, and the lawyer had never argued before. I thought he was just wonderful. And I've seen men and women getting up before the Court who have lived in instances with the issue and with the case and they don't have to worry about knowing the issue. They know the issue and they've seen it from the ground all the way up, so their challenge is to understand the dynamics of the Court, how the precedent works and that this is the Supreme Court. They're not bound by any precedent but their own, so when a justice says "Well, what about this?" you're not supposed to say, "But you can't do that. You decided such and so . . . "

The Court is a pretty secret place in all the best senses of the word. There have been leaks, but probably four or five in twenty-five years or so. The sense is that the Court understands the importance of its deliberations. It understands how its decisions will affect the society politically, socially, medically, and they work very hard to keep that information inside the building. There have been a couple of exposés, if you want to call them that, by clerks. There were a couple a few years ago; some years ago now, probably fifteen years ago.

But I think that's very important, that the lawyers who appear before the Court and the general public know that these people are really working hard. They're serious people trying to do a job and not looking for headlines and not trying to aggrandize themselves as they carry out their responsibilities.

Q: There have been requests now for years to bring cameras into that courtroom like we have in Congress. The White House is covered wall to wall with cameras. What is your opinion on whether that would work for this branch of government?

DAYS: The short answer is, I don't know. I think that the concern that lawyers would play to the camera is probably a less serious concern than it has been made out to be by some people. I do think that the sampling issue is a serious one; that is, the Court hears a lot of cases and one can understand the Court best by seeing it work through a tax case or a labor case. Then you've got one of the blockbusters, and these are the same justices, doing the same job that they were doing when it was a tax case or a labor law case. Yet by pulling out those high profile cases, I think there's a risk that a misimpression, a very serious one, is left with the viewer. . . .

Justice White used to say, "It will affect my anonymity." Here's a guy who's 6 foot 3 inches, an all-American football player. I think he was identifiable when he went around town. I thought the radio feeds [of oral argument] were pretty good. I think they were very positive in educating the people about the Court, but with fixed cameras, you can't really get that dynamic in the way that I think is very important. . . . When you've got nine justices, there's got to be some camera panning. Otherwise you're looking at the chief justice all day long.

That's a very long and rambling answer, but I think every effort ought to be made to determine what technology will make the Court more familiar to more citizens and non-citizens in the United States; indeed around the world.

Q: Well, thank you, again, so much. We appreciate your time.

DAYS: My pleasure.

LYLE DENNISTON

Reporter, *SCOTUS Blog*

*L*yle Denniston, dean of the Supreme Court reporters, has been cover-ing the Supreme Court for more than fifty years—nineteen of them for the Baltimore Sun. *His homebase now is* SCOTUSblog, *an online site for Court-watchers. A Nebraska native, he is the author of a book about the Court, and is a frequent contributor to discussions about the Court for publications, broadcasts, and seminars. Mr. Denniston was interviewed on July 14, 2009, by C-SPAN's Mark Farkas.*

FARKAS: We have seen you [in the Court's press room] on opinion re-lease days; could you describe what's happening? What are we looking at on these days?

LYLE DENNISTON: The Court releases opinions usually on scheduled days. We know in advance approximately when opinions will be com-ing out. They usually don't start coming out in any great number un-til late December into January because the Court takes some time to prepare them. When they are ready for a release, we don't know what's coming down until the chief justice announces from the bench, which we can hear on the internal audio in the press room. [He announces] the docket number of the case and the title of the case and which member of the Court, if not himself, is going to be an-nouncing it.

Reporters wait for an opinion in the Public Information Office. Inset: Lyle Denniston.

At the moment that the chief mentions the docket number, the staff of the Public Information Office hands out copies of the decisions to us, and we then go rushing, some of us faster than others, to write about it, or to the telephone to let the world know what the Court has done. For a veteran of the Court, it's a fairly easy thing to handle because by the time a decision comes down, ultimately or finally resolving a case, you will have had several opportunities to become acquainted with what's at stake. Particularly, if you've been covering the law a long time, you know the wider perspective that potentially is involved in it. So, within a range of reasonable possibilities, you know what the Court is going to decide. It's very seldom a real surprise, and there is going be a decision on the merits. They may duck some issues, but it's fairly easy to discern quickly what the Court does, because each opinion is released with not only the text of the opinion itself, what the Court is actually saying; it's released with what are called "head notes," which are prepared by the reporter of decisions, who is an officer of the Court, summarizing what the Court has done. If you scan the syllabus at the top of the opinion, you very quickly know what the Court has done. As time allows, then you dip into some parts of the opinion. After you've done it for a while, you know which parts of the opinions to jump to quickly. . . .

We also get from the Public Information Office a release of orders—actions that the Court has taken on new cases or already pending cases. Usually what we care about most is which cases among the new ones the justices have agreed to hear. They have almost complete discretion whether to hear cases or to simply deny review.

Some of us also pay a fair amount of attention to what the Court is not going to decide, because there are always major cases that come up that some of us think are newsworthy. And we would think that they are likely to be heard by the Court, and they're not.

One that I think of as a classic one was the case that came up over the rights of the detainees at Guantanamo. The issue was whether or not they could challenge their continued detention. The Court denied review of that the first time it came up. That was in April of 2008, and we were all very surprised because we thought clearly that the Court was going to take that case. As it turns out, the Court sat on the case without finally disposing of it for another four or five months, and then granted it. That illustrates that the Court has really very wide discretion in composing its docket for decisions.

Q: Who is in that room on opinion release days? The Public Information staff and the reporters? There seems to be a fair amount of anticipation and energy as you're waiting.

DENNISTON: The rhythm of the Court's term is such that the major decisions are often held until the last two or three weeks of the term, that is, beginning somewhere around the 10th to 12th of June of each year. . . . The term builds up quite slowly. The decisions don't really start flowing out of the Court until the middle of the winter, and then they come out fairly slowly. When the Court finishes hearing public arguments, usually by the end of April, that's when it goes to work seriously to write the opinions in the remaining undecided cases. Usually the undecided cases at that point include many of the major ones that are going to come down. So, we get more excited about opinion release days because as the Court focuses in on the remaining decisions, we begin expecting the really big ones. For example, in the term that completed in June of 2009, the Court was about to announce a major decision on the constitutionality of a very important part of the Federal Voting Rights Law. We were anticipating that all the way from the early part of June up through the time when the Court finished for the summer and did decide that case just before going away.

There is a lot of tension in the room because people are eager to get at the opinions. Sometimes when one justice is announcing one opinion and you're anticipating more that day, you get antsy waiting for the justice to finish so that the next one can be announced and you can go with that one.

The people in the room will be the staff of the Public Information Office, who have in front of them closed boxes with the copies of the Court's "slip opinions," as they are called at that stage. As the chief justice announces the title of the case, the staff then hands them out. The only people in the room at that time will be members of the press who are covering the Court and the Public Information Office staff. The public doesn't have access to that part of the building.

Q: What is the biggest challenge for you as a reporter in covering the Supreme Court?

DENNISTON: It's a challenge that was bigger for me when I worked for daily newspapers than it is now that I work for a legal online entity because my audience for my blog work now is much more legally sophisticated than the general newspaper audience was. Then, the challenge was always to try to make a Supreme Court decision intelligible to people who are really not going to spend very much time with you and probably have no real legal knowledge or legal perception. And so, I made it a habit when I was in the newspaper business, of avoiding the use of any legal terms, always finding a phrase that would describe in lay terms or, if you will, the language of the street what the Court has done, rather than using terms of art. I assumed in the news business, particularly the newspaper business that you don't have very much of your reader's time and so you don't want to waste any of it.

Now that I work for an online entity, the audience for which is largely lawyers, legal academics, and other kinds of academics, I can use some of our legal terms of art. But I still carry on the old newspaper habit of much preferring to write so that if a lay person happens to read our blog, he or she will be able to discern immediately what's actually happening.

Q: I have this impression after doing our documentaries on the Capitol and the White House that the Supreme Court is visited less often than those two places and that the Court itself is this mysterious place to many in the public. Why do you think that it is?

DENNISTON: Most Americans tend to focus on institutions that are publicly responsive, if you will. The Court is an institution that really doesn't do things because of the way the winds of politics or cultural norms are blowing. The Court is supposed to be, and when it's working right, successfully, is a detached institution. As a consequence, the public is not as aware of it, and moreover the Public Information Office of the Court is not a part of the public relations community the way the White House Press Secretary is. They do not engage in spin control. They do not engage in promotional work so that the public is more aware of the Court's activities and its decisions. So, the Court sits there up on Capitol Hill, away from the center of public attention.

Another factor is that in recent times the Court is deciding about half of the number of cases that it did some twenty-five or thirty years ago. The Court in the 1982–83 term decided, I think, 155 cases. An average number these days is seventy-five cases a year. So, in some real respect, the Court itself is withdrawing from the center of public attention. But I think the main factor is that it's a specialized institution that often speaks in a specialized language, and so, it probably is an institution that depends for its communication with the general public much more on the capacity of the press to translate what it does into understandable English for the average American reader. . . .

Another factor in this is that the Supreme Court does not allow immediate broadcast coverage of its public sessions. No cameras are allowed. No recording devices of any kind are allowed in the court-room when it's holding its public sessions. And so, the Court, has made choices about not to being as visible as it might otherwise be, though I must warn people who are so anxious to get the Court on television that if you hear an oral argument from the start to finish in a case involving the Employment Retirement Income Security Act of 1974, you are going to lose your audience after about the first thirty-eight seconds. A lot of what the Court does is quite detailed and some of it is very highly technical. Maybe no more than about one-fourth of its decision output is the kind of popular information that the general public is going to be interested in.

Q: Can you talk about the human side of the Court and the collegiality there? Is that important?

DENNISTON: The Court is really an inward-focused institution. It's a very closed community. Even those of us who are not employees of the Court, who are regularly in the building, are accepted as a part of the Court community. We're not allowed to sit in on the justices' private deliberations, of course, though some of us would like to do that. It's an institution where virtually everybody knows everybody else. And among the justices—and this really depends on the pattern that the chief justice sets—if the chief justice wants a really collegial court, the chief justice can do things that bring that about.

Chief Justice Warren, for example, had a largely collegial Court. Of course, he always had to deal with the feud that never seemed to end between justices Black and Frankfurter, but Earl Warren himself was very warm and friendly and ran a Court that was agreeable with each other.

The Court under Warren Burger, the late Chief Justice Burger, was not a happy place. The relationships between the justices tended

Portraits of Chief Justices Earl Warren and Warren Burger in the Court's West Conference Room.

pretty rapidly to deteriorate; there was a lot of internal resentment among the justices, and the chief justice didn't work very hard at trying to dispel that. In fact, the way he ran the Court at times contributed to that kind of internal dissension because he would play favorites in the way he assigned opinions. He would sometimes cast his vote one way in order to have control over the assignment of the functions and then change his vote later on. He ran the court in a way that contributed to the internal divisions.

Now, Chief Justice Rehnquist, on the other hand, ran a very happy Court, a very collegial Court. Remember that I'm talking about a Court during the Rehnquist years that was very deeply divided along philosophical and ideological lines. Nowhere is it defined that the chief justice should be the principal caretaker of the emotional state of the Court. But he has that capacity, using the functions of the office and his leadership of the Court, to make the Court a harmonious place or has the capacity to do just the opposite.

It's apparent that Chief Justice Roberts is trying very hard to follow the example of Chief Justice Rehnquist and have a collegial court. He has a bit of a disadvantage because, unlike Rehnquist, he was not on the Court to establish relationships before he became the chief justice. I think that helped with Rehnquist, having been one of the nine before being the leader of the nine. Justice Roberts didn't have that opportunity. Also, he is considerably younger than a lot of his colleagues, which makes it a little more challenging for him to establish the kind of leadership potential that I think he ultimately will have.

Within the Court building, it's an easy relationship between the Court and their staff members. The only group that is completely out of touch for us in the press is the law clerks. The Court admonishes them very severely not to talk to the press. There have been times in the past when law clerks were sources of leaks about the internal deliberations of a Court, and the Court doesn't like that. When new law clerks come on board, they usually get a pretty stern lecture about not talking to the media. Kenneth Starr, who is now at Pepperdine and former solicitor general, former federal judge, and one-time law clerk, used to say that they had a thirty-second rule, which was: thirty seconds after you are seen talking to a member of the press you are out of here. It's now such a restrictive environment for the law clerks that if you see one in the cafeteria line at the lunch hour, and you greet them socially and say nothing more than hi, you won't get a response. I suspect that they are all concerned that any form of communication with identifiable members of the media will be looked down upon.

. . . We have some access to the justices. That depends, now, from one justice to the next. You can go upstairs and sit down and talk with a good many of them. It's always off the record. You don't learn anything that you can publish. I'll be frank: You don't very often learn anything that's terribly newsworthy, but you do use the opportunity to get some flavor for the person. And you get to look around the chamber to see the kind of physical environment in which they function day to day.

Q: You've got nine distinct personalities on the Court. Are there one or two that stick out for whatever reason?

Retired Associate Justice David Souter in his C-SPAN interview, June 2009.

DENNISTON: On the Court that has been sitting since 1986, there is one highly colorful personality who always attracts a lot of attention, and, I think, frankly, loves the attention: That's Justice Antonin Scalia. He is technicolor in spades in terms of high visibility as a justice. He shines during all argument. He really loves that kind of atmosphere. But each justice has a different personality. Most of us are really going to miss Justice David Souter now that he has retired, because he brought to the Court a kind of a dignity and even more important a kind of human civility. In an institution that at times can be really contentious internally, Justice Souter brought those qualities, which improved the overall humanity of the institution itself. One justice can make that kind of difference. Justice Souter also was the best prepared justice for oral argument that I have seen in all the time I have covered the Court. He really was capable of going immediately to the heart of what was at issue in the cases before the Court. So, he is extremely intelligent and very perceptive, while appearing to be a shy and withdrawn person.

Justice O'Connor was always a really visible presence on the Court, because she was such a dominant figure. Not dominant in the sense of wielding her power over other people, but so much of the jurisprudence of the Court, the actual results of what they did particularly on constitutional issues, was very much a product of the thinking of Sandra Day O'Connor. She was unbelievably important to the Court's modern history.

Justice Steven Breyer is one of the most lovable members of the Court, at least in his public persona, because he's kind of like the absentminded professor. He will be talking in one direction about something, and then he'll appear to lose his train of thought, and then he'll move off. . . . Sometimes I have teased him that the Court wouldn't need to have arguments as long as they do if he didn't participate as much as he does, because he tends to ask very long questions. He's also just a delightful human being to know. He serves wonderful tea in his chambers.

Q: It does seem like the justices are on different sides of one case, and on another case they are on the same side. How important is collegiality up there?

DENNISTON: The most important part of the collegiality within the Court is that when you've decided a case you've got to move on. However much you may have resented the way your colleagues on the other side have decided the case, there is going to be another tough case coming up right afterward. And so, if the prevailing atmosphere in the Court is one of collegiality, then you are able to have a real tussle over a case, but then once it's decided, put it aside and move on. If it were an institution that harbored grudges, that nursed bad feelings over and over again, it would be very, very difficult to move from one of these huge controversies to another one. And because it's the Supreme Court of the United States and because it is so selective in what it does, it really gets only the toughest cases. . . .

I think it's awfully important for the Court to be able to talk with each other and to remain largely civil. I understand that in the private conference when the Court is behind closed doors, the discussion can get fairly lively and even heated at times. If it were a Court like the Court when Chief Justice Burger was there, one that doesn't get along very well, the potential for disrupting the process would be much greater.

Q: So, obviously, the chief justice can set a tone. On the other hand, you've got eight other individuals who don't have to answer to the chief justice.

DENNISTON: The justices who sit with the chief justice do not want to have any of the administrative duties that the chief justice has. They will defer to the chief justice to decide things like when they should start a construction project or what they should put in the budget that they send across to Congress. Anything of administrative nature, they will just defer to the chief justice. But when it becomes an issue in which the institutional operation or stature is important, the other justices want a major part in that. For example, when the issue came up during Chief Justice Rehnquist's tenure—and it came up repeatedly—about whether the Court would allow broadcast coverage of the public proceedings, that was not a decision that the other justices were willing to let the chief justice make by himself. They wanted a part in that. Rehnquist was never going to have an order allowing cameras to come into the courtroom to cover the public activities if he didn't have the concurrence of his other justices.

The chief justice's control over the assignment process is very much a unitary control. The chief justice doesn't ask the advice of the others. He doesn't say, "Would you like me to assign you this case or that case?" . . . The chief justice has pretty awesome powers to make the assignment of who gets to write the majority opinion, if he's in the majority, and who gets to write the dissent if he's in the dissent. But the chief justice generally . . . doesn't consult with his colleagues about how you would get these assignments. And it's not a good idea for another justice to lobby to get the right to do a particular opinion, because the chief justice guards that power pretty jealously. There aren't very many decisions that the chief justice gets to make unilaterally. There are nine votes on every substantive decision that the Court has, and the chief justice only controls one of those votes. Obviously there could be inter-

The Supreme Court's official photograph, 1986–1987 term.

Top row, left to right: Justice Sandra Day O'Connor, Justice Lewis F. Powell, Justice John Paul Stevens, and Justice Antonin Scalia.

Front row, left to right: Justice Thurgood Marshall, Justice William J. Brennan Jr., Chief Justice William Rehnquist, Justice Byron R. White, and Justice Harry A. Blackmun.

Collection of the Supreme Court of the United States.

The Great Hall is the ceremonial space leading up to the entrance of the Supreme Court Chamber. Lined with busts of past chief justices as well as artwork symbolic of the law, it is used for significant events such as memorial services for deceased justices. Here, the body of Chief Justice William Rehnquist lies in repose, September 2005. *Collection of the Supreme Court of the United States.*

When a justice joins the Court, part of his or her investiture includes signing an oath card in the justices' Conference Room. **Right:** John Roberts and Justice Sandra Day O'Connor during Chief Justice Roberts's investiture, October 3, 2005.

All photos this page: collection of the Supreme Court of the United States.

Left: Chief Justice Roberts and Justice John Paul Stevens with President George W. Bush, also during Chief Roberts's investiture. Justices O'Connor and Kennedy are in the rear.

Right: Justice Alito signs his oath card during his investiture with Chief Justice Roberts, February 16, 2006, as Justices David Souter and Ruth Bader Ginsburg look on.

The Supreme Court Chamber. On days when court is in session, "the procedures are high ceremony, very traditional," according to Maureen Mahoney, who has argued twenty-two cases before the Court. A short distance separates the attorneys from the justices on the bench. Justice John Paul Stevens says, "You're right in the conversation with the people on the other side of the bench. And it's a very, very interesting experience." Each side is given thirty minutes for their argument; a system of lights on the podium helps keep time.

Justice Stephen Breyer shows one week's petitions for cases to be heard by the Court. Each year, about 8,000 petitions are made to the Court. Each is summarized into a memo by a law clerk. The justices read the memos and vote whether to take each case. If four justices vote yea, it comes before the Court.

The Court grants about eighty cases each year. For each case that is granted, a box sits on Justice Breyer's shelf. The boxes include color-coded briefs from both sides of the case, a brief from the government (gray, pictured here), and briefs from other groups interested in the case, known as *amicus* briefs, meaning "friends of the court."

Regarding the volume of reading, Justice Breyer says, "Briefs follow me around." He carries them with him wherever he goes to keep up with the workflow.

The justices' Conference Room, accessible only to the justices themselves; it is the job of the most junior justice to answer the door when the justices are in conference. As cases are discussed following argument, justices speak in order of seniority. After discussion, a tentative vote occurs and the most senior justice on each side assigns a justice to write the opinion and dissent. *Collection of the Supreme Court of the United States.*

Above: Justices' Dining Room. On days when the Court hears arguments, justices gather in this private second floor room for an informal lunch. Justices say the only rule is not to discuss cases. The custom of these lunches is credited to Justice Sandra Day O'Connor.

Below: Interior Courtyard. Four such courtyards surround the area near the Supreme Court Chamber and are accessible only to the justices and staff. The courtyards feature statuary symbols of justice, such as lions' heads representing authority, and turtles representing the slow, steady pace of justice.

West Entrance Pediment. The phrase "Equal Justice Under Law" was suggested for this space by the architects and approved by Chief Justice Hughes. It has come to symbolize the Court itself. The frieze above it represents the history of the law and people integral to the building's construction—architect Cass Gilbert, Chief Justice Taft, and sculptor Robert Aitken.

EQUAL JUSTICE UNDER LAW

nal trading in which you persuade somebody to come on board when you're writing an opinion by making a concession to something that they want in it. So the negotiating process does go on when you're writing an opinion. But still the chief only has a single vote. . . .

I suppose that the justices do make little alliances. If you have somebody on the Court who thinks ideologically some of the same ways that you do about something, you might want to put your votes together, put your heads together, and try to jointly have more influence than one of you could have alone. They are not cabals, but there are these little concentrations of justices working in blocks to try to influence each other.

But in the decisional process itself, the justices that I've known about, they do not defer to the chief justice very greatly on that. The chief justice has the power to control how the discussion goes, in the sense that the chief justice will open the discussion. But once the conversation is opened in the conference, then it's fair game. Anybody can take part in it.

Q: Do you find it interesting that after that conference where they battle it out individually . . . and after the writing has been assigned, there's very little human interaction?

DENNISTON: Yes, that's a surprise that you discover if you pay close attention to the Court. If you look at the past papers of justices that are now often available in some kind of collection, perhaps at the Library of Congress or at various universities around the country, the decisional process is very much a paper process rather than one in which one justice walks down the hallway and tries to persuade another justice. Now, there are exceptions to that. For example, in 1992 the court was re-examining *Roe v. Wade*, the 1973 abortion decision. Three justices put their heads together, justices Kennedy, Souter, and O'Connor, and fashioned a way by which the Court could resolve that case. That was quite unusual to put together a trio that was managing the case and controlling the outcome of the case. And they were able to get a majority to sign on to what they had chosen to do.

Q: Can you get us to the point where they announce the decision? Once the person who has been assigned the majority opinion finally gets their five, then do they report to the most senior justice on that side of the case?

DENNISTON: Well, no. . . . If the chief justice is not in the majority, then the most senior justice who is in the majority gets to do the assigning. Again, that senior justice only gets to do the assigning function; he or she doesn't keep control of it afterward. What happens is that the justice who has had the opinion assigned to him or her will go through a series of drafts and get responses from the other colleagues and will keep control of the opinion throughout the process. Unless of course it happens—and it sometimes does—where the opinion loses its majority support. It then becomes potentially a dissenting opinion, and the majority switches to the other side. . . .

There can be a dozen, fifteen, eighteen drafts over a period of time. And the justices often take four or five, sometimes six months to decide a case. The easier cases they can decide more quickly. But an opinion goes through many drafts, many revisions.

Though if you look at past opinions of the Court in the Library of Congress where you can see the earlier drafts, it's remarkable how little change is made from the beginning draft to the concluding draft. There are exceptions where there are wholesale changes. But by and large, case in, case out, there is not much change between the opening draft and the concluding draft. There are little phrases, nuances, new shadings. But it's seldom that it really takes a totally different turn.

Q: Justice Souter is leaving, and we're about to get a new justice in the fall. What does a new justice potentially do to the Supreme Court?

DENNISTON: Justice Bryon White used to say—and everybody repeats this now because it's conventional wisdom, but it's conventional wisdom that is quite true—that each new justice changes the whole court. I think what he meant by that was that because it's a Court of nine very particular individuals, there is a dynamic that develops in the group of nine and the new justice can change that dynamic, can come in with a different attitude, a different approach. I remember, as a matter of fact, that Justice Harry Blackmun said to me at one point—and he was quite resentful about Justice O'Connor—he said, "That woman came here with an agenda, and she means to carry it out." He was unhappy with her because his perception was that a new justice should come into the Court and not be very visible for a couple of years until they knew the ropes.

Justice O'Connor came into the Court, and she was kind of throwing her weight around. She was very self-confident. I recall that before the end of November—she came to work in October—she was filing opinions, dissenting from the Court's decisions not to hear cases. Dissent from a denial or a review is a bold thing to do, particularly if you're brand-new to the Court.

A new justice comes into the Court and brings a personality, brings a history, brings a style of judging, a style of writing, and because there is this constantly changing internal dynamic, the addition of a new ingredient in that dynamic changes the whole. Now, it doesn't cause other justices necessarily to change their views, but it does open up the possibility of shifting majorities, shifting blocks within the court.

I remember when Justice Breyer joined the Court. A lot of us anticipated that Justice Breyer would be quite liberal. He was a Clinton appointee, and we expected from his experience on the lower court that Breyer would be a dependable member of what's called the liberal block, or, if you will, progressive members of the Court in ideological terms. But he's become quite a centrist. On a Court that's dominated by conservatives, he looks as if he is a member of the liberal block, but he's very much a member of the centrist, the dynamic center of the Court. When the Court is divided, as the present Court is on ideological terms, the center really has a lot more control because they can throw the Court one way or the other. Steve Breyer plays a very important role in that dimension. I suspect Sonia Sotomayor will be able to change the dynamic, too. On a divided Court, she's much more likely to try to become a member of the dynamic center rather than being predictably lined on one side or the other. Most people would expect that as the nominee of a Democratic president, she would be a liberal member of the Court. Well, people may get a bit of a surprise. . . .

Q: How long, in your observance of these new justices, does it take them to hit their stride, understand the traditions, and fit in?

DENNISTON: I'm not sure this is my perception, but it used to be a convention and, ten or twelve years ago it was always said that a justice doesn't really have any influence for about five years. I think Justice O'Connor's experience suggests that maybe that's too long a time span to have an impact on the Court's work.

The Court is very much aware of history. It's much more aware of history than any president would be. The presidents can read about prior presidents or they can have some historic sense about prior presidents, but there is a continuity in the Court because the membership evolves so slowly. There are only about 110 people who have ever served on the Supreme Court. And so the place is one where continuity is very important. History really does influence the way the Court works.

There are a lot of people who believe, for example, that *Bush v. Gore,* the big decision in 2000 that resolved the presidential election, was driven by partisan consideration in the Court. If you pay close attention to the Supreme Court of the United States, you know that that opinion was driven in large part by history. The Court was acutely aware of what had happened in 1876 when the country did not have a president until the night before Inauguration Day. And that kind of awareness of the role of the Court, the role of the politics of the presidential election, that was very much in the mind of the Court when it felt as an urgent matter the need to resolve the presidential contest. The Court didn't see it as a political thing; it saw it as a constitutional thing. This country was confronted with the possibility of a constitutional crisis. The Senate was controlled by the Democrats, the House was controlled by Republicans, and one of the candidates for the presidency was the presiding officer of the Senate. I think the Court looked across the street and said, "Whoa, we're not sure that we can let this run all the way through the political process." So it was a constitutional decision.

If you read almost any constitutional decision—and some decisions interpreting statutes as well—there is always a large dimension of history. I was chatting with someone the other day who is on the staff at James Madison's home at Montpelier, in Orange, Virginia. I was saying that it's remarkable how often these days you see James Madison and his work relied upon and cited in Supreme Court opinions. We recently had a case out of Alaska involving the little city of Valdez putting a tax on the big oil supertankers that come in and out of its port. That case was resolved on the basis of the Constitution's tonnage clause, which nobody has heard of. But in the course of writing that opinion, James Madison was quoted at length. Or you can have a case about bankruptcy, not exactly a lively topic. Within the hands of a Supreme Court justice, a bankruptcy decision goes back to the founding era and looks at what the founders, the framers of the Constitution, intended to do about bankruptcy.

History is very much a useful medium of debate, of intellectual commerce in the Court. That gives the Court a sense of having not only a present personality, but a continuous personality that's very much linked to the past. Because of those kinds of things, the Court is a place that doesn't change very quickly in almost any dimension. The Court is still behind the times, one supposes, in terms of media of communications. It won't allow cameras in the courtroom. But it changes very slowly not because it's content being what it is and not because it's just stubbornly resistant to change, but because it understands the value of continuity, the value of constancy, in a way that the politically responsive branches don't have the capacity to do.

Q: You've covered the Court long enough to see so many protests having taken place out there. Obviously, the right of free speech is in the constitution. Can you talk about being out on the west front some of those days and connecting what people were able to do with what goes on inside that building?

DENNISTON: What happens outside the building in the political community almost never has any effect inside the building. The one exception is where there has been an ongoing, prolonged, and angry national conversation over something, for example abortion rights. The Court's decision in 1992, in the Casey case, from Pennsylvania, which partly reaffirmed *Roe v. Wade*, was a decision animated by the Court's institutional concern about bowing to the opposition that had developed outside. But I think that was a rarity. Every January we have protests in the streets in Washington coming up to the Court about *Roe v. Wade*, and I don't think that has one whit of impact on what goes inside the building.

The Court works the way that it always has, and maybe the way that it was really intended to work [with a sense of] detachment. You don't want an institution that is immediately responsive to political change, or political dynamics. You want an institution that has the capacity to sit back and say, "Wait a minute, what we're about to do here is terribly important, and we want to be able to say as persuasively as we can that this was decided on the basis of legal principle, on the basis of tradition, on the basis of those kinds of guiding sentiments that people will regard as contributing to justice."

Politics can be very unjust. Ideally—and I don't think this is naïve to suggest this, I think this is the nature of the institution—you don't want the dirty, homely atmosphere that prevails in the political community to be dictating outcomes in the Court. If you watch Congress, for example, when it takes hold of something that is agitating out in the public, or at least Congress thinks it is, Congress reacts quickly, and then it reacts another way. . . . Well, the Court always looks to the larger context. Obviously, I'm very much a partisan of the Court in the three branches of government, but that comes out of a half century of watching it do its work very, very well.

Protests will come; protests will go. And with the rarest of exceptions, I don't think they make a difference. The Court under Earl Warren was very impressed by the civil rights movement, but in the sense that they could feel that there was a paradigm shift. What was happening in the culture, what was happening in the larger social and political community was trending towards a necessary change in constitutional perception. There's always a little bit of lag between a major historic shift in public sentiment and a constitutional response to it. The Court doesn't leap into changing the constitutional understanding just because there's a new fad in political conversation. You really want the constitution to lag behind the flow of the political winds at the moment. . . .

I wanted to mention an opinion that Justice Souter wrote; it may have been his last opinion before this Court. It was a separate opinion when the Court was facing the issue of whether to give an individual who has been convicted of a crime and who really believes that he's innocent, a constitutional right to demand that the DNA evidence used at the trial be newly tested to see whether this person could establish his innocence. The court said, "No, there is no constitutional right to demand this. If you've had a fair trial, you don't get an opportunity later on to demand that the DNA evidence be examined anew."

Justice Souter wrote a separate opinion, and it's a masterful piece of work in terms of talking about the role of the Court in recognizing constitutional change. What David Souter's opinion says is that we should be very cautious when we give the Constitution a new meaning when we are not sure that the culture has shifted enough to justify that kind of new meaning. If you want to understand why the Court doesn't leap onto the latest political bandwagon, cheering with the band and all the noise, read David Souter's opinion in the *Osbourne* case. That tells you why the Court lags behind the election returns sometimes.

Q: We've learned much about the Court's many traditions. These traditions, are they important? They're not some anachronism that's not needed anymore?

DENNISTON: The traditions of the Court are worth continuing because the justices understand that they do contribute to the nature of the institution. I don't think one serves on the Supreme Court or observes what the Court does without realizing that tradition is in the Court's bones. It's what the Court really is like when it is aware of its institutional self.

These days the Court has a lot of critics, because the modern Court has been very aggressive at times, or at least energetic, in the uses of its constitutional power. For example, during the Rehnquist years, they struck down more federal laws than they ever did in any comparable time period in history. And so people talked about judicial triumphalism or a jurist-centric approach to the law, as if the Court were simply throwing its weight around.

Those pejorative assessments of the Court mistake the fact that the Court is an institution that is very much aware of itself. It's very much aware of its role in our political, our social, our legal order. Anybody who doesn't understand what the Supreme Court means when it follows a tradition should go back and read, for example, Justice Kennedy's opinion for the Court in what's called the *Boumediene* case, which was the June 2008 decision on the rights of the detainees at Guantanamo Bay. This is an opinion that speaks volumes about the Court's awareness of itself. We don't like people to be self-absorbed, and I suppose we don't like institutions of government to be self-absorbed. But that's not what I mean. I mean an awareness of what the Court has meant to the country, an awareness of its institutional responsibilities as well as its institutional energies. And tradition contributes to that.

This isn't a Court that was born yesterday. If it were purely a modern creation, if it were a Court that dated its history to 1995 or 1997, it would be a very different place. It would be simply a much more modern, reactive institution. . . . It's kind of like Plato's cave, if you will. The modern Court is looking at the wall and seeing its own shadows on the wall. Of course, what's really important is what is out there casting the light. I don't know whether that metaphor works for anybody else, but it does for me. All of that light that is coming from the rear, which illuminates the Court's present work and illuminates the institution of the Court and casts shadows on the wall is its tradition. It is the history of the Constitution. No one can understand the history of the Constitution without simultaneously understanding the history of the Supreme Court. They are ham and eggs. They are bread and butter. They always go together. You can't understand the Constitution unless you understand the Supreme Court.

Q: Have you ever taken a moment to be in that courtroom when no one else is there and contemplated the momentous things that have come out of there that have affected our country?

DENNISTON: Now and then, I've done that. The other place that I like to go is the Old Supreme Court Chamber in the Capitol. There, I imagine what it was like when *Plessy v. Ferguson* was decided in 1896. . . . There were momentous decisions decided in that room. . . . You can go to the Supreme Court chamber and have that feeling. This is the chamber where *Brown v. Board of Education* was decided. This is the chamber in which the big steel seizure case was decided, the most important decision in our history defining presidential power; it was decided in that room by human beings sitting on that bench after having listened to arguments by other human beings.

The aura of the place is always present. If you go into that room, it doesn't make any difference how badly a given lawyer is doing. There are some lawyers who appear before the Supreme Court who just aren't up to the task. But there's something about the feel of the place that tells you that something important is going on here. And to my mind, it's very much different from watching, let's say, a debate on the floor of the House and Senate, where you realize that what may be going on on the floor at any given moment really doesn't have anything to do with the legislative process. It's somebody making a speech about how important Mother's Day is or how we should honor a certain kind of animal husbandry or something. Everything that goes on in the Supreme Court is related to something important, and it's a part of a process that is working from beginning to end and will result in a substantive outcome. It's all meaningful.

In the atmosphere of that courtroom—and the atmosphere of the hallways, too, if you wander around the hallways and know what goes on upstairs—you're aware that you're in the presence of something that is really, really unusual. The power of the place is unmistakable from the moment you walk into it.

There have been critics in the media who say that the press corps at the Court is essentially there on bended knee. We're a part of the institution, we've become apologists for the justices and treat them as if they were untouchable gods, that sort of thing. Well, that kind of criticism simply misunderstands the role. Even though we try to be as detached from the Court as the Court is from the political winds, it doesn't hurt—in fact, I think it helps enormously—for a reporter who's covering the Court to be aware of the atmosphere. [It's useful for reporters] to have some sense—not simply being an apologist for the Court—but to be able to experience the awe of the place, the grandness of the place, and the majesty of the place. That's awfully important in order to be able to translate what the Court does to your readers.

Q: When you're in the courtroom for oral argument, do you sometimes get a sense that you're watching history unfold?

DENNISTON: Of course, you do. There are some cases that you know aren't going to make history. But with the Court granting as few cases comparatively as it does now, every case you would think, or you would hope at least, is among the most important issues of the day. When you go in for a big case, what we in the press think of as a big case, one with high visibility, where the stakes are really large, where you can feel the tectonic plates of the Constitution potentially beginning to shift . . . you would just be brutish if you didn't have a high level of sensitivity to the importance of that moment.

The term that ended in June 2009 [was one] where you heard the Court debating whether to strike down probably the most important civil rights law passed since the civil rights revolution began in the forties, the most important act that Congress had ever passed. The Court was genuinely confronting the possibility that it was going to find that law to be unconstitutional. To sit there and not have lingering in your mind the images of the March on Selma, the murder of the three young civil rights workers in Mississippi, to not have that somewhere moving around in your contemplation of what was going on in the courtroom at moment would mean being totally unaware of why you were there. It wasn't just a case, it was a moment. And it was a historic moment. Hopefully the good reporters that were there will be able somehow to convey the importance of that moment to their readers and listeners.

Q: What was Chief Justice Rehnquist like?

DENNISTON: I had known him since he was in the Justice Department. He seemed, when you were in his presence, like a big, physically clumsy guy. Because he always had back problems, at least when I knew him, he walked in a stilted, stiff way. He was very formal, but other times he was very informal. I recall that at his funeral service, which was held downtown in St. Matt's Cathedral, the stories that were told about him were wonderfully warm and embracing kinds of stories. There was that character of Bill Rehnquist; to the people who knew him in his public presence on the Court, he was stern a lot of the time; he really kept control over his courtroom. To some, he would insist rather brusquely on quiet in the courtroom, when there really wasn't that much noise going on. And he was pretty hard on counsel.

But the people who knew him personally were almost without exception very fond of him. He was a very friendly, open fellow in private—very different from what he was in public. He was very, very conservative. But ultimately in his approach to Constitutional meaning, he became more a chief justice interpreting the Constitution than a maverick individual justice going his own way.

Q: When he passed away, there was a ceremony in the Great Hall. Did you attend that ceremony?

DENNISTON: Yes. A funeral for a justice in the Supreme Court is a remarkable event. They've come to take a number of common approaches. They always use the Lincoln bier, the black-draped platform on which Lincoln's casket rested after he was assassinated. That's the centerpiece with the casket of the chief justice or the justice on it. The law clerks set up a vigil. The people who had served that justice post themselves around the casket, and do so in shifts so that they're there as long as the lying-in-state continues.

There's always a very moving ceremony in [the Great Hall]. It also is a room of jollity and good feeling, because that's where the Court always has its big Christmas caroling party. Its main function, when the Court is engaging in its daily business, is simply as the anteroom to the courtroom, because you must go to the Great Hall in order to get into the courtroom from any entrance. . . .

Each justice gets a memorial service, which is sometimes months after the funeral. There will be a conference at which invited guests will come and sit in chairs while various eulogies are spoken about that justice, and his or her career will be celebrated.

Q: You must, as you walk through there, stop to consider Earl Warren. It must bring back some memories of what he was like.

DENNISTON: People have often referred to Earl Warren in the same way, as a big teddy bear. Warren was a very friendly fellow. He loved to speak with people in a direct, personal way. He was very friendly on the bench. He wasn't very judicial in the sense of seeming to be up there above the fray. He was always intimately and emotionally involved in the cases before the Court, particularly if they involved somebody who was an object of his sympathy. He would always ask the question, "Is it fair? Is it fair?" He really meant that in a very fundamental, perhaps non-Constitutional way.

We used to tease that if you wanted to take Earl Warren anywhere, like to a ball game, you had better be sure there was a sandwich or a hotdog involved because he loved to eat. Food was always an attractive opportunity for him. It was awfully important that he had been in political life before he came to the Court; that really contributed to his capacity to lead the Court. To a degree, it's probably unfortunate that with Sandra Day O'Connor's retirement, we had nobody with an active career in political life before [coming to the Court]. Justice Souter, of course, had been an attorney general in New Hampshire for a fairly brief period of time. But the Court probably needs someone who has spent some of his life in the political arena and can bring that dimension to the Court's work.

Q: One day, John Roberts's bust will be in that Great Hall. From what you know now, how would you describe him?

DENNISTON: Well, John Roberts is a bit different as a chief justice than I expected him to be. He's more ideologically oriented than I expected him to be. People who have known John Roberts for a long time say that he's no more conservative than they thought he would be. He is more conservative than I thought he would be. He also seems to be more, if you will, agenda-driven than I expected. The Court under John Roberts is an institution that's very bold about re-examining long-standing precedents. It's interesting, because the popular perception of him, particularly in the media, is that he's a chief justice who wants the Court to move in more incremental ways, to take smaller steps. And there's that dimension to him. I think the chief justice in some ways genuinely does want to have a minimalist jurisprudence.

But there are times when his conservative orientation, which is deep, deep inside him, leads him to want to push the Court to try to take really bold steps. I think, for example, of a case two terms ago—these were cases from Louisville, Kentucky, and Seattle, Washington—involving voluntary programs in public schools to try to increase the racial diversity of the student body. Now, in the past, the Court had often encouraged people in public education to voluntarily take actions to try to increase racial opportunities and equity of racial opportunities, rather than being driven to do so by court orders. These communities had done that, and the Court reached out and grabbed that controversy to bring it in and to strike down what those communities had done.

Whatever you think about what was right or wrong in some kind of moral equation about the decision, there is no question that the

Court's reaching out to do that was quite adventuresome. The conventional case that the Court grants to be reviewed involves a division between lower courts, and it's the Supreme Court's role to try to sort that out. Here there wasn't any division that they had to resolve. So they reached out and grasped that [case].

In the big case [this term] involving the question of the role of the federal government in monitoring campaign spending and political campaigns for the presidency and for Congress, the Court under Chief Justice Roberts's leadership was reaching out to make fundamental changes. That's not necessarily wrong in any kind of moral terms. But what does that tell you about the nature of the Roberts Court? It is a Court that is prepared to re-examine, and to re-examine on ideological grounds, much of what the Court has been devoted to for a long period of time. That's going to upset some people, because the Court will be throwing over some of the precedents. Maybe not as many as, let's say, Justice Clarence Thomas would like, because Thomas is clearly the most adventuresome of the justices. He would like to throw out a lot of jurisprudence and start all over again, believing that it was wrongly decided. But he doesn't have five votes to do that most of the time. The Court under John Roberts is much more, "energetic" I suppose that's a more neutral term, much more energetic in its willingness to reach out for opportunities to change the law in fundamental ways. So that tends to contradict the perception that is often more appropriate, that when the Court makes changes, it's probably the best when it does so incrementally rather than wholesale.

Q: You spoke about Clarence Thomas, obviously an African American. You spoke about energy. This makes me think of Thurgood Marshall . . . an African American justice with high energy. Do you remember going into that Conference Room for his retirement announcement?

DENNISTON: I do. I remember that I offended him because I asked him if he was leaving because of ill health. He reacted very negatively to that. . . . I was asking what I thought was a straightforward question, but he resented it. It was an encounter that was in some ways deeply sad, because his physical health had deteriorated so markedly. If you know anything about Thurgood Marshall, [you know that he] was a giant of an American who had at great personal risk taken on some of the most seemingly foolhardy causes to try to win in court. He was a master strategist in them all. And it isn't a pleasant experience to see a person who has become literally a giant in American history in a state of visible, obvious decline. But there was the wonderful part, this jollity that was in him, the old storyteller, the guy who loved to tell catfish stories as they were called around the Court. Then, even as a very sick older man, he still had that internal sense of humor, that gaiety about him. And so it was a mixed kind of thing.

A departure from the Court, a personal departure, a human departure from the Court is always deeply saddening. Even when a justice does it for reasons having nothing to do with health. Justice O'Connor's health was excellent when she retired. It was mainly because of her husband, who was quite ill, that she wanted to have an opportunity to [retire]. Justice Souter, of course, was leaving in what would appear to be the prime of his life. But there's something sad to see the end of a career of a Supreme Court justice because there haven't been that many of them. Watching one of them voluntarily depart is usually a quite sad experience.

Q: What's the biggest part of the learning curve for a new justice?

DENNISTON: Part of it is suddenly being aware that you are at the top of the heap, that this is where ultimate judicial power resides. I don't know how soon that becomes evident to a new justice. I suspect it takes a little while to realize that this is where it all ends. It probably takes a new justice awhile to appreciate the enormity of it. The question is, is that a humbling experience, or is it a liberating experience? Do you go in there and say, "Whoa, now I have all this wonderful power, I'm going to start using it"? I suspect that this is an osmotic process; slowly you become aware that you are one of the nine most important judges in this country, and you have the capacity to make major changes in the law. If you're on a lower federal court, you have to be constantly aware of the fact that there's somebody higher than you. Anything that you do is subject to being second-guessed. But for the Supreme Court of the United States, of course, you can be second-guessed by Congress when you're passing on a meaning of a law, or you can be second-guessed by the Constitutional amendment process. But it's much harder to be second-guessed that way. I suspect that it takes a good deal of time to become aware of how much power you really do have and what you're going to do with that.

Q: In the Justices' Dining Room, there are portraits of Marbury and Madison next to each other. Why is something like that important to have there?

DENNISTON: Probably in all of the Supreme Court's history there is no one case that says as much to a justice about what it is like to be a justice. *Marbury v. Madison* is the embodiment of judicial review, the concept that in the understanding of what the Constitution means, we [the Court] are the ones who say that. When you say it is the Constitution that we are expounding, that means the Constitution that we as justices of the Supreme Court are expounding. To have [those portraits] in a place, you're frequently reminded of the enormity of the task that's given to you.

There's no quotation in all of the history of Supreme Court writing that justices more prefer to repeat than the phrase in *Marbury v. Madison,* which says that it is emphatically the power and the duty of the judiciary to say what the law is. That's a quote from John Marshall. It's the absolute quintessential statement of what it means to have the last word on what the Constitution means, subject always, of course, to the amending process. But in terms of articulating what the existing Constitution means, that's where the power lies. It's in the group of nine that sits together. . . .

Q: What do you think the future will hold in terms of press coverage of the Supreme Court?

Lyle Denniston in his July 2009 interview with C-SPAN.

DENNISTON: My sense about the press in the Court is that we are in the early stages of a perhaps profound shift in the press attention to the Court. The press awareness of the Court—if I can put it in those terms—is going to be so much smaller over time. Maybe the American people will in time find the Court even more of a stranger to them. The newspaper industry's decline is something that probably is not going to be reversed. One cannot imagine an economic model that will keep that medium viable or restore it to its former prominence at any foreseeable time in the future given the changing nature of electronic media in this country. So the question arises, who will be the chronicler of the Supreme Court of the future? Who will tell the American people what their Supreme Court is, what it's doing, where it's going, who's on it? Who will be paying attention? I'm not sure I know the answer to that. To some degree, the electronic media—as it is and as it will develop over time—can take up the slack. But the pressure in the electronic media for constant twenty-four-hour coverage enhances the importance of brevity. And in covering the Supreme Court of the United States, brevity can be the enemy of clarity. Brevity can be a contradiction of the substance of what the Court does because it takes a little bit of space, a little bit of time, a little bit of language, to tell what the Supreme Court's doing when it's deciding issues that are intensely complex.

It's easy, for example, to think of high-volume press coverage for something like *Roe v. Wade* or *Brown v. Board of Education*. But is it as easy to imagine high press coverage of something as important as whether workers will have an easier time or a harder time bringing claims of age or race or religious discrimination in the workplace?

The work of the Court that tends to be somewhat more technical— who will cover that? You can imagine that there will be technically oriented Web sites that will do that. But will there be any medium of general circulation that will pay attention to that? I can tell you, just by my own observation in the last ten years, the American newspaper scope of coverage of the Supreme Court of the United States has declined markedly. If someone doesn't take up the slack, if there is no way by which other media of mass communication can emerge, then does the Supreme Court look smaller and smaller and smaller in the American governmental landscape? I suspect that it might. Will Americans take it upon themselves to find alternative ways to learn about the Court? When it isn't served up as easily as it has been in the American newspaper, will Americans go looking for places to learn about the Supreme Court? Some will. Maybe in the future people will learn more about it in union halls or in civic meetings or in public lectures; maybe something like the Chautauqua would have to come back to provide a place where the Supreme Court can be learned about.

I'm a little bit despondent about that because to my mind—maybe this is the view of a traditionalist—there is no substitute for mass communication attention to a governmental institution in order to keep it visible. If America in the future is going to have to depend upon haphazard or per chance opportunities to learn about the Supreme Court, will people make the effort to do so? I'm not sure they will.

. . . During an age when one can be perhaps satisfied by a 140-character Twitter message, can you describe a complex Supreme Court decision in 140 characters? You probably can't. So if the trend in modern electronically based media is towards ever more brevity, everybody "a Twitter," for an institution like the Supreme Court that does things that take some explaining to do, will it get the coverage it needs? I suspect not. It probably just won't. Perhaps then it will become an institution that's—in a manner of speaking—owned by the people who care about it only, and not by the general public.

Q: The White House has its press staff. The congressmen and senators have their press people. But the Court's press people, they have a little bit different role.

DENNISTON: The Public Information Office of the United States Supreme Court is a facilitator of the work of the press much more than it is a location of attempting to influence the press. The public information officers don't hold press conferences themselves. They don't explain the work of the Court.

If you went in on a decision day, and you had in hand an opinion by the Court, and you went to Kathleen Arberg or Patricia McCabe-Estrada and you said, "What did this mean?" they would look at you in the most peculiar way and wonder what in the world you think you're doing asking about that. The Court does not explain itself, and therefore the Public Information Office feels no obligation to explain itself.

There is a public education function that goes on. They answer all the mail from all the Americans who write in and want a copy of this opinion and that opinion. It's very much a service-oriented institution. The reporters who cover the Court could not function without the Public Information Office because they are our medium of communication between the press corps and the workings of the Court, the clerk's office and the marshal's office and the justices themselves. . . .

A lot of people say that the Court is a very secretive institution. No, it isn't. It's an institution that virtually does most of its work in the open. And as they like to say, the work comes in the front door and goes out the front door. You know the cases that come into the Court, and when they do, if you're in the press room and an important case is filed there, you instantaneously get a copy of it. . . . Now you can get an electronic copy of it if you want as soon as it's scheduled for argument.

In Canada, the Supreme Court's Public Information Office holds briefings, closed door briefings, before opinions are handed out to explain what the Court is about to tell you it's deciding. That would never happen in the Supreme Court of the United States because the press office is not perceived by itself or by the press corps as being an explainer of the Court's work. The Court's work speaks for itself....

It's very nice if you're a member of the press not to have the sense that somebody's trying to spin you, because everywhere else in Washington you know that in addition to the substantive documentary material what you're also going to get is somebody telling you how you should react, how you should read that material. That doesn't happen at the Supreme Court of the United States.

Q: When you go into the courtroom, even after all this time, do you still get an adrenaline rush when you hear the "Oyez, oyez"?

DENNISTON: I suppose so.... More Americans should try to watch the Supreme Court in action.... If you go in and sit in on a committee hearing in Congress, you know the aides are sitting behind the members, feeding them information and feeding them questions. There's nobody behind the Supreme Court bench doing that. They're doing their own work.

When they depart, the nine of them will sit together with no aides in the room, no presentations being made to them by staff to try to persuade them what to do. The nine of them work it out on their own.

If you come into the courtroom and see that process working, it's something you don't see anywhere else in Washington. It's something you don't see in corporate America. You don't see the people with the power actually doing the work. That's something that I think a lot of people are appreciative of when they come into the Supreme Court.

Sure, there's a lot of pageantry there. But what you're actually witnessing is the process of judging unfolding before your very eyes. And it's terribly exciting.

Q: Would it work if it were televised?

DENNISTON: I don't think television cameras in the courtroom would make any difference whatever. There is an ongoing debate—and it's probably never going to end—as to whether the presence of cameras in any court changes people.

I suppose that debate was a reasonable debate a long time ago. But we've had so much experience now in state courts, in particular, with cameras in the courtroom, that it doesn't make any difference at all. Even in the federal courts now where they're experimenting now and then with big cases, they will allow the cameras in.

I think that judges are sufficiently aware of the craft of judging that having an observer is not going to be different in terms of how it affects the process, whether or not the observer has a notepad—as I do—or a camera taking images of what the court does. That's a debatable point. I will concede that.

But I think judges who are aware of what they are supposed to be doing will not play to the cameras. I don't think lawyers will play to the cameras. A lawyer gets up in the Supreme Court and knows that he has one task: to persuade five people because that's all it takes to win is five of the nine. If you get up there at the podium and you're playing to the cameras because of the audience out there, the chances are fairly good that you will lose the focus on the five that you're trying to persuade up in front of you.

If you're one of the nine sitting on the bench and you are thinking about what the audience out there looking at the camera image is thinking, you're going to lose a focus on what's happening in front of you.

The dynamic of an oral argument is such that you've got to participate in it to make it work for you because the justices use oral argument very often to try to persuade each other. The oral argument, when properly understood, is an agenda-setting function. What is discussed in that one hour of time is going to very heavily influence the conversation that the justices are going to have when they retreat from the bench and go back into their private conversation.

Q: Why the resistance to the cameras, do you think?

DENNISTON: Part of it is a security argument. Justice Souter, for example, has often said that he does not want to become a visible public personality because he believes that might be threatening to him. He says that if the justices become noticeable personalities then when they travel, they'll have to have more security with them.

There is still a residual sense that somebody would react to the camera, that somebody would ham it up. Justice Scalia has said that one of his reasons for opposing it is that he thinks that somebody would play to the cameras. If, among the nine justices who have been most recently sitting in the Court, if anybody would play to the cameras I suspect the one most likely to do so would be Justice Scalia because he's a bit of a thespian.

I suppose this is another facet of the Supreme Court, that it doesn't change easily. It's set in its ways and not just because change is always bad. They've done pretty well doing it this way for a long time, and so there is a kind of inertia against change.

I suppose another part of it—though I've not heard it well articulated—is that the Court is concerned that what the media will do with the images will be to skew the public's perception. In other words, little snippets will be used and that will be passed off as if that's what the case was all about.

But the Court already runs that risk. When I was a print reporter I used selective material. Doing newspaper work, I'm not going to give you the entire thing. I'm going to select from them what I want you to know about it. So I think that's an argument that long ago lost its capacity to persuade.

But there is a resistance. There's no question about it. Among the justices now sitting, I don't know of anybody who is eager to have television coverage of the Court. I think that's unfortunate.

Q: Lyle, thank you, so much.

MAUREEN MAHONEY

Attorney and Former Supreme Court Law Clerk

*M*aureen Mahoney, a partner in the law office of Latham & Watkins in Washington, DC, founded the firm's appellate practice. She has argued twenty-two cases before the Court, winning twenty. After graduating from the University of Chicago Law School, she clerked for Justice William Rehnquist and Seventh Circuit Judge Robert Sprecher. Ms. Mahoney served as United States deputy solicitor general from 1991 to 1993. She was interviewed by C-SPAN's Mark Farkas on May 27, 2009.

———————

FARKAS: For all of those people who don't get a chance to go into the Supreme Court chamber, visit Washington, visit the Supreme Court, can you describe the experience of being in that chamber and arguing a case? Do you remember your first time in that Supreme Court chamber when you were about to argue a case?

MAUREEN MAHONEY: I do. When your first argument arrives, I think the uniform reaction among everyone is, "I can't believe I'm here." Beyond that, though, what I really remember was enormous pressure to perform, and that's what I feel every time I'm there. It was probably most intense the first time, though, because I understood that if I didn't do well, I probably wouldn't get to come back. It is, for many lawyers, the crowning achievement of their careers to argue before the

Supreme Court, and I wanted to do it more than once. So it was intimidating, but it went pretty well.

Q: In your eulogy of Justice Rehnquist, you quoted him as saying, "Lawyers should be nervous in front of the Court." Now, why is that?

MAHONEY: I think that sometimes it's important for lawyers to be nervous because anxiety helps to improve performance. It's very much like being an athlete, and for athletes, I think having some anxiety before the meet begins helps you to perform at your highest level. That's what you want to do when you go to the Supreme Court. I feel that way about other courts, too; you want to perform at your best. They deserve it; it helps with the development of the law if the justices are fully prepared and if the advocates are fully prepared, and if you deliver a performance that will help them do their job and hopefully help your client win their case.

Q: Can you describe walking up to that podium?

MAHONEY: When you look at the courtroom, you see that unlike many other courtrooms, you don't really walk very far [to argue]. You're seated right next to the podium. So you just stand up and slide over a few inches. For me, anyway, it's about taking a deep breath and saying, "Mr. Chief Justice, and may it please the Court." That's what you have to say when you start your argument.

Q: And the first argument that you had before the Court, who was the chief justice at the time?

MAHONEY: The chief justice was Rehnquist, and I had been appointed by the Court to do the argument. This is something that happens maybe once a year; for one reason or another, a party will decide that they don't want to defend the judgment below, usually because there's not enough money at stake, or something like that. The Court will appoint counsel by special invitation to defend the judgment below, and for my first argument, the Court appointed me to come and argue. So I owed my maiden argument to the Court and to the chief justice whom I had clerked for.

Q: Was there any added pressure on you because of doing that?

MAHONEY: I think so because I certainly felt that he had bestowed an honor on me. The clerk's office thinks I was the first woman who had ever received an invitation from the Court to appear as counsel in that way, and I certainly wanted to vindicate his choice and make the other members of the Court think that his confidence in me was deserved. So, yes, I did feel a lot of pressure.

Q: What's it like up there? What happens?

MAHONEY: It's very intense. That's what it's really like. Once you start, you're certainly in the moment, and it's all about just fielding those questions and using the time strategically so that you respond to the questions. It's essential to answer the questions. You can't persuade a justice if you don't answer what they have asked. But you also have to remember that you have a limited amount of time. At most, you're going to have thirty minutes; often the argument may be ten or fifteen, depending on whether you had to split it with another party. So you have to cover a lot of ground in the time that you have. While answering the question and getting across points that are responsive but also that are helpful to you, you're also trying to change the subject if you need to, but trying to do it in a way where you still feel like you've addressed the concerns that have been expressed by the justice.

Q: For people who have watched a courtroom battle on television in lower court or even in a courtroom drama, how much different is it?

MAHONEY: It's very different because it's not made for TV, and the answers that you're giving are usually not wonderful soundbites that the press would love to report and that an audience would love to cheer over. It's a much more scholarly exercise than what we typically see on television, and it's really designed to persuade them, based on the facts, and the record, and the case, and the precedents that the Court has to deal with, or the language of the statute. It's designed to bring all of those materials to bear in a concise and persuasive way and to do it in a very small amount of time.

So you have to be extremely well prepared if you're going to do well. You have to know your case backward and forward, inside and out. You better know it better than anyone in the courtroom [knows it]. You have to be able to recall it very quickly and weave it into a narrative that you're giving to the Court while responding to their questions. It's very challenging. The justices all are brilliant. Americans should be enormously proud of their Court. The Supreme Court is excellent—all the way across the bench—and so it's very challenging for advocates to argue at that level and meet their expectations, very challenging.

Q: Explain that process where the justices can pepper you at any time and interrupt you at any time, so you never know whether you're going to get a chance to talk for five minutes or twenty-five minutes.

MAHONEY: It would be very rare to be able to talk for twenty-five minutes. Ordinarily, yes, you get peppered usually within the first minute or two. It used to be sometimes within the first twenty seconds, but lately they seem to be giving advocates a little more time. So yes, you can get questions from any justice at any time, and your job is to answer the questions. It's really not about coming with a prepared speech. Most of the time that I spend preparing for argument is spent anticipating the questions and preparing answers that I think I would like to give to those questions. Sometimes that involves thinking of hundreds of questions that they might ask, even though they'll probably not ask you more than fifty or so. I once had an argument where I think they asked fifty-six questions in thirty minutes.

So there are a lot of questions, and yes, they interrupt each other, even. In fact, there was one time when I was arguing—I don't remember what case it was now, the chief justice was Rehnquist at the time. I was answering the question from one justice, and another justice cut in and asked another question, and Rehnquist leaned over and looked at the justice and said, "Let her finish her answer." I thought that was a great day because it was, in effect, the chief umpiring for me. My reaction to it was as if he had said: "She's worth listening to." So that was a great day for me.

q: How often do you feel like they are having a conversation back and forth among themselves through you?

MAHONEY: I think they always do. I think that's part of what oral argument is about; it is for them to test their ideas about the case. It doesn't mean that they're necessarily signaling what they think about the case with every question because I think all of the justices are interested in answers to a variety of questions, whether they have a formed view on that or not. But I think virtually all arguments involve some conversation among the justices, and that's appropriate, and that's what you want as an advocate. You want to hear what they're thinking and what they're saying to each other so that you have a chance to chime in and hopefully persuade them.

q: Have you ever had a time where you completely had to change your strategy on the fly as you came into it?

MAHONEY: Completely change strategy—I don't think so. Often when we're preparing it, you can't be sure which way the argument is going to go, and so you'll have fallback positions. You have the argument that you'd love to win if you could get the votes, and you may see early on that that's not likely, and so you need to fall back to a position that's more likely to garner five votes or six votes. Sometimes you'll have to make that judgment early on in the case, but that's not completely changing strategy; it's typically something that you've thought about in advance.

Q: How well do you have to know the style of each one of those justices up there as you prepare?

MAHONEY: It's helpful, and the more you know about the Court and about their precedent and the way they do their jobs, certainly the more of an advantage it is. But there are many advocates who show up for the first time who have never been to an argument before who do a wonderful job simply because they've mastered their case and they have anticipated questions without knowing precisely what questions Justice Breyer might ask or Chief Justice Roberts. Mastering the case is the most important thing.

Q: Before you go up there, where are you in the building? Are you in the courtroom for an extended period of time?

MAHONEY: I usually start at the cafeteria in the morning. I like to arrive early and get to the cafeteria and settle in, have a cup of coffee, and talk to the lawyers and my colleagues, the people that I'm working with on the case. Then after that, we go to the Lawyers' Lounge, where the clerk of the court and usually the deputy clerk come in and give practical pointers. They try hard to put people at ease. It's a fun place to be before going into the courtroom because there's a lot of camaraderie in there. You get to meet your opposing counsel if you haven't met them already. It's friendly; there's a lot of nervous energy in there. Then after that, we go to the courtroom.

Q: Have you ever seen someone in there so completely nervous that it's noticeable to you?

MAHONEY: No, not as if they were ready to fall on the floor or something like that. Most advocates are nervous before arguments. They may try to put on a visible face of calm, but most advocates are nervous, quite nervous.

Q: You're sitting in there before the justices have come in. Talk about that process when they come in. What happens? What gets said?

Where do they enter from? Describe that for someone who's never been there.

MAHONEY: When you're sitting in the chair getting ready to argue, they come in from behind the bench through the curtains. It is a very formal entry, and everyone rises, of course, to show respect. Then the gavel is pounded, and people sit down, and the Court is called into session. It's always very ceremonial. The building is majestic, the procedures are high ceremony, very traditional; there is nothing informal and modern about the way the Court conducts its proceedings; it's very, very traditional. I like it that way. I wouldn't change it. I have never heard an advocate say they'd like to see the Court's proceedings modernized in some way. It instills enormous respect for the institution, for the processes, a lot of reverence for the Court.

Q: When you're sitting in there, you must be so focused on the case. But when your portion of the oral argument is done, have you ever had the time to soak in that chamber itself?

MAHONEY: I soak in the chamber always in some sense, but you're correct that I am so intent on what I'm doing that day. If you've gone first, you're waiting to do rebuttals, so you still have to be completely focused on what is being said. Even when I'm sitting there waiting for Court to start, I am rehearsing up to the last second. So, I unfortunately don't have a lot of time to enjoy my surroundings. I enjoyed it much more when I was a clerk, and there was more time for reflection and more time to really look around and see the majesty of the building.

Q: When you were there as a clerk, you must have had time to go in there for lectures or other types of things over the years. Do you think about *Brown v. Board of Education*, some of the history that's unfolded there?

MAHONEY: Yes, and of course I've had to think about a lot of those things in connection with preparing for the cases that I've argued.

Brown v. Board of Education was certainly very important to an affirmative action case that I argued, for example. So often you have to think about the history that has transpired in a court, and even more when you're sitting there arguing a case, you'll have to think about it because you have to deal with that history as part of the argument that you're giving. But for me, it's really more about the advocacy in that case. It's about how to win the case, how to persuade the justices. That's the focus. Historians, I'm sure, come and probably have a different set of thoughts about the building and about what's transpired, but mine is about usually how to win.

Q: Have you had a least favorite experience?

MAHONEY: Oh, sure. I had a least favorite experience in a case that I lost 8–1. The justices were just merciless at the argument, so it was not fun. It's fun when it goes well; it's not fun when they seem very unpersuaded and not particularly interested in what nuanced answers you might be giving. That's a very difficult thirty minutes.

Q: That was definitely something you could feel?

MAHONEY: Oh, I could definitely feel it, yes. I could feel it, and as much as I may have prepared for it, it still was unpleasant. So it's much more fun when you either think you're winning or you at least think you've got a fighting chance.

Q: So you've had far more positive experiences, it sounds like, than negative.

MAHONEY: Fortunately, yes. I've had a lot of positive experiences.

Q: You have talked about your least favorite experience, an 8–1 decision. Do you know when a case is going really well? Is there a particular case or two that you look back on?

Maureen Mahoney speaks to the press after the June 23, 2003, *University of Michigan* decision.

MAHONEY: It's usually when you have a very strong case. So I don't want to take undue credit for that. But, for instance, I argued a case on behalf of Arthur Andersen. It was a case arising out of the collapse of Enron. I thought it was a very important case, and the argument went really well, and my mother was there that day. And it was Chief Justice Rehnquist's last argument, and so that was a very special argument for me.

Q: Could you talk about the *University of Michigan* case?

MAHONEY: The *University of Michigan* case was certainly the most historic case by far that I have argued, and the whole day was different because when I arrived at the Court, there had been people sleeping on the steps. They were awake by then, but for days they were waiting to get into the courtroom. There were demonstrators with placards, a very large congregation of people, intense interest in the case. The president of the United States had gone on television to talk about his views of the case. So there was a lot of public attention. The whole issue of affirmative action is not only divisive, but it is also one that people experience in their day-to-day lives, frequently students applying to college and people in the workplace watching promotions. So everybody had an opinion about that.

So that day for me coming to court was definitely like the whole world was watching, which of course is an overstatement. But more people were watching than usual, anyway, and that was a day that stands out. It was very different from any other day that I've argued before the Court.

Q: It seemed like a particularly interesting exchange you had with Justice Scalia.

MAHONEY: Certainly there were a lot of questions that day. But Justice Scalia decided to essentially tackle me on the question of whether or not the University of Michigan's program was too focused on the numbers such that it crossed the line and became a quota. There is no question that quotas are unconstitutional, and so it was my job to try to persuade him that the program really was about the use of numbers based upon goals, not quotas. And under the law, that was a very significant difference, one that made the difference between legality and illegality. And so that exchange, which surprised a lot of people, was him pushing hard on why he thought my position didn't really hold up and my efforts to withstand his battering. NPR played some of that on the radio that afternoon, and I got a lot of e-mails and calls from people who were expressing their sympathy about how mean Justice Scalia had been to me. I didn't feel that way about the exchange at all. He was in fine form. Many of the justices are getting very demanding, as they should be. That's their job. It's a very challenging exercise.

Q: You've argued cases for large corporations, for universities, for individuals. I read a quote of yours on liberty. On the east pediment of the building is written, "Justice, The Guardian Of Liberty." This notion of liberty you mentioned in one of those articles is so important to you. Can you tie that into your thoughts behind the law and what that building and that courtroom are there for?

MAHONEY: Certainly liberty is the foundation of our whole form of government, and one of the most important things that the Court does is ensure the liberties that have been given to us by our Constitution. I think all of the justices understand that this is one of the core missions of the Court and that they do an elegant job of ensuring our liberties. They differ about what liberties are guaranteed and which ones aren't, but it's all done in a very, very professional way. I would love for people to know just how much integrity our system of justice has in terms of how gifted these Supreme Court justices are, how dedicated they are. Clerking gives you the ability to see how the Court works, and it's really inspiring.

Q: The president is on television all the time. The House of Representatives is on TV, and the Senate is on TV. But the Court remains off limits to cameras, which is a whole other topic of discussion. But it seems to me that there's a mystery surrounding the Court with a lot of people. Why is that?

MAHONEY: They're not a mysterious body. I don't know why people would view them as mysterious. It is true they don't get to see the proceedings on television, something that I [wouldn't] welcome because I don't like the idea of everything being televised. But I also think it's great for the justices because they don't have to be the same public persona of someone who's on television all the time and is quickly recognized. I think it has that advantage as well.

I don't think of them as mysterious. Yes, they deliberate in private, but that's true of all courts. There's really no court that I know of where they do their deliberations in public. So, I'm not sure why they would be regarded as mysterious. They're not. They're just excellent at what they do, and their decisions are all public, obviously, and the proceedings are public, and people can come if they want. They should come to Washington, DC, and see the Court in action so they can see the building in person.

Q: What about the building itself most impresses you? Is there anything that stands out?

MAHONEY: Overall, it's the majesty of the building. I suspect it's the marble.... I don't know how much marble is in the building, but it's a large quantity, and when you have a very large, imposing structure done in a classical style in marble, it's awe-inspiring. It is majestic. It does promote reverence, and I love the building. There are beautiful courtyards I hope you'll be showing the viewers. Those are wonderful spots. There are very tranquil fountains, and when the weather is lovely in the spring and the fall, sometimes a little bit in the summer, you can have lunch out there; you can read and you can think and reflect. But for me, I think the part of the building that I love the most is the courtroom because that's where—at least as an advocate—the work is done. That's the space that I like to be in the most.

Q: I know you clerked for Chief Justice Rehnquist, but other than Chief Justice Rehnquist, do you have a chief justice or two that you look back in history and admire?

MAHONEY: I'm just a one-chief-justice girl.... Chief Justice Rehnquist was my boss, he was my mentor, he was the chief justice who presided over virtually all of my arguments. I have an honest respect for the current chief justice, so I don't mean to diminish him in any way. But I know he shares my fondness for his predecessor, so he'll forgive me.

Q: How well did you get a chance to know Rehnquist?

MAHONEY: He gets to know his clerks very well, all of them, and so I got to know him very well, and he certainly helped me with my career. He was responsible for getting me my maiden argument before the

Court when I was appointed to do my first argument. I think that with all of his clerks, he was always very supportive. It was just a joy to work with him and know him for all of those years.

Q: We're going to see some of the chambers of the justices. I'm assuming that's where some of the clerks do their work as well. Describe those quarters, and what is the job of Supreme Court law clerk.

MAHONEY: The job of a Supreme Court law clerk—mine was thirty years ago, but I don't think it's changed that much. One thing that is a little bit different is that Justice Rehnquist at the time just had three clerks. We all worked in the same office suite with him, in fact, the same chambers. It was essentially three large rooms. One was his quarters, and then there was a room where the assistants worked, two secretarial assistants, administrative assistants, and also a messenger, and then one room where the three law clerks worked. We all sat together at desks in the same room, which promotes camaraderie.

Whenever he wanted to talk to us, he would walk in, and he'd talk to all three of us. Often he would grab one of us, and we'd go off and walk around the block. He wore Hush Puppies so that he could be comfortable walking around the block with his clerks, talking about the cases. Then we would eat Oreos with him. The clerks, both for Justice Rehnquist, but also in other chambers, are sounding boards for their justices in terms of discussing the cases, and then they help draft those opinions. Their job is to help the justice screen the cases to figure out which ones to select, and then help to implement his or her views by drafting the opinions.

Q: There are lots of other things going on in that building. What do you wish people got a chance to see that you've been privy to that might inform them a little bit about how their tax dollars are getting spent?

MAHONEY: I suppose what I would like them to see the most is just how hard they work, how dedicated they are, how much time they

Maureen Mahoney in her May 2009 C-SPAN interview.

spend on these cases, the camaraderie and respect among the court personnel, and also among the justices themselves. That changes a bit over time, but certainly in the last few decades it's been excellent. It would be great for people to know just how dedicated and how smart and how careful these justices are and how well they work together to try to answer the toughest legal issues of the day. I think people would be very proud of this institution if they could really see them at work.

Q: Let's talk about the question of television. You're an advocate of televising those proceedings?

MAHONEY: No, I'm not. I won't say that it would be horrible. We would adjust. I recently did a televised argument in the New York Court of Appeals, and I prepared the same way that I prepare for a Supreme Court argument. But I think we need to leave it to the justices. I can see why they may not want it televised, and we should honor their wishes. That's my view. . . .

Q: When you argue before the Court, how many people are usually with you on your team? Is the person you're representing or their corporation, are they there with you? Do you have a team of lawyers with you?

MAHONEY: At the argument, the counsel table is limited. Oftentimes, I can only have one person with me. Four counsel can be seated at the table, but if there are two parties arguing, for instance, that just means two counsel at that table. So often it's only one lawyer, and it's usually the lawyer who has worked most closely with me on the brief. The clients are almost always in the courtroom, but they are not any place nearby that they can prod you or ask you why you didn't answer that differently.

Q: There's a certain light system in there. Could you explain that?

MAHONEY: The way the light system works in the courtroom is that it will tell you, when a white light goes on, that you have five minutes remaining, and when your time is expired, a red light goes on. In the Supreme Court, when the red light goes on, you are supposed to stop. When Chief Justice Rehnquist was presiding, you were really supposed to stop. I remember one time where Justice Scalia had asked me a question, and the red light went on just as he was finishing his question. I hadn't had a chance to say a word. I looked up at the chief justice, and he said, "Counsel, I think you can consider that a rhetorical question." And so I just sat down. In fact, the press didn't know that the red light was on, so they reported that I was speechless in response to Justice Scalia's question. But that's the way the light system works. Now sometimes we get a little bit more leeway, but you're really supposed to stop, finish your sentence, and sit down.

Q: When you go into certain cases, do you have a sense where the justices are going into that case and who the swing justices might be? And do you try to ever tailor your argument to those you think might be the swing vote?

MAHONEY: When I'm preparing for argument, I certainly try to anticipate where the votes are going to come from. Your ability to predict that really depends on whether it's an area where a lot has been written or not. Sometimes, they'll be interpreting a statute that they haven't interpreted ever before. It's very hard to predict how the justices might view language in a statute that's never been construed. On the other hand, if you're doing a case involving equal protection and affirmative action, these justices have written many opinions that deal with that subject.

So you have a very good idea going in what their basic views might be on the proper approach to the resolution of an equal protection case, a case where there's a conscious use of race, for instance, in decision making. In an argument like that, yes, you would have to prepare knowing where those justices have been. In the *University of Michigan* case, for instance, it was pretty clear that while I was trying to get every vote, I understood that we would have to get Justice O'Connor to win. We had to be especially careful to make sure that the arguments that we were advancing fit with the decisions that she had already issued in that area.

Q: Have you ever been completely surprised by a line of questioning or a question that you did not expect to come from a particular justice?

MAHONEY: Well, you try not to be surprised, but there was an argument I did in the case involving Haitians who were fleeing Haiti in an effort to get to the United States. It was really about the president's power to interdict and return fleeing Haitians. In that case Justice Blackmun asked me whether or not I had ever read a novel by Graham Greene called *The Comedians*. I have to tell you I did not anticipate that question, nor had I read the novel. It was a novel about repression in Haiti, and he was really just exploring issues relating to the humanitarian aspects of the president's policy, and doing it through literature. But that would be an example of a question that would be extremely difficult to anticipate. If I had been better read, I would have been able to respond, but I wasn't. So the moral of the story is read more fiction when preparing for argument.

Q: How hard do you think it is for the public who is in attendance to understand what's going on there?

MAHONEY: It is often difficult for the public to understand what is happening at argument because the issues tend to be very complex, and they are often about statutory interpretation. They are unraveling different words in the statute and talking about the enactment history and how different sections of the statute intersect and maybe how they interact with other federal laws. I think a discussion of that type is difficult for the public to follow. There are other cases that are easier for the public to get their arms around. I had a case about recruiting eighth-grade athletes and First Amendment protections that would apply in the recruitment process, and a lot of that was really about the potential for a coach to unduly influence an athlete by making calls to the home. In a case like that, people could listen to and nod their heads more because it wasn't as arcane.

Q: Does it say something about our country that the public is allowed into these proceedings?

MAHONEY: I think it shows the openness of our proceedings, certainly of all the courts. It's rare for a courtroom to ever be closed to the public. Occasionally it happens under very limited circumstances, but the whole notion of a democracy is having openness and having the public see our government at work. That's true of when Congress is debating, when the Court is hearing argument. I guess the executive branch is accessed more through the Freedom of Information Act, although the public can attend agency proceedings when they're having hearings on rules. So most of our proceedings are open.

Q: Between the time you've argued the case and the decision, how long can that take, and what is that time like for you?

MAHONEY: It can be many months, six months sometimes, sometimes only two or three. You'd think it's tense waiting for the decision, but it's really not because after I complete the argument, I'm on to the next, and if not in the Supreme Court, in some other court. I treat every case like it's the most important case I've ever had. So the memory of the one I just argued will fade. Of course I'm thrilled if I win and horrified if I lose. But it really is not foremost in my mind after I've completed an argument.

Q: Do you have any idea when the decision is going to come down on a case that you argued?

MAHONEY: Usually, you'll get a sense of maybe the month that it may come down. At the end of the term it becomes much easier to predict because there's only so many cases left. . . . You could actually start going to the Court to hear the decisions announced, and you might get the chance to be there when one of your decisions is announced. I was able to do that one time. I was in the courtroom when they announced the decision in the *University of Michigan* case because it was coming toward the end of the term, and so I could figure out the odds were high. But usually, most advocates don't have time to go sit in the courtroom, listening to decisions coming down, because they don't know which day it's going to be. They could be going there a lot of days.

Q: Now, some attorneys do come out of the front steps after they've made their oral argument.

MAHONEY: Ordinarily, after the arguments, I will come out in the front of the Court and go down the steps and leave that way . . . probably because that's the beautiful side of the building. We have to enter through the Maryland Avenue side, which is much more functional, but leaving the courtroom, especially if you've had a good day, coming down the steps makes you feel like you're queen for the day. It's a great feeling. I ordinarily don't talk to the press. Some advocates do, and I will under certain circumstances if my client really wants me to. But typically, that's not something I do.

Q: You mentioned the day you argued the *Michigan* affirmative action case. There were people out there who had been out there all night, and there were protests. When you see that, do you get a sense of the gravity of the function of what goes on in there and your role in it?

MAHONEY: When you see people at the courthouse with signs, chanting and singing, as they did the day that I did the *Michigan* case, you certainly have this very strong sense of the role of the Court in our society and your role as an advocate in helping the Court do its work. It feels like a very important job. The Court could function without advocates. But I like to think that we help them do their job and do it so well.

Q: Now, you've clerked there, you've argued cases there in that time period in which Sandra Day O'Connor came on the Court. What difference, if any, do you think it made having a woman on the Supreme Court?

MAHONEY: I think having Sandra Day O'Connor join the Court was very significant for the public and for generations of women. I don't think anyone should say otherwise because role models are important in our country. I'm not saying how that translates into how you interpret the Constitution. But I think it filled young girls, young women with pride to have Sandra Day O'Connor on the Supreme Court, and I shared that view. It was great to have her there.

I think the justices thought it was great to have her there, too—at least that was my impression—that no one was interested in having it be a male bastion forever, that that wasn't by design. It's still very difficult to find the women who meet the qualifications, but they're there, and there will be more of them every year. I think O'Connor crossed that divide for us and that there is a lot of equal opportunity in the United States now.

Q: You have argued twenty-two cases and only lost two. Why have you had such a great success rate in front of the Court?

MAHONEY: They're cases that I should have won. I think I've been really fortunate getting strong cases. Many of them are cases where I've filed a petition asking the Court to take the case, and if the Court grants a petition you're more likely to win than if you are defending something that they've decided to take. So I don't know why I've won that many cases, but I would say I'm lucky and I work really hard. I'm very grateful.

Q: Thank you, very much.

MAHONEY: Thank you.

JAMES B. O'HARA

A Supreme Court Historian

James B. O'Hara, a retired professor and administrator at Loyola University in Maryland, is a historian and lawyer. He is a trustee of the Supreme Court Historical Society, chairing the society's Publications Committee. Mr. O'Hara was interviewed by C-SPAN's Mark Farkas on May 12, 2009.

———————

FARKAS: How did you get interested in the Supreme Court?

JAMES B. O'HARA: Lots of things that happen in Washington, [the justices'] histories are sort of open books. But while lots of authors write about the constitutional history of the Supreme Court, the actual history of the Court as an entity, as an institution, hasn't been written about that much, and I just became intrigued by it.

I went to law school when I was in my fifties, and I obviously did not intend to practice law; you don't start a law practice at that age. So while all my classmates were studying how to write a contract, I was more interested in how the law of contract developed. When I was reading cases and saw that the case was written by Justice [Ward] Hunt or perhaps by Justice [George] Shiras—justices whose names have completely been forgotten in history—I became interested in who those folks were. I started to read about it, and what began as a hobby ended up as an avocation and then partly as a vocation.

Q: When you're approaching the Supreme Court building itself, do you have certain thoughts that always run through your mind or particular ideas about it, about what that building represents?

O'HARA: I think it makes a statement about the law and its importance. It's almost a mantra that this is a nation of laws and not of men. I think the Court is trying to make that statement. It's a relatively small building in comparison to other important government buildings, but it stands out in a way that still impresses me as I face it. . . .

One of the things I like about the building is those front steps. Although I am at an age now where I usually go in the side door, I am still impressed by the steps going up and the statement, "Equal Justice Under Law," that's at the top. . . .

The architect was trying to find statements to engrave into the building, and that was one that he came up with. I don't think anyone knows where the statement comes from, but it's one that has been repeated in democratic societies. By the time that they were ready to do those engravings on the front and on the back, Chief Justice [William Howard] Taft had died and Chief Justice [Charles Evans] Hughes was asked to comment on the architect's suggestions. He bought into [the statement] "Equal Justice Under Law" and approved it.

Q: You mentioned Chief Justice Taft, and on that pediment, one of the figures is Taft as a young man. I would be interested to hear a little bit about his story and his connection to the building.

O'HARA: Chief Justice Taft was the dynamic force that made the Supreme Court building possible. He's the only president who ever served on the Supreme Court. Although a few earlier presidents were nominated, none ever served. He was determined that the Supreme Court should not be an afterthought. The Supreme Court was working out of rooms that were very constricted in the Capitol building. The courtroom itself was the former Senate chambers. For some purposes they would have to borrow hearing rooms from the Senate. The justices' library was the old chambers in the basement. Taft felt that the Court should have a place of its own. It was, after all, constitutionally a co-equal branch of government. Some of the other justices didn't agree with him, but he forced the issue.

Q: Why do you think some of those other justices didn't force the issue? Now, it seems you look at the White House, the Capitol, and the Supreme Court and just assume that it's been there forever, but why wasn't it?

O'HARA: Early on, when Washington was being built, [Pierre Charles] L'Enfant at one point mentioned that there should be a hall of justice for the Supreme Court. But it was never built, and the Supreme Court always had been using the Capitol, often basement rooms. The justices met on Saturdays, when the Senate didn't meet, so that they could discuss cases. And the justices worked out of their homes, and they would have messengers who would go from one justice's house to another house with drafts of opinions. . . . Some of the justices were happy with that arrangement. They could work at home. They could eat lunch when they wanted to. They would come to the Capitol when a case was being heard, but it was an afterthought.

Q: Could anyone else have done what Taft did to get that building off the ground?

O'HARA: Maybe another chief justice who was fixated on a building could have pulled it off. But the fact is that Taft was the tenth or eleventh chief justice and none of them before had been able to do it, even though some of them were highly respected figures and had been chief justice for a long time. I suppose there was a time when the justices were happy with that arrangement because many of the justices did not live close to the Capitol building, so coming over to the Capitol was not an easy thing. And many of the justices lived relatively close to each other. A lot of them lived in the area along Connecticut Avenue or in the area immediately near Dupont Circle. But Taft had in mind that the Court needed to have a building of its own. He believed that when he was president, and when he became chief justice, it became almost an obsession.

Q: How much was he involved in the actual design of the building?

O'HARA: Taft was interested in that building to such an extent that when he initially went to Congress to the appropriate committees of Congress to ask for the money, he immediately ran into a little problem in that the architect of the Capitol wanted to have the chief role. Taft almost insisted that the legislation that Congress passed would make him chairman of the commission. There was a special commission for the Supreme Court building. Taft and one of the other justices were on that commission. The architect of the Capitol was on it, too, but Taft controlled the commission because he was friendly with the appropriate chairmen of the committees in the House and the Senate and made sure that other members would be members of the House and the Senate. Taft packed the committee, and he was responsible for choosing the architect. He liked Cass Gilbert, the architect who was chosen, and felt that of all the architects in America this was the one to build this building.

Q: Taft did not live to see the building completed. Was it built to his specifications?

O'HARA: Chief Justice Taft died well before the building was completed. Indeed, he died before the laying of the cornerstone. However, he was thoroughly familiar with the plans, and I think he died quite happy with the building that he knew was going to be built. He and Cass Gilbert corresponded regularly and talked regularly. As a matter of fact, when Taft

Architect Cass Gilbert. *Collection of the Supreme Court of the United States.*

Left to right: Justices Brandeis, Van Devanter, Taft, Holmes, Butler, Sanford, and Stone view a model of the Supreme Court building, May 17, 1929. *Collection of the Supreme Court of the United States.*

was president, he had appointed Gilbert to a fine arts commission for the Capitol, and then Woodrow Wilson re-appointed Gilbert. So Gilbert knew what the Capitol was about and he knew what visions Jefferson had had for the Capitol, and he also knew intimately what Taft wanted out of that building.

Q: What was the reaction of the nine justices at the time when that building actually opened up?

O'HARA: When the building opened up, some of the justices didn't like it very much. Some of the justices, as a matter of fact, continued to work out of their homes. The chief justice at that time was Charles Evans Hughes. The office that was provided for him in the Supreme Court building he used more as a ceremonial office to greet distinguished visitors and so forth while he continued to work out of his home. Most of the justices at the time did not even claim the office space. The first justice who used that building extensively as his office was Hugo Black, who was Franklin Roosevelt's first appointment to the Supreme Court. He was appointed to the Court after the building was completed.

Q: What did the justices say about this place?

O'HARA: The Supreme Court justices were not shy and some of them felt that the new building was grandiose. Justice [Harlan F.] Stone, who later became chief justice, was an associate justice when the building was built and is alleged to have said that the justices were like nine black beetles in the Temple of Karnak and maybe they should ride in each morning on elephants. He also made the comment that the building was too grandiose for nine old guys who were on the Supreme Court.

The other thing about the building—aside from the fact that it had an awful lot of marble in it and an awful lot of oak and awful lot of bronze, which the justices were certainly not accustomed to in their borrowed quarters in the Capitol building—was that the building was very large for them. Gilbert and Taft felt that unlike many other office buildings in Washington, they should build for the future. They recognized that the Court would grow. So there was a lot of space there, and I think the justices who came to the Court at the time that it opened felt that there was a lot of wasted space.

Q: Justice Black must have been a bit lonely over there.

O'HARA: Justice Black probably felt a little lonely when he came in, but after Black was appointed, Franklin Roosevelt had a lot of appointments in a relatively short time. Black was almost immediately joined by Justice [Stanley Forman] Reed, who was a Roosevelt appointment. Then Roosevelt had another quick appointment with [Felix] Frankfurter and [William O.] Douglas and then [James F.] Byrnes. So in a short period of time, Black was joined by lots of other Roosevelt appointees, and they all used the offices that were provided for them in the building. . . .

Justice [Louis] Brandeis never moved into the building. He was perfectly happy with working in his home. Justice Brandeis, for all of his superb mental abilities and for his superb legal mind, was a very gentle and simple man. Maybe he felt that the building was not the kind of building that he could write his opinions in and feel at home in, so he never moved in.

Q: What did these chambers look like? How did they divvy up the space?

O'HARA: The justices' chambers consist of three rooms. There's an ante-room, where secretaries would work, where visitors would be greeted as they came in. Then there would be a second room where clerks would work. Then the third room is the justice's chambers. The original chambers were very ornate with lots of wood, wooden book-shelves that are built in. They were very beautiful rooms. There have been additional chambers that have been carved out of the building, which don't have as much oak but are still very pleasant rooms.

Subsequently, the number of clerks assigned to justices has grown. Back when the building was built, each justice had one clerk, except the chief had two. . . . Now each justice has four clerks, and the chief justice has five. So that means that for some of the junior justices, the rooms for the clerks are not immediately accessible to the justices' of-fices and might not even be on the same floor. Of course, there is im-mediate access back and forth, and it's not a difficult thing for relatively young clerks to come down to the justice's chambers if they're needed.

Q: [Can you talk about how different justices approach oral argument?]

O'HARA: Some justices ask lots of questions, and some justices rarely ask questions. That is not only a phenomenon of the present day; it has been a phenomenon in the past, too. Justice [William O.] Douglas, one of the Roosevelt appointees, almost never asked a question.

Justice [William J.] Brennan Jr. rarely asked questions. Justice [Hugo] Black did not ask that many questions. Justice [Felix] Frankfurter used to pepper the lawyers with questions. The style of individual justices during that question-and-answer period will vary. It doesn't mean that a justice who doesn't ask questions is unprepared, and it certainly doesn't mean that the justice is uninterested in the case. But some justices do not feel that oral argument is where they want to work out the issues they have with the case. They do listen, of course, to the questions and answers that come from the other justices.

Q: When you're sitting in there watching and listening to a case, do you sometimes find yourself looking around the room, at the artwork and the architecture that's meant to be there to uphold the purpose and the activity that's happening in there?

O'HARA: I think that when you're sitting in the courtroom for a case . . . particularly if the case is a case that is of interest mostly to lawyers, it's not a case that has a constitutional issue that's central to it, you let your eyes wander around the room a bit. The room is very high with an ornate ceiling. There are allegorical figures above the justices and in the back of the courtroom, and there are historical figures in friezes high above the courtroom, great figures in the history of law. You'll find Moses there. You'll find Mohammad and Hammurabi and Justinian and Augustus Caesar; great figures who were responsible for either codification of law or for edicts of law. For example, King John who was responsible for the Magna Carta is one of the figures that's there. The idea behind the decoration of the room is again to make clear that the law has a certain majesty that is exemplified in this Court and that this Court has a rightful place with all of these great figures of the past who were responsible for enormous contributions to the development of the law for earlier generations.

Q: Do you find yourself sitting in that Supreme Court chamber thinking about the cases that have been heard in there, cases that have changed the course of our country?

O'HARA: It's difficult to be in the courtroom without being aware of the fact that there's a lot of history there. Of course, the Supreme Court building was not opened until 1935. But you can think of the cases in the 1930s in which New Deal operations and New Deal laws were judged to be either constitutional or unconstitutional. Or you think of *Brown v. Board of Education.* I rarely am in that courtroom when I can't see in my mind's eye Thurgood Marshall not as a justice, but as a lawyer standing there and arguing the great civil rights cases that culminated with *Brown.* He argued many cases before the *Brown* decision. I can see Brandeis sitting on that bench, and I can see Frankfurter sitting on that bench or Douglas or Earl Warren sitting on that bench. Even for somebody like myself who has become somewhat immersed in Supreme Court history, walking into the room is still an event—even if it's not for a case, even if it's for a lecture, it's an event.

Q: Can you describe the Court's Great Hall for people who have never seen it?

O'HARA: If you walk up the steps of the Supreme Court and then walk into the building itself, you see the courtroom way down at the other end of the hall. There is an impressive marble hall, the Great Hall, that separates the front door of the building from the doors that lead into the courtroom. It's characterized by marble columns. Between the columns are busts of earlier Supreme Court chief justices, all of the chief justices up to and including Chief Justice Burger. The bust of Chief Justice [William] Rehnquist has not yet been added. You see as you walk through, you see John Jay and then John Marshall and then [Roger B.] Taney and then up to Taft and then Charles Evans Hughes and then Earl Warren. You're, in a certain sense, walking through the whole history of the Court. That room is also used when a justice dies. The body of the justice is laid there ceremonially, for people to pay their respects to the justice. But it's also used for other [events]; there are dinners held there. The Supreme Court Historical Society has an annual dinner each year, which is held in the Great Hall. It's, of course, an extremely impressive entrance into the courtroom itself.

Q: So, in a sense, you really walk the history of the Court and the history of the country as you make your way down that hall.

O'HARA: You are walking through the history of the Court with amusing little sidelines. For example, when Chief Justice [Roger] Taney died—he had written the majority opinion in the *Dred Scott* case, which I think all court historians would say was the worst case in American history, the worst mistake of the Supreme Court in all of history. And when he died, Congress refused to appropriate the money for a bust of Chief Justice Taney. Now, they were in another building at the time, and the busts were in another place. It was not until a later date when things had quieted down that Congress appropriated money for a bust of Chief Justice Taney so that the collection could be complete.

Q: Among those other chief justices, do you have particular favorites, or are there any whom you dislike for particular reasons?

O'HARA: There are no chief justices that I dislike. But there are several that I have a great admiration for. Everyone admires John Marshall, who may well have been the greatest judge in the history of the English language. He stands as a towering figure in the development of law. But there are other chief justices whose busts are there whom I have a great deal of respect for. One is a justice whose name has now been forgotten by the general public. His name is Melville Fuller. He was appointed to the Supreme Court by President Grover Cleveland and was chief justice for twenty-five years. He died somewhere around 1910. He was so short that when they did the portraits of the justices together—you're familiar with the picture of the nine justices with the chief in the middle—they would have to put a hassock under his feet because they did not quite reach to the ground. He was a man with a great sense of humor. Oliver Wendell Holmes thought he was a great chief justice because his temperament was such that sometimes when different points of view would become sharply in disagreement in conferences of the justices, it seemed that Chief Justice Fuller always had a way of lightening the situation. He ran a very happy court. I feel sad that he hasn't been remembered. He was chief justice for so long, and when you have a figure as great as Holmes think of him as a great chief justice, it just seems sad that he's been forgotten.

Then there are other chief justices. Harlan Stone is there. Harlan Stone was chief justice when I was a little boy. I can remember Stone swearing in President Truman when Roosevelt died. Truman was called over to the White House, and the chief justice was there to swear him in. The chief justice died not long after that. But he had served as an associate justice for many years and then was appointed chief justice by President Roosevelt. He was one of the few chief justices who went from being an associate justice to being a chief justice. Most of the chief justices are appointed from outside the Court.

Q: You had a quote for me on the phone that I found very apropos of the Supreme Court, which is basically that in this building the president is not the chief.

O'HARA: The first three articles of the Constitution tell who is in charge of a particular branch of government. Article I says that Congress with a House of Representatives and a Senate shall be the legislative branch. And then it says the president will lead the executive branch. Then it says the Supreme Court will lead the judicial branch. So, technically speaking, when the president is visiting in the Supreme Court building, he is an honored guest. Of course, he's still president of the United States. But he is not the head of the judicial system. The Court is. You can see this when on the rare occasions that a president is present in the courtroom, the justices are seated in the higher place. The president sits in an honored place as the chief of the people visiting today, just as when the president gives a speech to Congress, the speaker of the House and the president of the Senate, who happens to be the vice president, sit in a higher place than the president's speaking dais.

Q: Now in *Bush v. Gore* in 2000, the Court was actually involved in selecting a president, and there were demonstrations outside the Supreme Court building.

O'HARA: There are occasions when you'll see demonstrations outside of the Supreme Court. And it seems to me to be a wonderful example of what democracy's about. Technically speaking, the justices and judges are supposed to decide cases on the basis of the law. They're not supposed to be moved by demonstrations on one side or another, particularly when there are demonstrations on both sides.

Yet the Constitution says that the people have the right to assemble peacefully to express their views. So demonstrations before the Court are in a way as common and perhaps even more common than demonstrations outside the White House or the Capitol building. Since the Court is closer to the street, demonstrators can get closer to the building than demonstrators at the White House can. With the White House, of course, there is an enormous lawn in the front, which is fenced. Demonstrators can really demonstrate in Lafayette Park, but they can't go up right to the steps, whereas at the Supreme Court they can come right up to the steps and demonstrate.

Q: You pointed out the bollards that are in front of the Court, put there, I assume, after 9/11.

O'HARA: There are now bollards to keep cars from being able to get close to the building. They were put up as a way of protecting the building from potential harm after 9/11. Even on those, you can see little symbols. There are little symbols all over the Court of the law. And those, each one of those individual bollards has written on it *Lex*, the Latin word for law.

Q: The site of the Court itself has an interesting history. There is, it seems to me, a very interesting back story to this grand building that sits there now.

O'HARA: The Supreme Court sits on First Street. It's an irregular site because Maryland Avenue cuts in at a rakish angle. And the site itself is an historic site. After the British burned the Capitol building and during the War of 1812—the fire was actually in 1814—a brick building was built here called the Old Brick Capitol. And that building was where Congress met until the Capitol could be repaired. During the Civil War, it became a prison where Confederate spies and Confederate personages were held. And then, subsequently, part of that building was developed, and there were some townhouses built there. A Supreme Court justice lived in one of those townhouses, a justice from California by the name of Stephen Field, [whose] townhouse was torn down for the building of the Supreme Court. One of those houses was the home of the National Woman's Party, and those buildings all had to be torn down for the building of the Supreme Court. The National Woman's Party fought that. They now are about two blocks away in a home that is itself a very historic house. It was the home of the man who was secretary of the treasury both for Thomas Jefferson and James Madison. They fought that, but they were fighting a former president of the United States who really wanted to build a Supreme Court building. So, they lost.

Q: The construction itself, when was the ground broken and how long did it take to build the court?

O'HARA: The building plans were completed around 1929. Construction was begun somewhere around 1930. Of course, Chief Justice Taft died in 1930. So, a cornerstone was laid around that time. The building was completed in 1935. And the first cases were heard there in October of 1935.

The Supreme Court always begins, in modern times, its term, or its year, on the first Monday of October. So, on the first Monday of October in 1935, the Court heard its first case in the new building.

Q: How do they assign chambers in the Supreme Court?

James B. O'Hara in his May 2009 C-SPAN interview.

O'HARA: Chambers in the Supreme Court are assigned by seniority. The senior justice has the right to choose chambers. Of course, the chief justice is always senior even though the other justices may have been appointed earlier. But after that a justice takes seniority from the date of the appointment confirmation and swearing in. So, if a justice retires and gives up chambers, and a justice who has sufficient seniority wishes to move to the evacuated chambers, the justice has the right to do that. Sometimes a retirement may occasion several justices moving, although often justices will stay in the same place for the entirety of their tenure. It once was true that all of the justices had their chambers on the same floor. But now because of the growth and the size of the number of clerks, some justices are on a level higher than other justices.

Q: Let's talk about Hugo Black. Here we have the first Supreme Court justice taking up residence in his chambers in this new building, but pretty quickly he comes under fire for his membership in the Ku Klux Klan. It seems like an inauspicious start to the building itself.

O'HARA: Justice Black had been in the Senate when he was appointed, and he did not have a home with an office. He had offices in the Senate office building. He lived in a residential hotel, a hotel then called the Wardman Park, so he needed an office space. The other justices had long since made arrangements either in their homes or even in the apartments where they lived, but Black needed that space. Shortly after his appointment and confirmation, while he was in Europe, it came out that he had been in the Ku Klux Klan. He came back from Europe and went on radio. He answered the charge and admitted that as a younger man he had been in the Klan. He promised that the Klan would play no part in his work as a justice and that he would do everything in his power to be honest and fair. I think his subsequent career proved that was accurate. He was one of the great figures in civil rights on the Court.

Q: Back to the justices meeting in the Conference Room, there are nine and only nine people in there. Do you think about the history that has unfolded in that room?

O'HARA: Yes, I do think of the history that goes on when the Supreme Court justices are there alone discussing cases. They've played with different ways of discussing cases. Under Chief Justice Stone, the argument back and forth was so free flowing that sometimes it would take several days to discuss one case.

Over time, the justices have limited themselves so that every justice speaks, and no justice speaks a second time until all of the other justices have had an opportunity to speak. I suspect that sometimes a justice's contribution may be, "I agree with justice so and so," and nothing more.

Some chief justices, Chief Justice Earl Warren comes to mind, would feel that the chief justice should write unanimous opinions in major cases like *Brown v. Board of Education*. Other chief justices, like Chief Justice Fuller, seemed to think that it was better to let other justices write the big opinions and for the chief justice to be, even in a nonpolitical court, even less political. And Chief Justice Fuller would seldom write the decision in a major case. Some say that that was because he was self-effacing and modest. I think he just felt that the case could better be handled by someone else.

Q: When I think about some of the historic appointments to the Court, obviously Sandra Day O'Connor comes up. In your study of the Court, did anything change in that building because of her? It could have been something from the mundane to the majestic, but did something change over there because of the first female being added to the Court?

O'HARA: Prior to the appointment of Justice O'Connor, when it was anticipated that the president might name a woman to the Supreme Court for the first time, the justices sitting at that time made a decision that from now on they would not refer to themselves as Mr. Justice, but simply as Justice. A lot of times when you're reading old books, or reading the reports of the Supreme Court, you will read that the opinion of the Court was given by Mr. Justice Brandeis or by Mr. Justice Frankfurter. Now the official reports will say the opinion of the Court was given by Justice Stevens or was given by Justice Ginsburg. It does not affix the Mr. or Mrs. or Madame, which I think the women justices would not have liked to have had. That was one change that came in.

There were other changes, too. The Court accommodations had to be changed. There was one rather amusing question that came up. There had always been in the Supreme Court a dining room for the spouses of the Supreme Court justices, and it had been called from the beginning of the opening of that building the "Ladies Dining Room." And suddenly you have a justice who is a woman, and her spouse is a man. Are you going to continue to call that room the Ladies Dining Room? For a while they did continue to call it that, but later on the name was changed.

There have been studies done to see whether or not women judges generally, not Supreme Court justices only, tend to decide cases differently from men judges. And the studies that had been attempted in this area indicate that there is no serious difference between men's opinions and women's opinions in legal cases, except in cases involving sex discrimination. Women judges, tend, as a group, to be more open to plaintiffs alleging sexual discrimination on the job than men judges are. So maybe the presence of women on the Court begins to influence the opinion of male judges on similar issues. I'm not sure what studies have been done in that area, but I think that the addition of women justices has been a wonderful addition to the Supreme Court.

Q: Now, you mentioned what used to be called the Ladies Dining Room. Where is it? What is it called now?

O'HARA: I think they had been looking for some time for a name for the room other than the Ladies Dining Room when at this point, there were already two Supreme Court justices who were women and who had living spouses. It was recommended that the room be named after Chief Justice Rehnquist's deceased wife, and it is now called the Dorothy Cornell Rehnquist Dining Room.

Q: Do the justices have their own private dining room?

O'HARA: There is a large dining room for justices with just nine chairs in it. That dining room is not used very often. Many of the justices work through lunch and will eat at their desk. There is a cafeteria in the Supreme Court, and sometimes you go to the Supreme Court cafeteria and you will see a justice in line, particularly at breakfast time. I used to come over to the Court quite often and have breakfast there. When Justice [Harry] Blackmun was still on the Court, almost every morning Justice Blackmun would be in the Supreme Court cafeteria, sitting there eating breakfast with his clerks. It was very amusing to see the clerks, these young people fresh out of law school or only a year out of law school, interacting with a Supreme Court justice with a lot of joking and laughter back and forth. Sometimes the justice would be laughing at something that the clerk had said, and often the clerks would be laughing at something that the justice had said. People who would be visiting the Supreme Court, tourists who would be eating breakfast there, wouldn't realize that that gentleman over there with the young people was a Supreme Court justice.

Q: Talk about that lower great hall; there's that distinct sculpture of John Marshall there.

O'HARA: That statue has a very interesting history. For many years it sat on the Capitol grounds, outside, and at the time that they were preparing the Capitol grounds for the inauguration of Ronald Reagan it was noted, first of all, that the statue stood in the way of some of the things that they needed to do to set up the grounds. Secondly, it was noted that the statue was showing some serious signs of deterioration because of being out in the weather for so long. So the statue was repaired and moved inside the Supreme Court building. The statue is interesting from another point of view: It was actually sculpted by William Wetmore Story.

William Wetmore Story was the son of Joseph Story, who was a Supreme Court justice, a contemporary on the Supreme Court of Marshall. So one can imagine the sculptor, the son of a justice, knowing Marshall. Now, of course, the statue was done after Marshall's death. The son, William Wetmore, was a lawyer who fairly late in life decided to go to Europe and study sculpture and then came back and from then on didn't practice law. He did sculpture, and he was a well regarded nineteenth century, late-nineteenth-century sculptor. He did that statue, and it is very, very impressive. Of course, everyone agrees that of all of the justices of the Supreme Court, John Marshall was the greatest. There's some disagreement about who might be next. Some people would say Louis Brandeis, some people would say Oliver Wendell Holmes, some people would say Earl Warren, but there's no question about who is first, and that's John Marshall.

So once again, as you're walking through that area, you become aware of the history of the Court and some of the great figures who have shaped that history over time. I think it's a wonderful thing that the curator's office, probably with prodding from the justices, have decided that there should be some modern portraits there. I think it's a wonderful thing to come in and see Justice Brennan's portrait or Justice Marshall's portrait because they played so important a role in the modern history of the Court.

Q: Talking about Justice Marshall, did anything change inside that building because you had the first African American justice?

O'HARA: I think there was a statement that was made by President [Lyndon] Johnson when he appointed Justice Thurgood Marshall. He said, "It was the right man in the right place at the right time." He was not only talking about Marshall, who was a superb lawyer, but saying, "I'm appointing a superb lawyer, but I'm appointing a superb lawyer who is an African American."

The time had come. When you think that the appointment came about one hundred years after the ending of slavery, the time certainly had come. Thurgood Marshall was unique. When they made Thurgood Marshall, they broke the mold. For all of his abilities as a lawyer, he not only was one of the greatest experts on civil liberties law in the history of civil liberties, but he also was a man with an utterly inexhaustible collection of stories. Some of those stories were stories of his own legal career, his own legal practice, his experiences trying cases in the 1930s in the South, sometimes having to move from house to house. He had to live in private houses because hotels were not open to him. Sometimes being in fear of his life, and so many of his stories were stories like that, but there were also the stories that one suspected that over the years the justice had maybe added a little bit to in order to make them more interesting. He was always good for a story. I think that in a way he insisted that the practice of the Court be less formal than it used to be because he just didn't know quite how to be formal. I think that there were subtle changes in the way the justices dealt with each other after Justice Thurgood Marshall joined the Court, and I think President Johnson was right; the time had come.

Q: We've talked a little bit about this, but why did it take so long for the Supreme Court to have its own place?

O'HARA: The Supreme Court perhaps more than the other two branches of government in Washington—I don't want to say the Supreme Court is a branch. It's the judicial branch, but the Supreme

Court is the Washington appearance of the judicial branch—the Supreme Court has perhaps evolved more than Congress has or more than the presidency has in terms of the way it does its work.

The Supreme Court, according to the Constitution, is an appeals court. But Congress, when it was enacting the legislation that set the Supreme Court in motion, seemed to feel that if the Supreme Court only did appellate work that the Supreme Court justices wouldn't be busy enough. So Congress added to the responsibilities of the Supreme Court the task of actually hearing cases around the country. So in the earliest days of the Supreme Court—I'm talking the 1790s, the early 1800s—Supreme Court justices did not live in Washington. They lived in their homes in South Carolina or in Maryland or in Connecticut. They would be assigned to hear cases in a district and would move around that district, and in a certain sense, being a Supreme Court justice could be a difficult job.

Supreme Court justices were not usually young—the life expectancy of an American male in the early 1800s was probably not even sixty—so you had relatively old people responsible for moving from place to place. This was particularly true in the southern districts. The districts are called circuits. In the southern circuit you might have a justice, for example Justice [James] Iredell, who lived in North Carolina and was expected to hear cases in Georgia and Alabama and Mississippi. So he was constantly traveling. When you were a Supreme Court justice, you were not only expected to come to Washington once or twice a year to sit in, as an appellate court, you were expected to move around. Remember, roads weren't paved, so in order to get from one place to another you might be on a barge going down a river. You might be on a stagecoach that was going on a road right after it had rained and was muddy so the coach could only go a couple of miles a day. You stayed at dirty inns, and you ate terrible food.

Anyway, the Supreme Court justices didn't come to Washington, and so there didn't need to be a building in Washington. When they were here, they were only here for a month; being in the Capitol building was fine. It was not until right before the Civil War that

Supreme Court justices began to live in Washington. And it was not until after the Civil War that all of them lived in Washington. So the period in which the Court was actually in need of a courtroom in Washington happened fairly late in the history of American government. Until the 1890s, Supreme Court justices were still expected to hear cases back in their home circuits.

By that time railroad travel had come in, roads were paved, riverboats were much more comfortable, and hotels were much more comfortable. Still, you'd have a case like Justice [Stephen Johnson] Field from California, who once a year had to get on a train, go all the way to California, spend several weeks in California hearing cases, and then get on the train for the long travel back. So it was not really until the 1880s that the need for something more permanent began to be felt and even then only by a few. And of course it was not until forty years after that with Chief Justice Taft that the present building came to fruition.

Q: Describe to me what it was like there in the Capitol, when Taft decided, this is too much; we need a place.

O'HARA: Using the rooms in the Capitol was a problem for the Court, even in its earliest days. That room in the basement, which is called the Old Supreme Court Chamber, was poorly lighted. They used oil lamps, so there was always a heavy oil smell from whale oil in the building. It was cold, although they had some fireplaces to heat it, and it was damp. Then, when they moved upstairs to the Old Senate Chamber, Taft noted that if the justices wanted to get together to discuss a case, they would have to borrow a hearing room from one of the Senate committees. The justices did not have a robing room, so the justices would be putting on their robes outside, but the space was cramped. And here was the real thing that Taft worried about: lawyers who perhaps were coming from distant places could not, when they got to the Supreme Court and were ready to go in and argue the most important case of their lifetime—and there might be three lawyers from the same law firm—they couldn't even go over their notes together; there was no place for them to meet except in a hallway where the lawyers for the other side might be trying to do the same thing.

The chief justice was a person who always felt that there was a certain dignity that should attach to the law and that the dignity of the Court was being violated. . . . The chamber that the Court had for the actual hearing of cases, the Old Senate Chamber, which was the room where Henry Clay, Daniel Webster, and John Calhoun had thrived, it was a very nice looking room, but aside for the room itself, there was no other space. It defies description to say that in the 1920s and early 1930s, justices of the Supreme Court did not have offices. These are people of tremendous importance in American government, and they had to work at home. Certainly for the 1920s and 1930s, having messengers take cases back and forth from one house to another was not exactly an exotic way to move in a modern world, so Taft was obviously right.

Q: Can you tell us more about Cass Gilbert?

O'HARA: Cass Gilbert was one of the best-known architects of his time. He was born right before the Civil War, in Ohio, but as a child the family moved from Zanesville, Ohio, to St. Paul, Minnesota. His father was an engineer; the Gilberts were well-to-do. Gilbert's father died when he was only nine years old, but he left Gilbert's mother with substantial income from properties and so forth. So Gilbert had the advantage of a very good education. He went to MIT and studied architecture, although he did not complete the entire program. He also had the advantage, as a very young man, of going to Europe for eight months for a grand tour to make sketches of buildings. When he came back, he joined the architectural firm of McKim, Mead, and White, which was probably the best-known architectural firm in the United States. He worked with them for a number of projects and then decided to move back to St. Paul where he opened an office with another architect.

Over time he developed an architectural practice of incredible importance. By 1900 the firm moved to its New York offices, and he designed major buildings in New York, including the Woolworth building, which was at the time the highest building in New York. He also designed the state capitols for two states—his home state of Minnesota and the state capitol of West Virginia. I don't think any other architect ever was the architect of two state capitols. He designed the Customs House in New York.

So here was a man who was accustomed to designing large public buildings that made a statement. He was definitely not a modern architect, but he was an architect whose practice had given him enormous experience in building the kinds of buildings that Chief Justice Taft felt fit in to the capital that Jefferson wanted built. So it was the perfect match of architect and employer. Taft wanted Gilbert, and Gilbert wanted the job. Years before Gilbert became the official architect of the Supreme Court, he was doing sketches and sending some of those sketches onto Taft so that Taft could get some idea of what was on Gilbert's mind. So when Taft began to chair the committee that was to choose the architect, Gilbert was very much the first choice that Taft had in mind. Neither Taft nor Gilbert lived to see the building completed. Gilbert died only a few months before the building opened. He was obviously present for much of the building, and there was a lot of correspondence between Gilbert and Taft's successor, Chief Justice Hughes, but he died a few months before it was opened. Gilbert was seventy-five years old at the time of his death.

Q: How much was Gilbert's input into the look and size of the building, and how much was Taft's?

O'HARA: I believe it was a partnership between Taft and Gilbert, although I think that Taft recognized that Gilbert was the architect he wanted, and he wasn't going to tell Gilbert how to be an architect. I think that Taft told him the kinds of spaces he wanted, and then Gilbert submitted back to Taft his ideas for those spaces. I'm talking about the inside spaces. On the outside, at one point there was a drawing that Gilbert did in which the Supreme Court building had a dome, not unlike the dome that is in the older building of the Library of

Congress. It was a much smaller dome than the Capitol building. At another point, the central part of the building was sort of boxy; it almost looked like a cake. Then it was decided to go with the present design, and when you look at those drawings you'd say that the architect made the right decision because the present building is much more attractive than those earlier drawings were. Whether Taft played a role in the elimination of some of those designs, I don't know, but I suspect that since there was a friendship between the two men and an extensive correspondence, that Taft played a pretty big role in that.

Q: We know that there was some dissension on the court on whether they even needed a new building. What about in Congress in terms of appropriating the money. Was there any back story to that?

O'HARA: There was some opposition in Congress to the construction of a new building. When Taft originally proposed the idea, he spoke to a couple of senators, and some of the senators were negative about it. But ultimately, Taft was able to deal with senators that he was comfortable with and whom liked Taft. Taft was a very likable man. And of course he was a former president of the United States who was now chief justice. Senators know how to deal with power. They respect it, and Taft had power. So Taft ultimately got the commission of Supreme Court committee together to supervise the building, and he got the cooperation of senators. The appropriation that Taft asked for was a little bit less than ten million dollars, which was a lot more money in those days than it is now. The economic problems of the Great Depression actually helped in that because what ten million dollars would have built when Taft asked for the money would have been a building. Taft would have had to go back to Congress to ask for another appropriation for the furniture and for the outfitting of the building. But during the Great Depression, there was a deflation so that money would buy more than it would have bought before. They were able to build the building, furnish it, and still turn one hundred thousand dollars back to the Treasury of the United States. It came in under budget. It may be the only government building in history that came in under budget.

Q: If it hadn't been for Taft, how long do you think it might have taken to get something like this done, if ever?

O'HARA: If Taft had not pushed for the building, I think that in a relatively short period of time a building would have been built. Here's why I think that. First of all, they were in the middle of the Great Depression, and Roosevelt seemed to understand that pumping some money into the economy was a good thing. It gave employment, and the money you put in had a multiplier effect. It was good for the economy to build buildings so a lot of buildings got built during that period. It would not have taken a lot of convincing of the Roosevelt administration that a Supreme Court building was a good idea.

Putting it where it was put might have been a problem. There was a proposal at one point to put the Supreme Court building over where the Jefferson Memorial is now, and the justices at the time objected to that. I think they wanted to be closer to what they thought was where the action was, near Congress, near the Capitol building. I also think there was a feeling that the Court should be fairly close to Union Station because of the attorneys coming in to argue cases. As it is now, the Court is within easy walking distance of the station or a very short cab ride. If it had been in any other location in Washington, that convenience would not have been there.

Q: Thank you, very much.

WILLIAM SUTER

Clerk of the Supreme Court

C-SPAN's Connie Doebele interviewed William Suter in his office on *June 15, 2009. General Suter has served as Clerk of the Court since 1991. He retired from the U.S. Army in 1990 at the rank of Major General, after a long career that included decorated service in Vietnam and service as an army judge advocate. His law degree is from Tulane University.*

———————

DOEBELE: Where have you been this morning?

WILLIAM SUTER: We had a session in court this morning. The business was to announce the orders from last week's conference, which only took a minute, and then we had the announcement of two opinions by the Court. One justice announced both of them, Justice Breyer, who wrote both of the majority opinions. Then we moved the admission of about eighty attorneys that were in different groups to become members of the bar, and they were sworn in. So, largely, today was a ceremonial day.

Q: And how you are dressed?

SUTER: This is a morning coat. It is a very traditional outfit, and here at the Court it is worn by the marshal of the Court and myself. The solicitor general of the United States and his staff wear it when they

General William Suter, clerk of the Court, in the traditional morning coat, June 2009.

argue cases here. Now, some of the women on his staff do not wear the morning coat. Here, our marshal is a woman, and she wears the morning coat, and one of my deputies is a woman, and she wears it also. We traditionally wear the morning coat, the marshal and myself, when the Court is in public wearing robes, so when we are in session upstairs, at the State of the Union message over in the Capitol, and at the inauguration of a president. It is very traditional, and years ago, all the attorneys arguing cases wore the morning coat. That has fallen into disuse, and now the attorneys wear traditional, formal attire.

Q: Do you know how far back that tradition goes?

SUTER: I really don't know. It's a long time. Things last a long time around here.

Q: And after you finish with the Court, what is your normal day like? What are your duties as the clerk?

SUTER: The clerk of any court—trial or appellate—is basically responsible for the legal business of the court. Not writing the opinions, but being the interface with the public—normally members of the bar of this court who are filling documents here, petitions, briefs and oppositions, merits briefs, applications to stay, whatever it might be. My office meets them, receives documents, analyzes them for correctness and legality, and enters them on the electronic docket, and then we deal with the attorneys with setting the argument dates, getting the briefs up to the justices, maintaining all the legal documents for the Court.

Q: What's the hardest part of that job?

SUTER: This is not a hard job. It's a great job. It's an honor to work in the Supreme Court. After all the years I had in the military as an army judge advocate, I missed leaving the army because the camaraderie of serving your nation; there are a lot of great things about it. But I really found the same thing here. This is a small organization with no politics; justices are appointed for life. There's no civil service system; the people that are hired here are the best qualified, and instead of just having a job, the employees here have a sense of mission to get the job done as a constitutional mission to the court. It's really a high calling. They look at it as more than a job. I am very happy here and honored to be here, so I don't find this hard. When the justices need something, when something needs to be done, we try to anticipate and get it done before it is asked, but whatever is asked, we provide it.

Q: How many people work for the clerk's office?

SUTER: For the clerk's office only thirty-two, and these are mostly paralegals. There are four attorneys, highly skilled individuals. . . . They cleaned the file room up because you are here today and the men and women that work there are dealing with many documents. Now we are highly automated here at the Court, but you still need to have a lot of hard copy documents. We've eliminated much of the paper, but there still is some paper and they're in there processing the petitions for *certiorari* that come in. Those documents have to be maintained in an orderly fashion. They have to be transported up to the justices' chambers. They have to be returned; documents that are not used are recycled and so forth. So we have a real system for handling every document that enters this Court.

Q: How often do private citizens bring cases before this Court, and have you ever worked with one in which they might not have the legal background that the people of the bar do?

SUTER: It happens every day. We have about eight thousand petitions asking this Court to review cases and hear cases. It's a court of discretion, which means there are very few mandatory appeals. It's basically *certiorari* jurisdiction. About two thousand of those cases are filed by lawyers who know what they are doing, law firms or state entities or the federal government; their briefs are printed, and they have to pay a fee. We have about six thousand individuals out there who are paupers. They are poor, about half of them are in prison, about half have an attorney. They, too, under the law can file a petition here asking the Court to hear their case. On the front of this building in marble it says "Equal Justice Under Law," so we really believe that here. Some of these petitions might be frivolous, but each one is looked at and reviewed very carefully. You have sometimes people who are called jailhouse attorneys and other individuals who just don't have an attorney. It might be a civil case; it could be dealing with something like adoption or child custody or income tax. Anyone can file a document here. Some are handwritten. One of our most famous cases from the early 1960s, *Gideon vs. Wainwright*, was written by a prisoner in Florida, handwritten on prison stationery. His case was granted, he was heard, and it was a very important decision [regarding] a right to counsel. Now not many of these individuals who do not have attorneys are successful in getting their case granted and heard as you might imagine because they are not skilled. But they can make a try at it, and maybe they feel better. We deal with them all the time, and one of our jobs in the clerk's office is to make it as easy as we can for a person to file a document here. Don't hide the ball, the rules of the Court are written in plain English so they can be understood. They are posted on our Web site. We have forms especially for use from people without attorneys, fill-in-the-blank forms to make it as easy as possible to get the case before this Court.

Q: Twenty years ago, if you would have said to somebody that this Court was highly automated or highly computerized they might have laughed.

SUTER: They should have laughed. I've been here eighteen years, and it's been a very enlightening period for me to be here because we have totally automated the place. The printing of the briefs, everything we do, the memos written by the law clerks, everything is online. We have very sophisticated equipment, and we have excellent employees in our automation department to help keep everything going. We never hear around here that the computers are down. It just doesn't happen, so we are very fortunate in that regard.

Q: This is also seen as a building of great tradition. How do you combine the high automation and still keep the tradition?

SUTER: We thrive on tradition and discipline. Those things go hand in hand. Part of the tradition is that before the attorney goes into the courtroom in the morning, I brief them in the Lawyers' Lounge so they know what to expect that day. I make sure no one forgot a tie or a shoe; rookies especially sometimes are forgetful. When they go into the courtroom the first thing they see on their table are quill pens. They are handcrafted; they are a memento, a gift from the Court for a remembrance of their day here at the Court. They don't get an automated pen; they get a quill pen they can take home and put it in a shadow box or something. We maintain the tradition. When an attorney approaches the bench he says, "Mr. Chief Justice and may it please the Court." That's gone on forever and ever. Each side of the Court gets thirty minutes, not thirty-one minutes. Thirty minutes means thirty minutes, so there's part of the tradition, but that's also discipline.

q: Let's go to that Lawyers' Lounge; walk us through that. When do you do this?

SUTER: The attorneys are instructed to be there at 9:15 in the morning, and the regulars all know to be there. Sometimes they don't know each other. Sometimes you don't know your opponent; sometimes it might be someone from New York or California. This is a national court, so it's not just a bunch of attorneys who all hang around the same courthouse; it's a little different from that. They exchange greetings; they are all glad to see each other. They take their seats, and I go over the events that are going to occur that day. I let them know if opinions are coming down, how many motions there are for admissions, note the absences of any justices who might be recused; answer any questions they might have. I offer them cough drops, aspirin, anything like that they might need to make them feel more comfortable. We have restrooms for men and women. The Lawyers' Lounge is a very intimate place. The feedback I have gotten over the years is the attorneys like it very much. Now the solicitor general . . . she and her staff do not attend because they are here so frequently they need not attend. When Chief Justice Roberts was the deputy solicitor general when I came here eighteen years ago, he did not attend the briefings. When he left office and went with a law firm, he attended the briefings. He has told me, since he's now my boss as chief justice, that he liked the briefings. He told me to continue them because it is sort of therapeutic. . . . Sometimes the attorneys have last-minute requirements. We want them to enter that courtroom prepared and ready so both sides have an equal chance of winning the case. That's our job; we don't take sides.

q: Do you go in, a little bit, as a counselor? Do you find some of them a little nervous about this day in their life?

SUTER: Yes. I'm not a legal counsel, but to speak to them privately sometimes, [encouraging them] not to worry, not to be nervous. Those that are really nervous all need a box of cough drops . . . and sometimes they want an extra glass of water. We take care of that. We're there to make sure they are ready. The lawyers who argue cases here do a tremendous job. I always like to say there are three secrets to successful appellate advocacy: preparation, preparation, preparation. And some counsel are so good they appear here and argue with no notes, no three-by-five cards, no nothing. I don't recommend that, but some who are highly experienced do that, and they're good.

Q: Will you have any one-on-one conversations with them prior to them arriving at the Court that day?

SUTER: I do on some occasions. I have one staff member, the merits assistant, [and attorneys] are instructed [that] once a case is granted, you deal with her. She sends you a care package with all the documents you need, everything you need, when your case might be heard, her phone number, her e-mail. We ask them to deal directly with her, so they don't hear things secondhand, thirdhand. And, they get to all know each other. The bar here, their word is good, whatever they say, you can go to the bank on it. It's that kind of a practice of law; it's very sophisticated, and the people are the best.

Q: So, they leave the Lawyers' Lounge and walk into the chamber itself?

SUTER: Yes. I make sure that the attorneys are at the right table, petitioners on one side, respondents on the other. . . . I check to see if there is anything they need. I then talk to the people who are making the motions for admission, to be sure they have their motion, that they know what to do, where to stand, when to speak. Those that are being sworn in, I brief them on exactly what to do. They don't want to come in the highest court in the land and stand up and not know what to say or do, so we go over it with them very carefully and explain what's required. I generally check around to be sure we are ready to go, and at 10 o'clock sharp we start.

Q: Ever late?

SUTER: Never.

Q: Once the actual session begins, what's your role?

SUTER: I'm there if the Court needs anything. Sometimes they'll need another document; sometimes they will tell the counsel to be sure to follow up and submit that to the Court later. I make a note of that to be sure I have it down. Otherwise I am just to be there to assist the Court on anything that it might be needed. Some strange things might happen. A counsel needs another document or something; we will get that for them. But again it's a part of the tradition.

Q: Where do you sit?

SUTER: I sit, as you face the Court, on the far left and the marshal is on the far right, just a little bit below the justices. I can reach out and shake the hand of the junior justice, so it's a good perch. I listen to the arguments, but I'm more attentive to those I'm more interested in. I've witnessed about thirteen hundred arguments since I've been here. I get to see a lot of good lawyering, and good lawyering from the justices. They ask a lot of questions; they are very, very well prepared. A journalist who's a friend of mine, who's covered this Court for fifty years, told me he thinks this is the best prepared Court as far as the justices being up to speed on the cases and really understanding them and asking penetrating questions, the best he's ever seen. In one case last term, they asked 102 questions. In another case, 106 questions. In an hour that's a lot, so the counsel have to be very well prepared.

Q: Talk a little bit more about the interaction between you and the justices in your normal, everyday work.

SUTER: I deal more with the chief justice than with any of the others. But I deal with the junior justice every week after conference; they take the notes in the conference and when they finish, we sit down together with some other staff members and a few other Court employees and [hear] what happened at the conference: "We granted this case, we denied these cases, we're going to call for views of the solicitor general on this case," and so forth. We then retire to our office, double check everything, and prepare the orders of the Court, which are released the next Monday. This morning, the first thing the chief said when the Court opened was that the orders of the Court are certified and filed by the clerk; they will not otherwise be announced. Those orders then are released; they go on the Internet. Public Information lets them out, and all the people that are interested, including journalists and members of the bar and the public, know which cases are granted that will be heard next term.

Q: When you get that briefing from the junior justice, do you know what happened in terms of the discussion?

SUTER: No, no, no. We just get the results, and it just takes a few minutes. It's a very pleasant time with Justice Alito. He's only done this for a couple of terms. Justice Breyer did it for about eleven and a half years. He got very good at it. He was junior justice for a long time. . . . [Editor's note: Justice Sotomayor is now the Court's most junior justice and has assumed the conference notetaking role from Justice Alito.]

Q: Sitting back in that courtroom in the chamber, tell us from your vantage point what you see when you are sitting at your perch, as you called it.

SUTER: I've got to tell you, I am still awed by the building and the institution. I've been a lawyer for a long time. Before, I went in the army JAG, and then I was a lawyer for almost thirty years, and as lawyer here I do legal administrative and clerical type of work, but I sit there and think of the disputes that are settled in the courtroom, rather than in the streets or a way that would be illegal. And I think of all of the landmark cases in this building since 1935, and of the cases that aren't landmark—they're important to someone out there; a bankruptcy case is not something that gets me too excited, but it's important to someone and to the legal community, which looks to this Court for the guidance, interpreting the law. I take it seriously every time. It's never old hat. I think a lot of lawyers and other people, scholars especially, feel the same way. It's almost a solemn place.

Q: As you're sitting there, is there some piece architecturally or something in that Court that constantly draws your attention, or has over the years?

SUTER: The rosettes in the ceiling. I've never seen them before. Now I look for them in any building. I saw some up in New York a few years ago and I thought, "They look just like ours." And I ran back here and told the curator that it must be the same architect. It wasn't. But you don't see them. They're on the elevator doors; they're all over the building. The rosettes, I'm told, the architect had nothing particular in mind, but he liked them just as much as I like them. So I find some comfort looking up, and they are always there. They are just beautiful.

Q: As you look around the room, what represents the tradition of the Court that you physically see in that room?

SUTER: For one thing, the robes. They're not there just as people in business or lawyers; the robe is a mark of anonymity. That's what they really are. They're not monks; they're people who interpret the law, and they do it fairly without political persuasion.

I like to look down also and see the members of the press there. We don't have secret courts in this country. They're there. Citizens can line up and come in. Anybody can come in and watch a case if they want to. I'm glad to see that it is so open, that we are all there hearing the case argued in public, even those cases that are of great national importance, *Bush v. Gore* for instance. Hundreds and hundreds of people were here, and they got to hear everything that the Court heard, and then the Court had to retire and make a decision. So, I find it democracy at its best.

q: When you're sitting in your chair, you have a bird's eye look at the people outside of the press, who are attending just to watch the oral argument. What do you see?

suter: I think I see the greatest people on earth. I think this is the greatest country on earth. Those who are here vacationing with children, or school groups, or anybody that's here, some might not all fully understand what all's going on up there, but they're at least there to see this is the court of last resort. This isn't my building. We don't own this building; you own it. The justices work for the people. They're up there trying to do the people's work, and the public is there watching it. Whether they understand or not, doesn't make that much difference. Sometimes we have the parties that are involved in the case, they come here; a lot of student groups, high school groups, law students. It's wonderful to sit and see America across the spectrum; all types are in the courtroom.

q: Do you have an opportunity to ever speak to any student groups?

suter: I've spoken to about thirteen hundred since I came here—two or three a week. Boy Scouts, Girl Scouts, students from all over the United States, high school groups. Many are repeaters; one interesting group is the Rugby School from the United Kingdom, where rugby was invented. I speak to lots and lots of student groups, and they're very interesting. They have questions. I especially like the high school students. I tell them about cases we've had here that deal with children their age. I'll read a part of the Constitution, explain what it is that the case deals with, and tell them what the facts were. Then I'll let them vote to see who wins. It's rather interesting. Their teachers are sometimes surprised at the results, too. By the way, the justices do a lot of public speaking. Not formal speeches, but they speak to groups, same type that I speak to. School groups, particularly bar groups.

Q: The history of your office. Tell us a little bit about that.

SUTER: The clerk was the first person appointed here in 1790. He was Mr. [John] Tucker whose portrait is on the wall behind me. They didn't do a lot of business the first few years because the Court didn't know exactly what it was supposed to do. Those who created the Constitution thought it was good idea, but they focused on the other two branches of government more than the third branch as we're called, because we are named in Article III of the Constitution. But the Court itself historically—the clerk's office under Mr. Tucker—was sort of getting organized. We've had some interesting clerks, one who stayed thirty-six years. One stayed only one year. Of course when I came here, I said, "I've got to last longer than he lasted." I did. The clerks have taken notes and written things; very interesting people have been the clerk. I know a lot about the history. I'm keeping a lot of documents with the aid of my college interns in the summer, who are gathering information for me. I'd like to compile some sort of historical

Portrait of John Tucker, first clerk of the Court in 1790.

document when I retire about all the clerks. There are some very interesting stories.

Q: How many have there been?

SUTER: Nineteen.

Q: Are there a couple of those nineteen who particularly jump out at you as interesting that you might be able to talk about?

SUTER: James Browning left here and was appointed to the Ninth Circuit Court of Appeals, and he is still on that court as a senior justice. I believe he was the last clerk to hold the Bible when a president was sworn in, and that was John F. Kennedy. I've met Mr. Browning; very delightful fellow. I've known about five of the previous clerks. They're interesting people, and each one is a little different. I'm the first [clerk with a] military background.

Q: Are there any artifacts from the early days?

SUTER: Oh yes. On my right, there is a rolltop desk that belonged to Mr. [Elias B.] Caldwell, who served as the clerk from 1800–1826. I have it displayed beneath his portrait. I have quill pens over there for him, too, if he ever wants to come back and use the desk.

Q: I want to ask you about your military background. What was it about the time in which you were in the military and being a major general that prepared you for a job like this?

SUTER: I went into the army right out of law school. I had taken ROTC. One colorful thing about it: I took my basic training and ROTC at Fort Hood, Texas, alongside Elvis Presley. I keep a picture of me and Elvis here in the office. So I came in the army because I had a requirement to come in right out of law school. I enjoyed it, and my

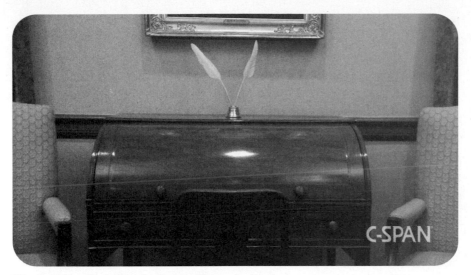

Elias B. Caldwell's desk in the clerk's office at the Court.

wife enjoyed it very much. I got a lot of experience early on prosecuting and defending cases. We lived around the world: Bangkok, Thailand; Vietnam; Charlottesville, Virginia, where the JAG is; the Pentagon, of course. I had many assignments in different places, and each time there was more responsibility and more challenges. I just enjoyed it all. In many ways I felt like I was getting ready to come here for this job. We had some things we wanted to get done over here; the Court let me know and we got those things done. And I think having the time in the army prepared me for that, where you're a worker bee and then you later are a supervisor and administrator, getting things done.

Q: What's your favorite part of this building?

SUTER: This office. It's very comfortable. It's a very nice place to greet visitors. It's a great place to work. Other employees come in. We have chats. I'm very big on delegating authority to everyone else to make decisions. There's no need to bring everything in to me. For instance, the law clerks work for the justices. They are wonderful young men and women, very dedicated and exceptionally bright, hard working, just the best. But they go see whichever deputy or person in my office is the one responsible for that area and talk to them. They don't have to come and see me. So I get to know a few of them, but not all of them.

Q: Do you remember your first day here?

SUTER: Yes. I was clueless. But I put on an air that I knew what I was doing and walked around and sort of got the lay of the land. I've done this before in the military. You go into a new job, and you have to be careful about making changes too quickly. Be careful about what you believe. Just take it easy. I went around and had interviews with all the justices. That was very interesting to me, to come in and talk to all these important people. I found out the staff was a great staff and the budget was fine. So, little by little we got moving. But, yes, I remember the first day. In fact, I wore one of my brand-new suits that day, too.

Q: Had you ever visited the Court as a tourist?

SUTER: I'd come over here as an army officer to hear military cases that were argued here. Several times I came over and heard cases we had a great interest in. There is something about a lawyer; you want to see the argument. All that counts is the opinion, but you want to see the inter-action that goes on because you know the law; you're very interested in it. I probably heard four cases over here, and I was admitted to practice here as an army lawyer, and had made some motions for admission, so I was not a stranger. I had had some friends over here that were clerks who'd been in the military. It wasn't a strange place for me, but I didn't know the ins and outs of the building. I was always lost.

Q: As you have said, not very many people actually get to see what happens in that courtroom. So walk us through: the Court begins, you've left the Lawyers' Lounge, you've come in and made sure every-one is ready, you've taken your seat. It's 10 o'clock; what happens?

SUTER: A lot of people are doing a lot of work, our police, the marshal, the aides. A lot of people are getting the lawyers in to be sure they are seated. The members of our bar, they are seated up front. All the spectators, everyone is there and ready. They're in there early. The press is even there on time, believe it or not. Everything is very orderly and respectful. There's a five-minute buzzer, and it means five minutes and we're ready to go. Then the justices appear behind the curtains. The curtains open in three places and the justices enter in groups of three. The marshal cries the court in with her traditional cry, part of which is "oyez, oyez, oyez," which is used throughout the country to announce the arrival of the court, and the justices take their seats. Everyone rises, and it's an inspirational moment. People say, "I couldn't believe it, there they are, they are really there." It's not like a Broadway production, but it does make the hair on the back of your neck stand up just a little because you feel, "This is really it." We stand, the marshal cries, brings the gavel down, we sit, and the business of the Court starts. It's a very orderly, very respectful grand moment for everyone who comes up there.

If it is a normal argument day, the chief will say motions for admission first, maybe an opinion coming down, and then he'll say: "Now we'll hear argument number 08410 *Smith v. Jones*, Mr. Holtz." And Mr. Holtz will say: "Mr. Chief Justice and may it please the Court." They know where to stand; nobody is wandering around. Everyone knows exactly what to do. The chief justice has a script, prepared by this office; even the names of the attorneys are spelled phonetically, so he can get the right name. We don't want to make any mistakes up here.

Q: That's about the last time you have any control, right? After he says, "May it please . . . "

SUTER: They're out of the gate and they're off. The attorneys are on their own, but they've practiced; they know what to do. They are glad to get on with it. Sometimes the counsel would rather go first than second because you're sitting there second, just waiting and waiting, but that's the way it is. Sometimes they will get up and leave the room for a minute and come back, just to take a little stretch or something. But they have to be back at 11 o'clock, and then we start our second case.

Q: General Suter, thank you.

PART THREE

SUPPLEMENTARY
MATERIAL

BIOGRAPHIES OF THE JUSTICES

Chief Justice John G. Roberts Jr., 109th justice, 17th chief justice
Appointed by: President George W. Bush
Sworn in: September 29, 2005

Chief Justice John G. Roberts Jr. was born in Buffalo, New York, in 1955. He graduated from Harvard a year early, with highest honors. He attended Harvard Law School (1979), and served as managing editor of the *Harvard Law Review*. Upon graduation, he clerked for Judge Henry J. Friendly, U.S. Court of Appeals for the Second Circuit (1979–1980) and in 1980, for then Associate Justice William Rehnquist, U.S. Supreme Court. He served in the Reagan administration's Department of Justice, 1981–1982 and the White House Counsel's Office from 1982–1986. He served as Deputy Solicitor General from 1989–1993, representing the government before the Supreme Court. He was a lawyer in private practice in Washington, DC, from 1986–1989 and again in 1993–2003. In 2003, he was appointed to the U.S. Court of Appeals for the District of Columbia Circuit. When he was named chief justice in 2005, John Roberts was the youngest chief justice since John Marshall in 1801, who was forty-five.

He married Jane Marie Sullivan in 1996 and they have two children, Josephine and John.

Associate Justice John Paul Stevens, 101st justice
Appointed by: President Gerald Ford
Sworn in: December 19, 1975

Associate Justice John Paul Stevens was born in Chicago in 1920. He graduated from the University of Chicago in 1941 and then served in the U.S. Navy (1942–1945) during World War II, earning the Bronze Star for his work as a navy code breaker. He attended Northwestern University School of Law, where he was named editor-in-chief of the school's law review and graduated with the highest grades in the law school's history. Upon graduation, he served a term as law clerk to Supreme Court Justice Wiley Rutledge. In private practice and as a law school professor, Justice Stevens focused on anti-trust law, which earned him positions as special counsel in both the House of Representatives and the U.S. Attorney General's office. In 1970, President Richard Nixon appointed him to the United States Court of Appeals for the Seventh Circuit where he served for five years before his appointment to the high court.

He married Maryan Mulholland in 1980. He has four children from his first marriage: John Joseph (deceased), Kathryn, Elizabeth Jane, and Susan Roberta.

Associate Justice Antonin Scalia, 103rd justice
Appointed by: President Ronald Reagan
Sworn in: September 26, 1986

Associate Justice Antonin Scalia was born in 1936 in Trenton, New Jersey. He graduated from Georgetown University, summa cum laude, and Harvard Law School, magna cum laude. He began his career in private practice but soon moved to academia: He was a professor of law at both the University of Virginia from 1967–1971, and the University of Chicago from 1977–1982. In between, he joined the Nixon administration as general counsel in the Office of Telecommunications Policy, from 1971–1972, and then served as chairman of the U.S. Administrative Conference from 1972–1974. Named to the Justice Department's Office of Legal Counsel, he served as an assistant attorney general from 1974–1977. He was a judge for the U.S. Court of Appeals for the District of Columbia, 1982–1986, before being named to the Supreme Court.

He married Maureen McCarthy in 1960, and they have nine children: Ann Forrest, Eugene, John Francis, Catherine Elisabeth, Mary Clare, Paul David, Matthew, Christopher James, and Margaret Jane.

Associate Justice Anthony M. Kennedy, 104th justice
Appointed by: President Ronald Reagan
Sworn in: February 18, 1988

Associate Justice Anthony Kennedy was born in 1936 in Sacramento, California. He earned his undergraduate degree from Stanford University and law degree from Harvard Law School in 1958. After graduation, he practiced law, first in San Francisco, from 1961–1963, and then in Sacramento, from 1963–1975, assuming his late father's law practice. He also taught constitutional law at McGeorge School of Law, University of Pacific, from 1975–1988. During the administration of then–California Governor Ronald Reagan, he worked on statewide propositions, limiting the state's spending. In 1975, he became the youngest-serving federal judge with his appointment to the U.S. Court of Appeals for the Ninth Circuit.

He married Mary Davis in 1963, and they have three children: Justin, Gregory, and Kristin.

Associate Justice Clarence Thomas, 106th justice
Appointed by: President George H. W. Bush
Sworn in: October 23, 1991

Associate Justice Clarence Thomas was born in 1948 in Pin Point, Georgia, and was raised by his maternal grandfather. He briefly attended a seminary in Missouri, then entered Holy Cross College, graduating ninth in his class. He attended Yale University School of Law and after graduation, he returned to Missouri where he worked with then-State Attorney General John Danforth; he was assistant attorney general of Missouri from 1974–1977. After a brief stint as a corporate lawyer, he joined John Danforth's U.S. Senate staff as a legislative aide. During the Reagan administration, he was named assistant secretary for civil rights in the Department of Education in 1981, and was later appointed director of the Equal Employment Opportunity Commission (EEOC). President George H. W. Bush appointed him to the U.S. Court of Appeals for the District of Columbia in 1990 and one year later, to the Supreme Court.

He married Virginia Lamp in 1987 and has a son, Jamal Adeen, by a previous marriage.

Associate Justice Ruth Bader Ginsburg, 107th justice
Appointed by: President Bill Clinton
Sworn in: August 10, 1993

Associate Justice Ruth Bader Ginsburg was born in 1933 in Brooklyn, New York. She earned her undergraduate degree from Cornell University and attended Columbia Law School, graduating at the top of her class. She then served as associate director at the Columbia Law School Project on International Procedure, and in 1963 she joined Rutgers University Law School. Justice Ginsburg served as general counsel for the American Civil Liberties Union from 1973–1980. During this time, she argued before the Supreme Court, including six cases on women's rights. In 1972, she was the first woman hired with tenure at Columbia Law School. In 1980, she was appointed judge on the U.S. Court of Appeals in the DC Circuit.

She married Martin Ginsburg in 1954, and they have two children, Jane and James.

Associate Justice Stephen G. Breyer, 108th justice
Appointed by: President Bill Clinton
Sworn in: August 3, 1994

Associate Justice Stephen G. Breyer was born in 1938 in San Francisco, California. He earned his undergraduate degree from Stanford University and his law degree from Harvard University; he later clerked for Justice Arthur Goldberg in the Supreme Court's 1964 term. He was assistant special prosecutor to the Watergate prosecution in 1973, under Archibald Cox. He was Special Counsel in 1974–1975 and, later Chief Counsel (1979–1980), to the Senate Judiciary Committee. His teaching assignments included Harvard Law School, 1967–1994, professor at Harvard's Kennedy School of Government, 1977–1980, and visiting professor at the College of Law, Sydney, Australia, and at the University of Rome. He also served on the United States Sentencing Commission from 1985–1989. In 1980, he was named judge of the U.S. Court of Appeals for the First Circuit where he served for fourteen years, four of them (1990–1994) as chief judge.

He married Joanna Hare in 1967, and they have three children: Chloe, Nell, and Michael.

Associate Justice Samuel Alito, Jr., 110th justice
Appointed by: President George W. Bush
Sworn in: January 31, 2006

Associate Justice Samuel Alito Jr. was born in 1950 in Trenton, New Jersey. He graduated from Princeton University and earned a law degree from Yale Law School, where he was editor of the *Yale Law Journal*. He clerked for Judge Leonard I. Garth, United States Court of Appeals for the Third Circuit. He was assistant U.S. attorney for the District of New Jersey, and later named assistant to the solicitor general, U.S. Department of Justice. In 1985 he was named deputy assistant attorney general for the U.S. Department of Justice and was then named U.S. attorney for the District of New Jersey. In 1990 he was appointed to the U.S. Court of Appeals for the Third Circuit, where he served until nominated to the Supreme Court.

He married Martha-Ann Bomgardner in 1985, and they have two children, Philip and Laura.

Associate Justice Sonia Sotomayor, 111th justice
Appointed by: President Barack Obama
Sworn in: August 8, 2009

Associate Justice Sotomayor was born in 1954 in the Bronx, New York. She graduated from Princeton University, receiving the school's highest academic honor. She attended Yale Law School, where she was an editor of the *Yale Law Journal*. She began her career as an assistant district attorney in the New York County district attorney's office, serving from 1979–1984. She then entered private practice where she focused on litigation and international commercial cases. In 1991, President George H. W. Bush appointed her to the U.S. District Court, Southern District of New York. In 1998, she was named as judge to the U.S. Court of Appeals for the Second Circuit. She is the first Hispanic American named to the Supreme Court.

BIOGRAPHIES OF THE RETIRED JUSTICES

Associate Justice Sandra Day O'Connor (Retired), 102nd justice
Appointed by: President Ronald Reagan
Sworn in: September 25, 1981
Retired: January 31, 2006

Sandra Day O'Connor was born in 1930 in El Paso, Texas, and raised on a ranch in Arizona. She received her undergraduate and law degrees from Stanford University where she served on the law review. She practiced law in Arizona, where she was named assistant attorney general, serving from 1954–1969. She was appointed to the state senate in 1969 and won election for two additional terms. She was chosen as the Senate Majority Leader, the first woman nationally to attain that position. She was elected judge of the Maricopa County Superior Court in 1975 and in 1979 was named to the Arizona Court of Appeals, where she served until her historic appointment as first female associate justice of the Supreme Court. She received the Presidential Medal of Freedom from President Barack Obama in 2009.

She married John Jay O'Connor III (deceased); they are the parents of three children: Scott, Brian, and Jay.

Associate Justice David Souter (Retired), 105th justice
Appointed by: President George H. W. Bush
Sworn in: October 9, 1990
Retired: June 29, 2009

Associate Justice David Souter was born in Melrose, Massachusetts, in 1939. He attended Harvard College and Magdalen College, Oxford, as a Rhodes Scholar. He graduated from Harvard Law School and practiced law in Concord, New Hampshire, from 1966–1968 when he became an assistant attorney general of New Hampshire. In 1971, he was named deputy attorney general, and in 1976, the state's attorney general. He was appointed to the Superior Court of New Hampshire in 1978 and in 1983 was named an associate justice of the Supreme Court of New Hampshire. In 1990, he became a judge of the United States Court of Appeals for the First Circuit and just months later was named to the U.S. Supreme Court.

MEMBERS OF
THE SUPREME COURT
OF THE UNITED STATES

Name	State App't From	Appointed by President	Judicial Oath Taken	Date Service Terminated
Chief Justices				
Jay, John	NY	Washington	October 19, 1789	June 29, 1795
Rutledge, John	SC	Washington	August 12, 1795	December 15, 1795
Ellsworth, Oliver	CT	Washington	March 8, 1796	December 15, 1800
Marshall, John	VA	Adams, John	February 4, 1801	July 6, 1835
Taney, Roger Brooke	MD	Jackson	March 28, 1836	October 12, 1864
Chase, Salmon Portland	OH	Lincoln	December 15, 1864	May 7, 1872
Waite, Morrison Remick	OH	Grant	March 4, 1874	March 23, 1888
Fuller, Melville Weston	IL	Cleveland	October 8, 1888	July 4, 1910
White, Edward Douglass	LA	Taft	December 19, 1910	May 19, 1921
Taft, William Howard	CT	Harding	July 11, 1921	February 3, 1930
Hughes, Charles Evans	NY	Hoover	February 24, 1930	June 30, 1941
Stone, Harlan Fiske	NY	Roosevelt, F.	July 3, 1941	April 22, 1946
Vinson, Fred Moore	KY	Truman	June 24, 1946	September 8, 1953
Warren, Earl	CA	Eisenhower	October 5, 1953	June 23, 1969
Burger, Warren Earl	VA	Nixon	June 23, 1969	September 26, 1986
Rehnquist, William H.	VA	Reagan	September 26, 1986	September 3, 2005
Roberts, John G., Jr.	MD	Bush, G. W.	September 29, 2005	
Associate Justices				
Rutledge, John	SC	Washington	(a) February 15, 1790	March 5, 1791
Cushing, William	MA	Washington	(c) February 2, 1790	September 13, 1810
Wilson, James	PA	Washington	(b) October 5, 1789	August 21, 1798
Blair, John	VA	Washington	(c) February 2, 1790	October 25, 1795
Iredell, James	NC	Washington	(b) May 12, 1790	October 20, 1799

Name	State App't From	Appointed by President	Judicial Oath Taken	Date Service Terminated
Johnson, Thomas	MD	Washington	(a) August 6, 1792	January 16, 1793
Paterson, William	NJ	Washington	(a) March 11, 1793	September 9, 1806
Chase, Samuel	MD	Washington	February 4, 1796	June 19, 1811
Washington, Bushrod	VA	Adams, John	(c) February 4, 1799	November 26, 1829
Moore, Alfred	NC	Adams, John	(a) April 21, 1800	January 26, 1804
Johnson, William	SC	Jefferson	May 7, 1804	August 4, 1834
Livingston, Henry Brockholst	NY	Jefferson	January 20, 1807	March 18, 1823
Todd, Thomas	KY	Jefferson	(a) May 4, 1807	February 7, 1826
Duvall, Gabriel	MD	Madison	(a) November 23, 1811	January 14, 1835
Story, Joseph	MA	Madison	(c) February 3, 1812	September 10, 1845
Thompson, Smith	NY	Monroe	(b) September 1, 1823	December 18, 1843
Trimble, Robert	KY	Adams, J. Q.	(a) June 16, 1826	August 25, 1828
McLean, John	OH	Jackson	(c) January 11, 1830	April 4, 1861
Baldwin, Henry	PA	Jackson	Jaaury 18, 1830	April 21, 1844
Wayne, James Moore	GA	Jackson	January 14, 1835	July 5, 1867
Barbour, Philip Pendleton	VA	Jackson	May 12, 1836	February 25, 1841
Catron, John	TN	Jackson	May 1, 1837	May 30, 1865
McKinley, John	AL	Van Buren	(c) January 9, 1838	July 19, 1852
Daniel, Peter Vivian	VA	Van Buren	(c) January 10, 1842	May 31, 1860
Nelson, Samuel	NY	Tyler	February 27, 1845	November 28, 1872
Woodbury, Levi	NH	Polk	(b) September 23, 1845	September 4, 1851
Grier, Robert Cooper	PA	Polk	August 10, 1846	January 31, 1870
Curtis, Benjamin Robbins	MA	Fillmore	(b) October 10, 1851	September 30, 1857
Campbell, John Archibald	AL	Pierce	(c) April 11, 1853	April 30, 1861
Clifford, Nathan	ME	Buchanan	January 21, 1858	July 25, 1881
Swayne, Noah Haynes	OH	Lincoln	January 27, 1862	January 24, 1881
Miller, Samuel Freeman	IA	Lincoln	July 21, 1862	October 13, 1890
Davis, David	IL	Lincoln	December 10, 1862	March 4, 1877
Field, Stephen Johnson	CA	Lincoln	May 20, 1863	December 1, 1897
Strong, William	PA	Grant	March 14, 1870	December 14, 1880
Bradley, Joseph P.	NJ	Grant	March 23, 1870	January 22, 1892
Hunt, Ward	NY	Grant	January 9, 1873	January 27, 1882
Harlan, John Marshall	KY	Hayes	December 10, 1877	October 14, 1911
Woods, William Burnham	GA	Hayes	January 5, 1881	May 14, 1887
Matthews, Stanley	OH	Garfield	May 17, 1881	March 22, 1889
Gray, Horace	MA	Arthur	January 9, 1882	September 15, 1902

Name	State App't From	Appointed by President	Judicial Oath Taken	Date Service Terminated
Blatchford, Samuel	NY	Arthur	April 3, 1882	July 7, 1893
Lamar, Lucius Quintus C.	MS	Cleveland	January 18, 1888	January 23, 1893
Brewer, David Josiah	KS	Harrison	January 6, 1890	March 28, 1910
Brown, Henry Billings	MI	Harrison	January 5, 1891	May 28, 1906
Shiras, George, Jr.	PA	Harrison	October 10, 1892	February 23, 1903
Jackson, Howell Edmunds	TN	Harrison	March 4, 1893	August 8, 1895
White, Edward Douglass	LA	Cleveland	March 12, 1894	December 18, 1910*
Peckham, Rufus Wheeler	NY	Cleveland	January 6, 1896	October 24, 1909
McKenna, Joseph	CA	McKinley	January 26, 1898	January 5, 1925
Holmes, Oliver Wendell	MA	Roosevelt, T.	December 8, 1902	January 12, 1932
Day, William Rufus	OH	Roosevelt, T.	March 2, 1903	November 13, 1922
Moody, William Henry	MA	Roosevelt, T.	December 17, 1906	November 20, 1910
Lurton, Horace Harmon	TN	Taft	January 3, 1910	July 12, 1914
Hughes, Charles Evans	NY	Taft	October 10, 1910	June 10, 1916
Van Devanter, Willis	WY	Taft	January 3, 1911	June 2, 1937
Lamar, Joseph Rucker	GA	Taft	January 3, 1911	January 2, 1916
Pitney, Mahlon	NJ	Taft	March 18, 1912	December 31, 1922
McReynolds, James Clark	TN	Wilson	October 12, 1914	January 31, 1941
Brandeis, Louis Dembitz	MA	Wilson	June 5, 1916	February 13, 1939
Clarke, John Hessin	OH	Wilson	October 9, 1916	September 18, 1922
Sutherland, George	UT	Harding	October 2, 1922	January 17, 1938
Butler, Pierce	MN	Harding	January 2, 1923	November 16, 1939
Sanford, Edward Terry	TN	Harding	February 19, 1923	March 8, 1930
Stone, Harlan Fiske	NY	Coolidge	March 2, 1925	July 2, 1941*
Roberts, Owen Josephus	PA	Hoover	June 2, 1930	July 31, 1945
Cardozo, Benjamin Nathan	NY	Hoover	March 14, 1932	July 9, 1938
Black, Hugo Lafayette	AL	Roosevelt, F.	August 19, 1937	September 17, 1971
Reed, Stanley Forman	KY	Roosevelt, F.	January 31, 1938	February 25, 1957
Frankfurter, Felix	MA	Roosevelt, F.	January 30, 1939	August 28, 1962
Douglas, William Orville	CT	Roosevelt, F.	April 17, 1939	November 12, 1975
Murpy, Frank	MI	Roosevelt, F.	February 5, 1940	July 19, 1949
Byrnes, James Francis	SC	Roosevelt, F.	July 8, 1941	October 3, 1942
Jackson, Robert Houghwout	NY	Roosevelt, F.	July 11, 1941	October 9, 1954
Rutledge, Wiley Blount	IA	Roosevelt, F.	February 15, 1943	September 10, 1949
Burton, Harold Hitz	OH	Truman	October 1, 1945	October 13, 1958
Clark, Tom Campbell	TX	Truman	August 24, 1949	June 12, 1967
Minton, Sherman	IN	Truman	October 12, 1949	October 15, 1956

Name	State App't From	Appointed by President	Judicial Oath Taken	Date Service Terminated
Harlan, John Marshall	NY	Eisenhower	March 28, 1955	September 23, 1971
Brennan, William J., Jr.	NJ	Eisenhower	October 16, 1956	July 20, 1990
Whittaker, Charles Evans	MO	Eisenhower	March 25, 1957	March 31, 1962
Stewart, Potter	OH	Eisenhower	October 14, 1958	July 3, 1981
White, Byron Raymond	CO	Kennedy	April 16, 1962	June 28, 1993
Goldberg, Arthur Joseph	IL	Kennedy	October 1, 1962	July 25, 1965
Fortas, Abe	TN	Johnson, L.	October 4, 1965	May 14, 1969
Marshall, Thurgood	NY	Johnson, L.	October 2, 1967	October 1, 1991
Blackmun, Harry A.	MN	Nixon	June 9, 1970	August 3, 1994
Powell, Lewis F., Jr.	VA	Nixon	January 7, 1972	June 26, 1987
Rehnquist, William H.	AZ	Nixon	January 7, 1972	September 26, 1986*
Stevens, John Paul	IL	Ford	December 19, 1975	
O'Connor, Sandra Day	AZ	Reagan	September 25, 1981	January 31, 2006
Scalia, Antonin	VA	Reagan	September 26, 1986	
Kennedy, Anthony M.	CA	Reagan	February 18, 1988	
Souter, David H.	NH	Bush, G.H.W.	October 9, 1990	June 29, 2009
Thomas, Clarence	GA	Bush, G.H.W.	October 23, 1991	
Ginsburg, Ruth Bader	NY	Clinton	August 10, 1993	
Breyer, Stephen G.	MA	Clinton	August 3, 1994	
Alito, Samuel A., Jr.	NJ	Bush, G. W.	January 31, 2006	
Sotomayor, Sonia	NY	Obama	August 8, 2009	

An asterisk (*) denotes that the associate justice was elevated to chief justice.

SOURCE: From a booklet prepared by the Supreme Court of the United States and published with funding from the Supreme Court Historical Society.

RECENT C-SPAN SURVEYS OF PUBLIC AWARENESS OF THE SUPREME COURT

What Americans Know About the U.S. Supreme Court and Want Changed About the Court

Timed with C-SPAN's Supreme Court Week presentation of an original feature documentary on the Court and a series of justice interviews, C-SPAN commissioned a poll to determine what Americans know about the Supreme Court and what they would like changed about the Court. The poll of 801 voters, conducted by Penn, Schoen and Berland Associates, LLC, showed that nearly nine in ten American voters said the Court has an impact on their everyday lives—but only half could name a specific case heard by the Court.

The poll, conducted on September 17, 2009, indicated the public supports major changes to the Court, most notably revisiting the concept of constitutionally guaranteed lifetime appointments, and nearly two in three (65%) would like to see cameras in the Supreme Court to televise oral arguments. Following are the results for each of the fourteen questions.

1. Do you strongly agree, somewhat agree, somewhat disagree, or strongly disagree that the decisions made by the U.S. Supreme Court have an impact on your everyday life as a citizen?

Strongly agree, 39%

Somewhat agree, 49%
Somewhat disagree, 10%
Strongly disagree, 2%

2. Can you name any case heard by the U.S. Supreme Court?

Yes, 49%
No, 51%

Of the 49% of those surveyed who could name any case heard by the Court, one case predominated: *Roe v. Wade* (named by 84%). A few respondents were able to cite other cases: *Brown v. Board of Education* (9%); *Plessy v. Ferguson* (3%); *Bush v. Gore* (1%); *District of Columbia v. Heller* (1%); *Marbury v. Madison* (1%). When specifically asked about *Bush v. Gore* (the case that decided the 2000 presidential election), 71% said the ruling did not affect their view of the high court.

3. Did the Supreme Court's ruling on the 2000 *Bush v. Gore* election affect your view of the Court?

Yes, 29%
No, 71%

The survey also indicated the public supports major changes to the Court, most notably revisiting the concept of constitutionally guaranteed lifetime appointments. Nearly eight in ten Americans knew there is no mandatory retirement age for Supreme Court justices.

4. Is there a mandatory retirement age for U.S. Supreme Court Justices?

Yes, 21%
No, 79%

Just over half of those surveyed said they would prefer that justices do not receive lifetime appointments.

5. Currently, U.S. Supreme Court justices serve lifetime appointments. Do you strongly agree, somewhat agree, somewhat disagree, or strongly disagree that Supreme Court justices should serve lifetime appointments?

> Strongly agree, 14%
> Somewhat agree, 31%
> Somewhat disagree, 36%
> Strongly disagree, 20%

Three out of four of survey participants said they would prefer eighteen-year terms to the high court, a proposal published in the *Harvard Journal of Law and Public Policy* and reported on by the *New York Times*, among others.

6. What if U.S. Supreme Court Justices served an eighteen-year term with possible reappointment by the president subject to Senate confirmation? Would you strongly prefer an eighteen-year term to a lifetime appointment, somewhat prefer an eighteen-year term, somewhat prefer lifetime appointment and not change to an eighteen-year term, or strongly prefer a lifetime appointment and not change to an eighteen-year term?

> Strongly prefer eighteen-year term to lifetime, 31%
> Somewhat prefer eighteen-year term to lifetime, 47%
> Somewhat prefer lifetime to eighteen-year term, 12%
> Strongly prefer lifetime to eighteen-year term, 11%

(In fact, the average tenure of the eight justices appointed before the summer of 2009 was seventeen years. The most recently seated justice, Sonia Sotomayor, replaced Justice David Souter, who served 18.6 years.)

Another major change to the Court favored by those surveyed was televising oral arguments. Nearly two in three said they wanted cameras in the Supreme Court.

7. The U.S. Supreme Court currently does not allow television coverage of its oral arguments. Please indicate if you strongly agree, somewhat agree, somewhat disagree, or strongly disagree that the U.S. Supreme Court should allow television coverage of its oral arguments.

Strongly agree, 30%

Somewhat agree, 35%

Somewhat disagree, 22%

Strongly disagree, 13%

(Every state currently allows at least some level of television coverage of appellate court proceedings. Cameras also have been officially permitted in the second and ninth federal appeals courts on a case-by-case basis since 1996. In addition, the Supreme Court of Canada first allowed a camera in its courtroom in 1981, and in October 2009 Britain's Supreme Court admitted television cameras.)

The 65% number favoring cameras tracked closely with a 61% finding in a June 2009 C-SPAN poll of 1,002 voters, also conducted by Penn, Schoen and Berland, immediately before the Sonia Sotomayor nomination hearings.

C-SPAN conducted both polls to gauge Americans' basic knowledge of the Supreme Court.

8. Can you name any justices on the U.S. Supreme Court? (Those that entered "yes" were prompted to enter the name of a Supreme Court justice; only correct answers were counted as "yes" responses; poll conducted before Sonia Sotomayor's confirmation.)

Yes, 46%

Clarence Thomas, 14%

John G. Roberts, 11%

Ruth Bader Ginsberg, 7%

Antonin Scalia, 6%

David Souter, 3%

Samuel Alito, 2%

Stephen Breyer, 1%

Anthony Kennedy, 1%

John Paul Stevens, 1%

No, 54%

9. Can you name the first woman to serve as justice on the U.S. Supreme Court? (Those that entered "yes" were prompted to enter the name of the first woman to serve as justice. Only correct answers were counted as "yes" responses.)

Yes (Sandra Day O'Connor), 41%
No, 59%

10. Over the years, how many women have been sworn in as justices of the U.S. Supreme Court?

Zero, 3%
1, 9%
2, 27%
3, 37%
4, 8%
5, 6%
6, or more 9%

11. Over the years, how many African Americans have been sworn in as justices of the U.S. Supreme Court?

Zero, 9%
1, 28%
2, 39%
3, 9%
4, 4%
5, 5%
6, or more 4%

12. Does a jury hear cases before the U.S. Supreme Court?

Yes, 19%
No, 67%
Don't know, 14%

13. How long is the average argument before the U.S. Supreme Court?

30 minutes, 10%
One hour, 9%
90 minutes, 10%
One day, 5%
Two days, 9%
Don't know, 58%

14. Is it currently a requirement for the chief justice of the United States to be a lawyer?

Yes, 48%
No, 52%

The full results of the C-SPAN/Penn, Schoen and Berland Associates polls are available online at the following Web sites:

The September 2009 poll is here:

http://supremecourt.c-span.org/assets/pdf/SC_
SeptemberPollin-depthAgendaResults(092209).pdf

The June 2009 poll is here:

http://www.c-span.org/pdf/C-SPAN%20Supreme%20Court
%20Online%20Survey_070909_6pm.pdf

NUMBER OF SUPREME COURT PETITIONS AND ARGUMENTS HEARD, 1980–2008

Year	Number of Petitions	Cases Argued
1980	5,144	136
1981	5,311	153
1982	5,079	157
1983	5,100	159
1984	5,006	150
1985	5,158	158
1986	5,123	154
1987	5,268	148
1988	5,657	146
1989	5,746	131
1990	6,316	117
1991	6,770	112
1992	7,245	111
1993	7,786	90
1994	8,100	85
1995	7,565	81
1996	7,602	93
1997	7,692	98
1998	8,083	83
1999	8,445	86
2000	8,965	87
2001	9,176	80
2002	9,406	78
2003	8,883	82
2004	8,588	80
2005	9,608	79
2006	10,256	73
2007	9,602	74
2008	8,966	82

C-SPAN REQUESTS FOR
SAME-DAY RELEASE
OF ORAL ARGUMENTS

Between 2000 and 2009, C-SPAN has made forty-two requests to the Supreme Court for the same-day release of the Court's audio recordings of its oral arguments. Twenty-one of the requests have been granted:

2000–2001
- *Bush v. Palm Beach County Canvassing Board*
- *Bush v. Gore*

2002–2003
- *Grutter v. Bollinger*
- *Gratz v. Bollinger*

2003–2004
- *McConnell v. FEC*
- *Rasul v. Bush & Al Oday v. U.S.*
- *Cheney v. U.S. District Court*
- *Hamdi v. Rumsfeld*
- *Rumsfeld v. Padilla*

2005–2006
- *Ayotte v. Planned Parenthood of Northern New England*
- *Rumsfeld v. Forum for Academic & Institutional Rights*
- *Hamdan v. Rumsfeld*

2006–2007

- *Gonzalez v. Planned Parenthood*
- *Gonzalez v. Carhart*
- *Parents Involved v. Seattle School District No. 1*
- *Meredith v. Jefferson County Board of Education*

2007–2008

- *Boumediene v. Bush & Al Odah v. U.S.*
- *Baze v. Rees*
- *District of Columbia v. Heller*

2008–2009

- *Northwest Austin Municipal Utility District v. Holder*
- *Citizens United v. Federal Election Commission*

For updated information, visit

http://www.c-span.org/CamerasInCourt/timeline.aspx.

EXCERPT FROM THE OPINION

MARBURY V. MADISON

William Marbury v. James Madison, Secretary of State of the United States, February Term, 1803

Mr. Chief Justice Marshall delivered the opinion of the court.

. . . The constitution vests the whole judicial power of the United States in one supreme court, and such inferior courts as congress shall, from time to time, ordain and establish. This power is expressly extended to all cases arising under the laws of the United States; and consequently, in some form, may be exercised over the present case; because the right claimed is given by a law of the United States.

In the distribution of this power it is declared that "the supreme court shall have original jurisdiction in all cases affecting ambassadors, other public ministers and consuls, and those in which a state shall be a party. In all other cases, the supreme court shall have appellate jurisdiction."

It has been insisted at the bar, that as the original grant of jurisdiction to the supreme and inferior courts is general, and the clause, assigning original jurisdiction to the supreme court, contains no negative or restrictive words; the power remains to the legislature to assign original jurisdiction to that court in other cases than those specified in the article which has been recited; provided those cases belong to the judicial power of the United States.

If it had been intended to leave it in the discretion of the legislature to apportion the judicial power between the supreme and inferior courts according to the will of that body, it would certainly have been useless to have proceeded further than to have defined the judicial power, and the tribunals in which it should be vested. The subsequent part of the section is mere surplusage, is entirely without meaning, if such is to be the construction. If congress remains at liberty to give this court appellate jurisdiction, where the constitution has declared their jurisdiction shall be original; and original jurisdiction where the constitution has declared it shall be appellate; the distribution of jurisdiction made in the constitution, is form without substance.

Affirmative words are often, in their operation, negative of other objects than those affirmed; and in this case, a negative or exclusive sense must be given to them or they have no operation at all.

It cannot be presumed that any clause in the constitution is intended to be without effect; and therefore such construction is inadmissible, unless the words require it. If the solicitude of the convention, respecting our peace with foreign powers, induced a provision that the supreme court should take original jurisdiction in cases which might be supposed to affect them; yet the clause would have proceeded no further than to provide for such cases, if no further restriction on the powers of congress had been intended. That they should have appellate jurisdiction in all other cases, with such exceptions as congress might make, is no restriction; unless the words be deemed exclusive of original jurisdiction.

When an instrument organizing fundamentally a judicial system, divides it into one supreme, and so many inferior courts as the legislature may ordain and establish; then enumerates its powers, and proceeds so far to distribute them, as to define the jurisdiction of the supreme court by declaring the cases in which it shall take original jurisdiction, and that in others it shall take appellate jurisdiction, the plain import of the words seems to be, that in one class of cases its jurisdiction is original, and not appellate; in the other it is appellate, and not original. If any other construction would render the clause inoperative, that is an additional reason for rejecting such other construction, and for adhering to the obvious meaning.

To enable this court then to issue a mandamus, it must be shown to be an exercise of appellate jurisdiction, or to be necessary to enable them to exercise appellate jurisdiction.

It has been stated at the bar that the appellate jurisdiction may be exercised in a variety of forms, and that if it be the will of the legislature that a mandamus should be used for that purpose, that will must be obeyed. This is true; yet the jurisdiction must be appellate, not original.

It is the essential criterion of appellate jurisdiction, that it revises and corrects the proceedings in a cause already instituted, and does not create that case. Although, therefore, a mandamus may be directed to courts, yet to issue such a writ to an officer for the delivery of a paper, is in effect the same as to sustain an original action for that paper, and therefore seems not to belong to appellate, but to original jurisdiction. Neither is it necessary in such a case as this, to enable the court to exercise its appellate jurisdiction.

The authority, therefore, given to the supreme court, by the act establishing the judicial courts of the United States, to issue writs of mandamus to public officers, appears not to be warranted by the constitution; and it becomes necessary to inquire whether a jurisdiction, so conferred, can be exercised.

The question, whether an act, repugnant to the constitution, can become the law of the land, is a question deeply interesting to the United States; but, happily, not of an intricacy proportioned to its interest. It seems only necessary to recognise certain principles, supposed to have been long and well established, to decide it.

That the people have an original right to establish, for their future government, such principles as, in their opinion, shall most conduce to their own happiness, is the basis on which the whole American fabric has been erected. The exercise of this original right is a very great exertion; nor can it nor ought it to be frequently repeated. The principles, therefore, so established are deemed fundamental. And as the authority, from which they proceed, is supreme, and can seldom act, they are designed to be permanent.

This original and supreme will organizes the government, and assigns to different departments their respective powers. It may either stop here; or establish certain limits not to be transcended by those departments.

The government of the United States is of the latter description. The powers of the legislature are defined and limited; and that those limits may not be mistaken or forgotten, the constitution is written. To what purpose are powers limited, and to what purpose is that limitation committed to writing; if these limits may, at any time, be passed by those intended to be restrained? The distinction between a government with limited and unlimited powers is abolished, if those limits do not confine the persons on whom they are imposed, and if acts prohibited and acts allowed are of equal obligation. It is a proposition too plain to be contested, that the constitution controls any legislative act repugnant to it; or, that the legislature may alter the constitution by an ordinary act.

Between these alternatives there is no middle ground. The constitution is either a superior, paramount law, unchangeable by ordinary means, or it is on a level with ordinary legislative acts, and like other acts, is alterable when the legislature shall please to alter it.

If the former part of the alternative be true, then a legislative act contrary to the constitution is not law: if the latter part be true, then written constitutions are absurd attempts, on the part of the people, to limit a power in its own nature illimitable.

Certainly all those who have framed written constitutions contemplate them as forming the fundamental and paramount law of the nation, and consequently the theory of every such government must be, that an act of the legislature repugnant to the constitution is void.

This theory is essentially attached to a written constitution, and is consequently to be considered by this court as one of the fundamental principles of our society. It is not therefore to be lost sight of in the further consideration of this subject.

If an act of the legislature, repugnant to the constitution, is void, does it, notwithstanding its invalidity, bind the courts and oblige them to give it effect? Or, in other words, though it be not law, does it constitute a rule as operative as if it was a law? This would be to overthrow in fact what was established in theory; and would seem, at first view, an absurdity too gross to be insisted on. It shall, however, receive a more attentive consideration.

It is emphatically the province and duty of the judicial department to say what the law is. Those who apply the rule to particular cases, must of necessity expound and interpret that rule. If two laws conflict with each other, the courts must decide on the operation of each. So if a law be in opposition to the constitution: if both the law and the constitution apply to a particular case, so that the court must either decide that case conformably to the law, disregarding the constitution; or conformably to the constitution, disregarding the law: the court must determine which of these conflicting rules governs the case. This is of the very essence of judicial duty.

If then the courts are to regard the constitution; and the constitution is superior to any ordinary act of the legislature; the constitution, and not such ordinary act, must govern the case to which they both apply.

Those then who controvert the principle that the constitution is to be considered, in court, as a paramount law, are reduced to the necessity of maintaining that courts must close their eyes on the constitution, and see only the law.

This doctrine would subvert the very foundation of all written constitutions. It would declare that an act, which, according to the principles and theory of our government, is entirely void, is yet, in practice, completely obligatory. It would declare, that if the legislature shall do what is expressly forbidden, such act, notwithstanding the express prohibition, is in reality effectual. It would be giving to the legislature a practical and real omnipotence with the same breath which professes to restrict their powers within narrow limits. It is prescribing limits, and declaring that those limits may be passed at pleasure.

That it thus reduces to nothing what we have deemed the greatest improvement on political institutions—a written constitution, would of itself be sufficient, in America where written constitutions have been viewed with so much reverence, for rejecting the construction. But the peculiar expressions of the constitution of the United States furnish additional arguments in favour of its rejection.

The judicial power of the United States is extended to all cases arising under the constitution. Could it be the intention of those who gave this power, to say that, in using it, the constitution should not be looked into? That a case arising under the constitution should be decided without examining the instrument under which it arises?

This is too extravagant to be maintained.

In some cases then, the constitution must be looked into by the judges. And if they can open it at all, what part of it are they forbidden to read, or to obey?

There are many other parts of the constitution which serve to illustrate this subject.

It is declared that "no tax or duty shall be laid on articles exported from any state." Suppose a duty on the export of cotton, of tobacco, or of flour;

and a suit instituted to recover it. Ought judgment to be rendered in such a case? Ought the judges to close their eyes on the constitution, and only see the law.

The constitution declares that "no bill of attainder or ex post facto law shall be passed."

If, however, such a bill should be passed and a person should be prosecuted under it, must the court condemn to death those victims whom the constitution endeavours to preserve?

"No person," says the constitution, "shall be convicted of treason unless on the testimony of two witnesses to the same overt act, or on confession in open court."

Here the language of the constitution is addressed especially to the courts. It prescribes, directly for them, a rule of evidence not to be departed from. If the legislature should change that rule, and declare one witness, or a confession out of court, sufficient for conviction, must the constitutional principle yield to the legislative act?

From these and many other selections which might be made, it is apparent, that the framers of the constitution contemplated that instrument as a rule for the government of courts, as well as of the legislature.

Why otherwise does it direct the judges to take an oath to support it? This oath certainly applies, in an especial manner, to their conduct in their official character. How immoral to impose it on them, if they were to be used as the instruments, and the knowing instruments, for violating what they swear to support!

The oath of office, too, imposed by the legislature, is completely demonstrative of the legislative opinion on this subject. It is in these words: "I do solemnly swear that I will administer justice without respect to persons, and do equal right to the poor and to the rich; and that I will faithfully and impartially discharge all the duties incumbent on me as according to the best of my abilities and understanding, agreeably to the constitution and laws of the United States."

Why does a judge swear to discharge his duties agreeably to the constitution of the United States, if that constitution forms no rule for his government? if it is closed upon him and cannot be inspected by him.

If such be the real state of things, this is worse than solemn mockery. To prescribe, or to take this oath, becomes equally a crime.

It is also not entirely unworthy of observation, that in declaring what shall be the supreme law of the land, the constitution itself is first mentioned; and not the laws of the United States generally, but those only which shall be made in pursuance of the constitution, have that rank.

Thus, the particular phraseology of the constitution of the United States confirms and strengthens the principle, supposed to be essential to all written constitutions, that a law repugnant to the constitution is void, and that courts, as well as other departments, are bound by that instrument.

The rule must be discharged.

BIOGRAPHY OF
JOHN MARSHALL,
THE "GREAT CHIEF"

Fourth Chief Justice of the United States, 1801–1835

John Marshall was born in a log cabin on the Virginia frontier on September 24, 1755—the first of fifteen children. During the Revolutionary War, he fought as a member of the 3rd Virginia Regiment. He studied law briefly in 1780, was admitted to practice the same year, and established a successful career defending individuals against their pre-war British creditors.

Marshall was elected to Virginia's House of Delegates; he also participated in the state ratifying convention and spoke out on behalf of the new Constitution to replace the Articles of Confederation.

Marshall was courted by the Washington administration but declined service as attorney general. President John Adams offered Marshall a position on the Supreme Court and also considered him as secretary of war. With former President Washington's encouragement, Marshall instead ran successfully for a seat in the U.S. House of Representatives, representing Virginia, but when offered the position of secretary of state for John Adams, Marshall accepted. In 1800, Oliver Ellsworth resigned as chief justice of the Supreme Court, and Adams turned to the first chief justice, John Jay, who declined the appointment. Federalists urged Adams to promote Associate Justice William Paterson, but Adams instead opted for Marshall, nominating him on January 20, 1801.

John Marshall accepted the appointment on February 2, 1801, serving as chief justice for thirty-four years—an unsurpassed record. During that time, he participated in more than one thousand decisions and authored more than five hundred opinions.

Marshall's groundbreaking opinions continue to guide the Supreme Court and the United States government. In *Marbury v. Madison* (1803), the Marshall court established the principle of judicial review, ruling that the Supreme Court had the power to declare invalid any act of Congress deemed in conflict with the U.S. Constitution. The Marshall court also ruled that state judiciaries could set aside state legislative acts if they conflicted with the federal Constitution, and that the U.S. Supreme Court could reverse a decision of a state court. Marshall's opinions are seen as increasing the power of the Supreme Court as a branch of the federal government. His opinions also helped establish the national supremacy of the federal government in the early years of the new U.S. government.

John Marshall died on July 6, 1835, in Philadelphia. He was buried in Richmond, Virginia, at Shockoe Cemetery next to his wife, Mary Ambler Marshall.

Sources: Oyez (www.oyez.org) and Library of Virginia (http://www.lva.virginia.gov/).

For complete audio, video, and transcripts of
the justices' interviews, plus additional material
on the Supreme Court, visit
www.c-span.org/supremecourt.

⁓

C-SPAN is directing all royalties from the sale of this book
to the non-profit C-SPAN Education Foundation,
which creates teaching materials for
middle and high school classrooms.

INDEX

Credit: Leslie Rhodes

Brian Lamb (right) is C-SPAN's founding CEO and chairman and longtime on-camera interviewer. **Susan Swain,** C-SPAN's co-president and also an on-camera interviewer, has been the editorial director for all six of C-SPAN's books. **Mark Farkas** (center) has been a lead producer of C-SPAN feature productions for a quarter-century.